Missouri Cowboy Poetry

The
M C P A
Anthology

Poems and Stories

By

The Missouri Cowboy Poets Association

The Missouri Cowboy Poets Association, Inc.
Rt 1 Box 155-A
Verona, MO   65769-9643

Book compilation, and design by Leroy Watts

Printed by:

Affiliated Lithographers
Phoenix, AZ

ISBN 0-9636993-5-0

INTRODUCTION

The Missouri Cowboy Poets Association, Inc was founded about midnight June 29, 1996, when Richard Dunlap of Louisburg, Missouri, Jeff Anslinger of Savannah, Missouri, Don Collop of Mexico, Missouri, and Leroy Watts of Verona, Missouri, met together to discuss their mutual interest in cowboy poetry, and the traditional cowboy lifestyle culture.

During this meeting, it was agreed that it was time for Missouri poets dedicated to the preservation of the history of the "Cowboy" lifestyle, to unite and establish their own organization for the purpose of promoting the "Cowboy Poetry" that had become so popular in the rest of the country. It was further agreed that this could best be accomplished by the formation of an association dedicated to promote and preserve Missouri's colorful history in the western development of America.

Missouri was "The Gateway to the West" when early settlers moved westward through St. Louis to the wagon train dispersing stations at Independence, Westport, St. Joseph, and other cities on Missouri's western border. Most certainly Missouri has a history in which to take justifiable pride, and it was with this intent that The Missouri Cowboy Poets Association, Inc. was formed.

Today the Missouri Cowboy Poets Association has become one of the most successful organizations of this kind in America, and have some of the finest talent that can be found anywhere in the country. When we promote our MCPA Cowboy Poetry Gatherings, we feature only the talent from within our own MCPA membership to fill the entertainment program. This however, includes a number of associate members from several other states as well.

Members of the MCPA enjoy the camaraderie that is so typically found in the companionship of the ranchers, farmers, and others of the agricultural society that is the very heart and soul of America. It is our purpose to generate more interest, support, and enthusiasm for Cowboy Poetry, and to promote cultural events to take place throughout Missouri.

The Missouri Cowboy Poets Association, Inc is listed as Missouri Charitable Organization #CO-196096, incorporated under Missouri statutes, and with tax free status under article 501(c)(3) of the Federal IRS code.

The Missouri Cowboy Poets Association, Inc.
Rt 1 Box 155-A
Verona, MO 65769-9643
417-498-6865   lwatts@mo-net.com

ACKNOWLEDGEMENTS

This anthology of the Missouri Cowboy Poets Association would not have been possible without the financial donations of the following organizations, and individuals. We wish to express our thanks and appreciation for their support in this endeavor:

AmerenUE Electric Company of St Louis, Missouri, for their very charitable donation to assist in the publication of this work.

The Missouri Arts Council for their donation of a grant to assist in this publication.

To Jennie Cummings, and LaVern Watts, MCPA Sec/Treas, who have spent many hours in the preparation of the necessaary documents for the application for the MAC grant.

To MCPA members John and Jeannie Beltz, Rex and Erma Lee Henderson, Judy Johnston, Jay and Debra Jones, Lowell Long, Lou Mahon, Leroy and LaVern Watts, and others for their anonymous donations to support this publication as well.

Neither would this publication have been possible without the help and assistance of many other individuals. We want to extend our particular thanks to fellow member Jimmy Couch, and the entire English Department of the Missouri Southern State College at Joplin Missouri for their assistance in retyping, and submitting finished computor discs for the insertion of many of the submissions of works for this effort. Among the particular individuals involved in that effort, other than Jimmy Couch, are the following: Charline Lewis, secretary of the MSSC English Depatment, and the following student employees who did the retyping and computor adaptations, Katherine Carlson, Carla Fairbanks, and James Thurman. Our most heartfelt thanks, and appreciation to all of you for your fine work. You certainly lifted a very considerable burden from this very thankful editor.

We also give a very special thanks to Leroy Watts, MCPA COB, without whose dedication for the many hours of compilation, and formatting of the materials submitted herein, this publication would not have been accomplished.

Comment:

This has been a labor of love, and I wish to express my personal thanks to all of the above, and to all of the members of the MCPA for their support and confidence during those times when their encouragement and sustaining inspiration was so very welcome.

Sincerely,
Leroy Watts

TABLE OF CONTENTS

MCPA ANTHOLOGY   CONTENTS

THERE WAS A TIME

There was a time when calves were drug to the fire,
    a hot branding iron awaiting to mark their hides.
There was a time that there was land to be had,
    and all a man needed to make his mark was
    determination, hard work, and a willing heart.
There was a time that indians, rustlers, and nature
    were all that needed to be fought.
There was a time when a boy was made a man
    by working the land.

But things are changing, the old ways forgotten,
    put away by time and progress.
Now the calves are pushed through clanging gates,
    and electricity replaces the fire.
Now the land can be had only by luck
    and a million bucks.
Now is the time that land must be protected from
    the banker, the environmentalists, and city dwellers
    who seek to escape the frightening world
    they've created.
Now the boys just grow into bigger boys
    and drift from the land.
Let us not forget the old ways altogether
    because they are what made us who we are.

******

Esther Ash
18665 Scott Road
Erie, KS
66733

Esther Ash is the mother of three, and the wife of one. She has worked in all aspects of the cattle industry and advertising, to the feed lot, to stockers, and cow/calf operations. She has a degree in Agricultural Education.

She made her debut appearance at "Old Cowtown Wichita Cowboy Gathering", and has performed at numerous events since that time. Esther is also a member of "Cowboy Story Tellers of the Western Plains", and has performed at several meetings for them. When she is not performing Esther stays busy with her full-time job as a mother, and as wife to her husband, Todd, who is a working cowboy on a ranch in Erie, Kansas.

ROPING EMUS

Ted's reaction to the Emus
    was a 'double', double-take.
He tried to herd them with his dog;
    they gave him 'shake-an-bake'.
Exotic birds were not his 'forte',
    though he knew of some around.
Ted predicted he might 'add value'
    if he could tie them on the ground.

"This pair of birds are valuable",
    Ted told his doubting wife.
"No doubt some breeder's frantic
    that this pair might lose their life.
No strays have been reported, but
    I'm thinking, then again
There might be a 'fat reward'
    for whoever brings them in."

Ted's life dream was of a country place
    that they could call their own.
Stocked with feeder calves and horses,
    with room for kids to roam.
Now, here was a chance for action
    at a fraction of the price
Of paying fees to rope in a rodeo;
    the challenge would be 'kind-of' nice.

The Emus were shadows to Ted's calves,
    alert and poised to run.
Their speed and agility promised
    roping Emus could be fun!
The birds fate seemed certain,
    what he needed was a plan.
Ted decided to build a 'chase-car',
    his kids shouted. "You're the MAN."

Ted took his 'trusty' Datsun
    to the welder down in town.
They built a 'brush-guard' bumper,
    with reinforcing all around.

Next, a seat and seat-belt
        was welded to the frame
That extended out in front
        of the truck, now dubbed. 'the flame'.

Ted would be the roper, but,
        who would drive the truck?
He needed skill and daring
        to run those Emus 'out-of' luck!
His kids were young and flighty.
        His wife refused to drive.
Neighbor Bob said, "I'll help.
        We'll bring 'em in alive."

The 'chase of the century' ended
        almost before it had begun.
You had to pay attention
        otherwise, you missed the fun!
The ropers had not reckoned,
        when they planned this daring deed,
How a Datsun 'extended' pickup rides
        in a pasture, at top speed!

When Ted cried, "faster, faster,"
        Bob put the pedal to the floor!
The Emus sprinted down a winding path
        through a patch of 'multi-flora'.
Bob grit his teeth and closed his eyes
        'til he reached the other side.
Ted'shirt and pants were shredded,
        he had DEEP scratches on his hide!

Bob helped Ted from his perch,
        saying, "I've got this much to say,
To catch that pair of speed birds,
        there must be a better way."
"There is a better way," Ted said,
        "and, it will give me some relief!
I'll put those Emus in my freezer,
        I understand that they taste a lot like BEEF!"

******

THE BLOATER
The Ballad of Ole' Texaco

Ted and Leon are regulars at the cattle sale.
>They hold a permanent buyers seat.
The passing stock gets a real close study,
>these boys are hard to beat.

They compete against the Masters!
>They play by all the rules.
They win some calves from the market setters.
>and other just plain assorted fools.

Sometimes though that special deal,
>is just too good to be true.
Like that fancy black baldy, he was a bloater!
>What should an honest trader do?

This calf gave new meaning
>to 'boys, he'll grow at night.'
He looked like he had gained 100 pounds,
>when Ted checked him at daylight.

Their calf couldn't belch, or
    (please excuse me) break wind like you or I,
But they must get the pressure off,
    anything is worth a try.

A small hose, down the gullet, to the paunch
    and the bloat - it is no more.
The calf gives a knowing, pleasant grunt,
    this trick has been performed before!

Our guys will play the cards,
    that come to them in any deal.
They wouldn't think of going to the sale,
    and lodging a 'foul' appeal.

No, they won't take him back;
    or slip him on a bunch,
To sell as a preconditioned calf
    by not giving the calf his lunch.

No! They will see this through!
    Everything has a silver lining.
This calf will be an asset.
    They won't spend their time a whining.

They build a pen in Ted's crew cab,
    with a little box to hold his feed.
Some water in his drinking cup
    then, rich clover hay is all they need.

A spigot in the bloaters flank
    with a shut-off valve in line,
Extends the mileage of Ted's truck
    and his engine is running fine!

Ted says "when a deal goes sour,
    you can't just cuss your luck!
The gas that critter's making
    he will use to run his truck!"

******

THE DROUGHT OF 2000
And The Cyber-Cow

The blazing sun burned their backs;
       heat waves shimmer across the land.
It's too hot for a breeze to stir,
       how much can these cows stand?

The water holes have turned to mud;
       the spring has ceased to flow
Grass is withered on the hills;
       the stock will have to go.

At dawn, we load the trailers;
       I'll sell, because I must!
They leave the ranch in single file,
       through pot-holes filled with dust.

A ranch without 'mama' cows
       is a lonesome place, at best.
Bank loans must still be paid;
       this is 'THE' survivor test!

Consultants are there to give advice.
       Good or bad, they collect a fee.
Ozark ranchers all believe
       that the best advice is free!

Livestock journals, now collecting dust,
       that never quite got read,
now beckon me from the shelf,
       I'll see what light they shed.

They point me to the internet!
       There, a guru will show me how
to convert the ranch from VIRTUAL beef
       to the 'lucrative' CYBER-COW!

Some say I have no need to treat for scours!
       I should 'log-on' to CYBER-VET;
somewhere, someone else does the work!
       How good can ranching get?

Others view the weekly auction as a dinosaur
        that will vanish bit-by-bit.
They say it's better to list cattle on the web;
        and, then wait for the CYBER-BUYER hit.

My cowboy would not sort and ship;
        That can be handled through CYBER-FREIGHT.
Weather, now, is of no consequence; and,
        they are guaranteed to not be late!

A micro-chip can replace the brand,
        to foil the CYBER-CATTLE THIEF.
A New York, steak can be 'trailed'
        back to 'certified' Missouri Beef.

If Cyber-Ranch gets up and running,
        the virtual-ranch can go to seed!
I can ride the range in a swivel chair.
        Web access is all the stock I'll need.

But, real-time ranching is my life;
        I don't understand the INTERNET!
Hands-on work is all I know:
        I have faith we will 'make-it' yet.

So, at the ranch we 'hunker-down';
        with RESOLVE to never accept defeat!
Believing, a six-inch rain could dent this drought,
        and a foot of snow MIGHT break the heat!

******

ELMO AND WILLIE
On The Grazing Tour

After weeks of preparation
        the time had come at last,
to board the bus out to the flint hills
        to learn about their grass.

Forty ranchers on a mission,
        to learn the latest grazing trends.
Total strangers on Monday morning,
        by Friday we were bosom friends.

We drew straws to determine
        our 'roomies' for the week,
a clever way to encourage
        reserved participants to speak.

Two 'outliers' on this tour
        were Elmo, a feisty, out-going guy,
and, Willie, a 'giant' young man in overalls,
        pleasant, but super shy.

Elmo volunteered he was a 'snorer';
        that he was an ex-marine 'snoring champ'.
He claimed that when on maneuvers,
        he bunked two miles from camp!

Elmo said, "his recorded snoring
        was played to keep starlings out of town;
that controllers at a jet airport called
        and asked that he please keep the noise down!

"The city trash pick-up crew
        won't work until he is up
They claim its' vital to their job.
        to hear the dumpster hit the truck."

"Willie, it's sure bad luck
        you having to room with me.
But, your young, you will recover;
        I'll go up and get the key."

As Elmo 'kibitz' at the desk,
        hands anchored to his hips,
Willie lifted him in a 'bear-embrace',
        and kissed him on the lips!

Then he took the keys from the clerk,
        did an 180 on his heel;
and said, "Elmo, lets get some rest.
        I don't want to miss the morning meal"

At breakfast, Willie was fresh and fit,
        but 'ole' Elmo appeared distressed!
Willie seemed to have rested well,
        while Elmo was a 'red-eyed' sorry mess!

Well, did Elmo snore last night?
      Or, did he pass the hours a'counting sheep'?
Did he sound like a bass-boat on the lake?
      Did Willie get his sleep?

Elmo said, "I never slept a wink last night,
      in daylight this may sound silly;
but, you don't snore if you don't doze-off,
      and, I was awake a'watching' Willie!"

******

THE GREAT BULL FIGHT
Or Why Cowboys Don't Wash Their Trucks

The cowboy was in his comfort zone;
    he planned to trade on up
from the used half-ton, two-wheel drive
    to a new 4-wheel, dually truck.

His color of choice was fire-engine red!
    With polished, aluminum trim.
The dash looked like a cock-pit!
    He shifted by the RPM.

He bought a special, added feature
    that none of his friends could beat.
He had a 'cattle-call' for a horn
    that sounded like a Jersey bull, in heat.

Honey, why don't you and the kids come along?
    There is plenty of room in this cab.
I want you to see this work.
    We will begin down at your dad's!

He eased his rig through the gate;
    drove carefully toward the shade.
Gave two long blasts on the 'cattle-call'
    before he recognized the mistake he'd made!

Multi-flora rose and brush began to boil!
    Then came a hideous, blood-curdling roar,
as a ton of sinew, muscle and hostility
    charged out aiming for that shiny door!

The door that mirrored the image of an angry bull;
    on the spot from where the call had come.
If this intruder wanted action,
    then 'the king' would give him some!

Around the truck the fighter sparred.
    The challenger attempting to retreat, but
the big bull pressed the attack
    trying to take his opponent off his feet.

Two doors, four fenders and the grille
    were casualties of this battle.
The cowboy now had a used, half-wheel drive,
    and no one to help him check the cattle!

******

THE WILD COW WORKING

As far as tall tales go,
    this one is pretty high.
But, it was told to me by an honest man,
    that I had never known to lie.

He never claimed to be the man
    embroiled in this frenzied fray,
but will admit that on occasion,
    he has had a cow working go astray.

The cow in question had not been worked,
    since she was a calf at her mothers flank.
For fourteen years, she had not been caught.
    She was wary, tough, and rank.

She has weaned twelve calves in a row
    and she didn't need a creep.
Now Jess decides she must be caught,
    he wants to worm her and check her teeth.

The plan was to rig the old corral,
    to hold 'buffalo' with ease.
It would surely hold one ole wild cow,
    'till they could work her through the squeeze.

She always came into the trap
    when they fed the grain and hay.
But, when the sorting started,
    she pulled all the stops to get away.

She liked to rear up against the fence,
    then begin her patented hop;
gaining height and leverage with each bounce,
    until she reached the top.

Today, things would be different.
    The boys plan seemed sound.
If she got loose, they were prepared
    to run her into ground!

Sam had the new ATV, and
    Jess was in the blue Ford truck.
If that cow missed this working,
    she'd need more than common luck.

Predictably, she did get away.
    Who forgot to tie the gate?
She leisurely heads back to pasture
    but, still it's not too late.

Sam is after her on the ATV.
    The boy is riding like a pro!
He bumps her heels each second jump,
    man, can that ole heifer go!

The ground is frozen hard and slick.
    Now, there is a sudden change of plan.
The cow falls down, then gets back up,
    and now she is after Sam!

Sam guns out across the frozen pond,
    he just never stopped to think.
That this cow would follow right behind,
    until they both were in the drink!

The cow is bent on mayhem!
    Jess can see she is trying to drown his man.
He drives as fast as he can go,
    to the pond to lend a hand.

Sam gets free and is running now.
    The cow breaks ice to shore.
Jess dives in behind the steering wheel
    as the cow comes through the door.

When she can extricate herself,
    Sam is back in her sights.
Now, she is after him again,
    and they are both down on the ice.

Jess knows now that it's up to him,
     to rescue Sam from this fix.
He goes behind the broken seat,
     and gets out the old ought-six.

In review, they rationalized,
     they had done the best they could.
They can always use the freezer beef,
     and, oh yes Jess, her teeth were good!

******

THE MACING OF OLLIE'S BULL

Thank God for neighbors,
  including kith and kin;
who, when they see a cow is out
  volunteer to put her in.

Those dreaded phone
  calls in the night
give my comatose brain a jar.
  "John, you have a cow on the road!
I almost hit her with the car."

That the cowman is in control,
  is the mind set of city folk.
To think cows are here to do his bidding,
  is an illusion or a joke!

True, feeds and waters;
  worms and treats for scours.
But, cows are mostly on their own,
  especially after hours.

Ollie's big, white charolais bull
  was content to stay at home.
He did get out, but that's no sign
  he was inclined to roam.

The motorist who call the 'Law'
  pulled-off to wait and see
how counties urban cops
  would handle this 'bovine' emergency.

This 'Good Samaritan' was rewarded
  for doing his 'good deed'.
With lights flashing and sirens whining
  the 'Law' responded at flank speed.

A curious bull that weighs a ton
  may appear menacing or mean;
when his attention is forced to focus,
  on 'strange' strangers on the scene.

The constable was well equipped
        to face a hostile mob.
His flack-jacket, cuffs and weapons,
        were over-kill for this job.

'Pierre' ambled toward the gate
        where the trailer had been set.
That he would load, on his own,
        was better than a 50-50 bet.

In the lot the bull nosed around
        checking out the place.
That's when 'the deputy' lost his cool,
        and MACED him in the face!

They said "the bull reacted!"
        Well, that should come as no surprise!
Ollie too, let out a scream
        when he got it in the eyes!

The man and beast are safe at home
        where they continue to SNORT and PAW,
whenever the sheriff's car goes by.
        Their BEEF is with the 'Law'!

******

PARTNERS

When 'Doc' bought the grazing land
        deep down, I was hopin'
he had no plans to sub-divide, but
        keep the spaces open.

He called me up one evening
        suggesting we should talk.
With all that grass on his place
        He sure could use some stock.

'Doc' was the kind of guy,
        I was certain who would enjoy,
a herd of cows of his own,
        sort-of like a 'grown'ups' toy.

But, then he told me about his plan
    to put MY COWS on his grass!
Why, I could hardly believe my ears!
    This opportunity shall not pass!

"But 'Doc', I protested weakly.
    Consider this alteration to your plan.
I will SELL YOU cows of mine
    to graze upon your land."

Nope, he wanted me to own the stock,
    if I was so inclined,
Besides, he could make his living
    repairing 'carnage' cows leave behind!

His declaration stopped me short!
    It cause me to reflect,
about times when doing chores,
    with cows we risk our neck.

If you climb upon a bucking bull,
    you expect to hit the ground.
But, try to tag a bawling calf
    and its mother will knock you down.

If you stand behind a swinging gate
    and slap 'bossie' with your hand,
her kick will knock you on your back.
    You have had a full 'body slam'.

When you use 'slightly worn' equipment,
    like a head-catch, here's a tip.
Don't lean across the handle,
    or you will get a busted lip.

Try to push a cow through a chute.
    She may step back in your cuff,
then slowly back the length of you!
    Cow care can get rough!

When the new-born can't find dinner,
    you, trying not to cause alarm;
guide him gently to the dinner-sack, and
    the cow tries to break your arm!

Folks report you had an accident,
    When your cows dish-out the pain.
But, you know its not accidental;
    they mean to hurt you if they can!

So, 'Doc' will not own the cows.
    He is wise to avoid that fuss!
Besides, his living is secure.
    He has a full-time job repairing us!

******

John Beltz,   Poet, Reciter, Story Teller
2790 So. Hwy 157
Willow Springs, MO   65793

John is a Charter Major Member of the Missouri Cowboy Poets Association. John was born on a farm in Texas County Missouri. His parents were Ruth and (L. E.) Elmer Beltz. John and Jeannie, his wife, have two grown children.

John served in the U. S. Navy aboard the U.S.S. Lafayette County LST 859 in the West Pacific. He attended Missouri State and the University of Missouri in Columbia, where he received His masters Degree in Industrial Education.

In 1976, after sixteen years as a teacher and administrator, John chose to become a full time rancher in Texas County. Using the training of an educator and his experience as a rancher, John has developed a unique avocation of writing, story telling, and after-dinner speaking.

He has one book published entitled "The Bungee Dog and Other Poems." John is also a member of the National Story Telling Association.

NOTE: The illustrations of "The Bloater", "Elmo and Willie", and "Wild Cow Working", were done by John Beltz's friend Merrel Breyer.

OLD PARD
1997

It was in late October in '39, I was broke and times were hard,
About sundown, crossing the JD Flats, was the first time I saw Ol' Pard.
Asked him where the Z Bell was camped, in a river bottom shack,
Said five miles south, across the river, follow that wagon track.

From that time we had a lot of good years, riding with rain or azure skies,
Oblivious of the stories we were caching behind our squinted eyes.
This is some of what happened in those days, to me and to Ol' Pard
There were times when all seemed good and some were awful hard.

Eating breakfast by lamplight...flap jacks, coffee and stuff
Ol' Pard was chewing on a piece of meat...it was kinda tough.
He rolled an eye toward the stove and that old black skillet
Wondering what the hell it was, just before I killed it.

Came my turn to jingle horses...I'd see'em heading north
I strolled out and caught the night horse, getting ready to salley forth.
I saddled up that Flea Bit Gray...things don't always to as planned
'Cause there I was, on my head, eyeball deep in sand.

We were putting in some river fences...seems 'twas only yesterday
The ol' Cheyenne rose up that night and swept them all away.
Without our boots, we'd been dragging wire, through water to our hocks
Then spent the night back in camp, drying pants and socks.

We were running wild horses, including Sky Pilot and the Ridge Running Roan
Their only home was the Bad Lands...they knew every pass and stone.
We corralled them at Ol' Pard's camp, not knowing what was in store
Sky Pilot escaped one dark night...wearing Pard's new hackamore.

Each winter came the blizzards and when our ears began to sting
We'd daily keep a'dreaming of those cherished days of Spring.
Of the winter softened days of April when new calves were everywhere
Then we'd raise our eyes in tribute...thankful we were there.

Pard and I were camping on the river, re-riding for the old "Z Bell".
It was cold, a north wind was blowing, half a century later I would tell
How the river was all froze over...we had to cross it twice
Breaking trail both ways...busting through that river ice.

My Ol' Pard is gone now...he rode over the big Divide,
But one day in the Big Pasture, we'll be riding side by side.
He was a true friend...a cow man with few peers
I humbly thank Almighty God for all those happy years.

His old saddle rides a partition in a horse barn stall
It hangs where he left it...that long ago year in Fall.
Nearly obscured in the dusky dark, by cobwebs and with dust
The old iron spurs he hung on the horn are now red with rust.

We enjoyed many good years together...my Ol'Pard and me
'Til the Father up in Heaven called him home, dontcha see?
I wish we were back there in that river camp tonight.
Gosh, it seems awful strange...how the years have taken flight.

******

ECHOES OF THE TRAIL
1998

He sits, dreaming of his yesteryears,
          of cowboy's song and tale,
Hearing not the squeaking chair
          but the Echoes of the Trail.
Bad horses and blizzards,
          dry camps and flooded streams
Were all a part of his cowboy life,
          as he fulfilled his boyhood dreams.

He never lived in towns,
          with churches and trees all in a row,
Oft times the realm he called home
          was buried 'neath winter's snow.
Out on the broad prairie
          between the mountains and the sea,
The grass flowed on forever,
          blending into Eternity.

Of several races and various ages,
          they were a motley crew
Who sat on those cow ponies,
          'til they wore their saddles through.

Came the settlers with their wagons,
    barbed wire and their plows.
All too soon, no grass was left
    to feed their hungry cows.

Though it was a new era,
    to them it made no sense
To turn good grassland wrong side up
    and surround it with a fence.
Never waste your pity on cowboys
    who never heard symphonic tones.
They had their prairie music
    out where they'd one day lay their bones.

Yes, he's a broke down cowboy
    with hoary head and body frail.
Now poignant memories cause
    his cowboy heart to swell
As he sits and rocks and listens
    to a coyote's mournful wail
While it joins the ever-fading voices
    of the Echoes of the Trail.

*[Written in memory of those who were old timers
when I was a young man.]*

******

AN ODE TO OLD FRIENDS
1936-1986

I remember old saddle horses that helped to mold my life
Through all those many years, fraught with toil and strife.
There was Tomahawk and Peace Pipe, War Bonnet and ol' Tin Can,
Kube and Denver, Tom and Casey, Yo-Yo and Big White Man.
There were sorrels and bays, apps and grays, several paints and blacks,
One or two with a blue "glass eye," some wore saddle tracks.
There was ol' Tanglefoot, on crooked legs he onward blundered
And a bald-faced black with many brands, good ol' Kills a Hundred.

A feller 'pined, "He may be good, but pardner, dontcha see?
With them white eyeballs and a dozen brands, he's trading stock to me."
Well, one by one, these ol' friends have drawn their last breath.
Each now dwells deep within the silent realm of Death.

Came the day when my rifle barked in the early dawn.
My heavy heart was "on the ground," ol' Grasshopper, too, was gone.
There was a roan appaluce, we called him Li'l Joe,
With his forebears, the old Nez Perce, chased the buffalo.
There's a lump in my throat, again my heart is full,
Li'l Joe died on the horns of a spotted Mexican bull.
Time marches on, Life's vein follows a meandering course.
Still I recall the halcyon days, spent with each ol' horse.

As I ride past those bleaching bones, each in their lonely spot,
A gentle zephyr seems to whisper, "Please, forget-me-not."
In your final resing place, ol' friends, whose lives were freely given,
There's trees and grass and water for you in Horse Heaven.
I'll not be hearing their nicker at the corral gate this day,
'Cause my ol' horses, like my years, have quietly slipped away.

******

WINTER SUNSET
1990

The falling sun of the winter shortened day, a red globe, appearing to be precariously balanced on the high blue horizon of the distant Black Hills, as it casts its last feeble rays over the snow covered landscape. A sliver of silver moon hangs low in the western sky.

A lone rider wends his solitary way out of the cedar dotted Cheyenne River breaks, as a covey of sharp tailed grouse zoom low overhead, the hard feathers of their cupped wings whining like so many miniature sirens in the cold winter air. Without reducing their speed, they fly headlong into a ten foot drift on a yucca studded hillside, disappearing in a cloud of white. Here they will rest through the long, sub-zero night, insulated from the cold by the snow.

From the southwest in the nearby Bad Lands, a lone coyote gives two sharp barks, closely followed by a long, mournful howl. Constantly alert, it is always watching for food and danger, life or death, depending on eyes and ears, nose and speed for survival.

The rider sways easily with the movement of the fast walking horse, listening to the squeaking saddle leather as it blends in rhythmical time with the squeaking of his horse's hooves on the hard snow.

At the corral he steps down and opens the gate, causing the hinges to screech in protest. The raucous sound invades the quiet of the coming night.   He unsaddles his horse and unties and removes the rawhide hackamore. Taking them into the barn, he soon returns with a gallon fruit can of oats and half a bale of Western wheat grass hay for the chuckling animal.

He slaps the line backed buckskin on the rump with a gloved hand as he leaves the corral and closes the gate behind him. He walks toward the house where a square of light seems to be peering through the curtained window into the deepening dusk that is fast over-riding the fading daylight.

He pulls his old brown hat lower against the biting wind that cuts his leathery cheek like a newly honed blade, as he turns a sun-squinted eye toward the red glow left by the setting sun. The jingling of his spurs is muffled by the snow. His steps are short and choppy, induced by a lifetime in the saddle. The delicate perfume of burning cedar wood permeates the cold evening air. Galaxies of stars far above, seem to twinkle cautiously as they begin their nightly vigil.

Pausing outside the door, he stoops to pet the ranch dog that greets him with wagging tail and laughing mouth. Opening the door, his nostrils are assailed by the pleasant odors of freshly baked cinnamon rolls and frying steak. A coffee pot bubbles and gurgles merrily on the kitchen counter.

He kisses the weathered cheek of his white-haired wife of half a century, as she busies herself about the kitchen stove. Hanging his hat and coat on a nail near the kitchen door, he makes his way toward the dull red warmth of the big box heater, well filled with dry cedar and cottonwood. Rubbing his cold, numbed hands together, he relaxes in his rawhide bottomed wooden rocker.

Another day had passed......another Winter Sun had set.

******

"WEEDS IN THE CORRAL"
1995

Boys, if you can spare a minute,
Hearken to the story I tell.
It's about a pasture with no cows in it,
AND WEEDS GROWIN' UP IN THE CORRAL.

I don't need a brandin' crew,
Gone is the cowboy's lusty yell.
I sit and think of friends I knew,
WHILE WEEDS GROW UP IN THE CORRAL.

With old time cowmen, I used to ride,
They've long since heard Death's knell.
Just drifted West, o'er the Great Divide,
AS WEEDS GROW UP IN THE CORRAL.

Was a time, there were daughters three,
But the future no mortal can tell.
In their city life, they cannot see
THE WEEDS GROW UP IN THE CORRAL.

All alone, the good years gone,
Life is an empty shell.
Day by day, Time marches on,
AND WEEDS GROW UP IN THE CORRAL.

Seems 'twas all too good to last,
And boys, it sure is Hell,
To sit and think of all that's past,
AND WATCH WEEDS GROW UP IN THE
CORRAL..........

******

"THERE'S NO ROMANCE IN RANCHIN'"
1985

There's no romance in ranchin', oh ye city snob.
We're a bunch of Bad Land cowboys, out here doin' our job!

Sittin' all this long cold day in a worn an' squeaking saddle,
We're headin' for the winter range with a thousand head of cattle.

With lots of grass and water, we went smilin' through the summer,
Comes a blizzard in October that sure was a bummer.

With winter comin' early an' the weather gettin' rough,
It's time for chaps an' long Johns an' cowboys gettin' tough.

Each weather prophet's story sounds worse than the one before,
Promisin' cold an' snow an' blizzards an' weather we abhor.

That cold north wind was whistlin' as we came down ol' Quinn Draw,
A-stingin' an' a-burnin', as each breath went down our craw.

While pickin' up a "bunch quitter" that was tryin' to go astray,
I could smell that beef a'roastin', though it was hours an' miles away.

Gotta cross the river ice, a crick an' snow filled draws,
A-listenin' to them bawlin' calves a-huntin' for their maws.

An' we're lookin' toward more blizzards, choppin' ice an' shovelin' hay,
We ain't a-huntin' "romance," just tryin' to make this ranchin' pay.

When this winter's history, an' a new calf crop is on the ground,
We'll jerk our cinches up one more hole, an' be ready for another round.

[Written for my cowboy friends.....published in Rapid City Journal, October, 1991]

******

THE DEATH OF DAKOTA BELLE
1984

Many long years ago, Ol' Buddy, we awoke to the cold and gray,
Wrapped in our army blankets, wishing the war would go away.
B-26 "Cowboys," renowned as a special breed
Who rode across the shell-torn skies, on an aluminum steed.
Known as a "hot ship," those stub-winged aluminum brutes
Called "Airborne Coffins," "Widow Makers," and "Flying Prostitutes."

Hurrying to the briefing room, to learn the target for the day.
"This one will be a tough one, Boys," they heard the Colonel say.
One by one, they climb aboard, each to his given station
One by one, planes lifted off, to make a box formation.
Who, on this fateful day, would drink of the bitter cup
As the Nazis in their flak towers, begin to open up?

Messerschmidts at nine o'clock, buzzing like angry bees,
While more came in at four o'clock, Ol' Belle was in a squeeze.
Dodging fighters, evading flak, grim looks shroud each face
As each breathes a silent prayer, "Please, take us back to base."
Ack-ack guns belching death, from far, far below.
Puffs of black surround the Dakota Belle, as the shell bursts glow.

Left engine's gone, the prop is dead, they're depending on its twin
While flak and cannon fire rip Ol' Belle's aluminum skin.
Smoke and flames trailed her, she bucked like "Angels Sing,"
Ol' Belle was in trouble, she shuddered like a dying thing.
The fifties were still chattering, as she slipped into a dive.
Of the parachutes that opened, they counted only five.

This day's channel crossing would be Ol' Belle's final trip
And you, Ol' Buddy, like the sea captain, went down with the ship.

No tears were shed at the family plot, none said a last good-bye.
A lonely spot in the channel was your destined place to lie.
Out there in "no man's land" without a grave nor stone.
You're always in our hearts, Ol' Buddy, you'll never be alone.
Many years have come and gone, but this story I must tell
About a good Ol' Buddy, who went down with Dakota Belle.

******

"OLD HOUSES"
1990

Are old abandoned houses lonely? Do they ever cry?
Are they sitting quietly as they mourn, as they slowly die?
Sad and neglected, so quiet and so still.
Do they remember those in eternal sleep, 'way up on the hill?

Does a vagrant breeze, emitting a gentle sigh
Bring memories of yesteryear, that slowly passed it by?
Rain drops like tear drops, streak each cracked and dusty pane
Not unlike tears of sorrow, always shed in vain.

Does it remember winter, its wind and driven snow
A balmy dusk in June, bathed in sunset's golden glow?
Ask as you drive past one, sitting on some grassy knoll
Are old houses just "old houses", or do they have a soul?

Are old abandoned houses lonely? Do they ever cry"
Are they sitting quietly as they mourn, as they slowly die?

******

CREATE A LEGEND
8-8-'92

While the waning moon slides down the slopes of
the western sky,
Leaving only night and stars in its wake,
And the morning sun of a new day reddens the dawn,
Delve deep into heart and soul
To create a legend,
That memory of you not cease at the grave,
But be cherished by unborn generations.

******

Arnold "Buzz" Benson,   Poet/Reciter/Story Teller
Box 502
Jasper, Mo. 64755

Arnold Benson is a Charter Major Member of the Missouri Cowboy
Poets Association. He was born on his father's homestead, November 10,
1916, near Cedar Butte, Northwest of Wall, South Dakota. In 1919
his parents moved to a ranch in Belcher Draw, Northwest of Owanka,
South Dakota. He graduated from the Owanka High School in 1934,
one of a class of two.

In October, 1934, he enlisted in the 793 Co., C.C.C. He
cooked at a "spike camp" in summer for the crews that built three
trails up the flanks of Harney Peak. In winter he fired the camp
boilers and worked in the timber.

After his discharge in 1936, he worked on ranches in Conata
Basin, Battle Creek, Spring Creek, Cheyenne River, and Pine Ridge
Reservation. Where he drove the Z Bell "Pie Wagon" and cooked for
the branding and trail crew.

At the outbreak of World War II, he enlisted in the USAAF,
serving with a B-26 Medium Bomber Group for four years, three
years in Europe. He was discharged in late 1945, S/Sgt., six
major battle stars and presidential unit citation.

In November 1945, he married Marie Winans of Carthage,
Missouri. They purchased a ranch on Hart Table, Northwest of
Scenic, South Dakota, where they ranched for fifty years. They
have no blood children. They raised three Lakota sisters and have
twelve grandchildren and six great grandchildren.

He is a cowboy poet, a member of the Missouri Cowboy Poets
Association. He has written four books about ranch life and has
entertained in several states. A rawhide and leather braider, he
has made numerous cow whips, rawhide hackamores, hobbles, and bronc
quirts.

They are now retired and live in Southwest Missouri at
Jasper, where he does some writing and braiding.

They are affiliated with the Southern Baptist Church.

Many of you may know that some of my poetic nonsense appears in "THE TOMBSTONE EPITAPH". A publication often described, by columnists who should know, as the "best western periodical" in America.

Christmas has always been a special time for us, and I usually write something meaningful for the remarkable season. My poem for the edition has become a tradition and appears each December in the same format as it did originally.

We hope the intended message is clear and that you will also rest contended in the palm of the hand of God. And we pray that you have peace; His peace.

- Gail T. Burton

A COWBOY'S CHRISTMAS PRAYER

The worn and wrinkled cowboy
slowly shaved and combed his hair.
He picked the finest clothes he had,
and then he dressed with care.
He stomped into his new bought boots,
and he shrugged into his coat.
The others would have questioned him,
but his thoughts seemed quite remote.

He stepped out of the bunkhouse,
and pulled his hat down tight,
Then climbed aboard his private horse
and rode into the night.
The single footin' gelding
ate the miles without a pause,
And seemed to know the rider
had a most important cause.

Twenty miles on through the night
with the rider deep in thought,
The stars came out to guide the way
to the goal the ride had bought.
His horse stopped on a gentle rise,
tho' the rider pulled no rein,
And the cowboy raised his head to stare
'cross the quite lonely plain.

He crawled down off the weary horse,
loosed the cinch so it could blow,
Then he walked a yard or two away
and knelt down in the snow.

He crushed his hat against his chest,
raised his face up to the sky,
And then he started talking
like a friend was standing by.

"Lord, you see I rode a piece tonight
'cause I knowed that you'd be here.
Course you wuz at the bunkhouse too,
but on this hill ya' seem s'near."
"As I look acrost' this prairie
and see the things you've made;
Why! comparin' things us men has done
really puts them in the shade."

"I thank you for the love you show
in everything you do,
And I'm proud to be a top-hand
with a loyal happy crew.
I've still got all my fingers,
my legs are bowed, but tough,
Rheumatiz' ain't touched my bones,
and my mind is sharp enough."

Your spirit gives me comfort,
and I know that when I die,
You'll let me rest forever
at that bunkhouse in the sky.
Forgive me when I wander off,
like a wild jug-headed hoss,
And I pray you'll not give up on me
'fore I learn that you're the boss."

"I've rode out here to tell you
I'm thankful for a Savior's birth,
And to send you MERRY CHRISTMAS
from your folks down here on earth."
Then he mounted up and rode away
with a casual good-bye nod.
A cowboy, with his heart at peace,
in the palm of the hand of God.

******

Down near the Southwest corner of Oklahoma is the little town of Temple. Three miles west of town is East Cache Creek. I've spent a lot of time along East Cache Creek doing what boys should be doing when there's country to be seen, and growing up to be done. Dreaming of such times, and places, has kept me contented while others were succumbing to the stress of life.

PASSIN' THROUGH

A hoot owl sends his unexpected call
through the rustling leaves of the cottonwood
and a hundred unseen eyes study your silent
form beside the dying fire.

The hobbled horses grazing nearby
seem grateful for your company;
tho' it's doubtful they'll welcome
your attention in the morning.

Your drooping eyelids feel
the warmth of reflected heat
while you contemplate the vibrant pyrography
of a single glowing ember.

A grau beetle, called from his hidden cave
by the unfamiliar light,
wanders precariously close to the heated rock,
then jolts with jerking movements
to the coolness of spittle
near your outstretched foot.

Your back is cold.

You ponder the need of another
stick of deadfall on the fire
as you wrap yourself in your tarp',
and pillow your dull contented head
on your rolled up jacket,
while the haunting trickle of Cache Creek
flows into your unremembered dreams.

******

COWBOY LINGO

I've never heard a cowboy
sing out "woopie ti yo".
I've thought this situation over
and there's things I'd like to know.
Where do these sayings come from
that no cowboy ever said?
I ain't never heard one say these things,
I just guess it's things I've read.

And "ridin' down the canyon
just to see the sun go down'?
Why! if he's ridin' out for pleasure
he'd just ride on in to town.
Cowboys get accused of things,
and some just ain't true of course.
I bet you've never seen a cowboy
stoop so low to kiss his horse.

No cowboy ever come back:
"When you say that to me, smile!"
It's most likely that he'd break his jaw
and just lay him in the aisle.
"Pilgrim" ain't a word he'd use;
he don't "mosey" anywhere.
His revolver only shoots six times,
and no cowboy packs a pair.

That guitar he's a-strumming,
as he rides along the trail;
I've always wondered where he puts it
when he "ties up at the rail".
I've never seen a cowboy
drinking "red eye" by the shot,
I believe cold beer's his usual drink;
bourbon also hits the spot.

I suppose some folks think they
need to sweeten up the pot,
And add some color to the cowboy
just to make him what he's not.

Cowboys don't need buildin' up
to show off their natural trait.
Although they're rough around the edge
that's the part that makes 'em great.

A TALE OF WOUNDED KNEE

For twelve long years they fought and died
        while led by Crazy Horse
'till their final stand in the Black Hill land
        they lost their home by force.

Then at the end the Sioux were led
        to a point of no return,
and a lonely death from winter's breath
        was all they'd ever earn.

Crazy Horse and his last small band
        went into Fort Robinson,
but a dirty cell was worse than hell
        and he tried once more to run.

A cold bayonet on a soldier's gun
        was the warrior's final wage,
he'd fought and died as white men lied
        and his death a sordid page.

His parents returned the warrior's bones,
        and the heart that beat so free,
to the sacred earth of the Peoples birth
        near a creek called Wounded Knee.

For thirteen years he rested there,
        in his sad and lonely grave,
while brothers died and others cried
        for a life they could not save.

Then a tiny band made camp one day,
        as the freezing winter blew,
they were all alone, their fight was gone,
        just three hundred fifty Sioux.

At dawn they gave their weapons up,
        no thought to fight or run,
surrounded then by mounted men
        they lay down every gun.

When someone fired a single shot,
        it signaled men to slay,
as minutes flew the death toll grew—
        near two hundred died that day.

The old and young lay still in death,
but at last their souls were free,
the stream ran red as children bled
near the creek called Wounded Knee.

******

A SONG OF WOUNDED KNEE

I can see the sinking sun
as evening marks the closing of the day,
Caught upon the mountains
as the earth tries still to make the night delay.
Searching for a resting place
where the evils of the night can never go.
Wandering through the darkened sea
and waiting for the morning wind to blow.

Once my soul was happy
as I roamed the forest mountains and the plains,
Living as the eagle
with the blood of freedom rising in my veins.
Trying to believe their words,
and hoping that someone would hear my plea.
Running from the future,
running to my final home at Wounded Knee.

Waiting still I listen
for the coming of the spirit of my friend.
Watching 'cross the prairie
for the buffalo to reach the journey's end.
Hoping as the seasons change
that once again I'll hear them passing by.
Knowing yet that they have gone
I know they've joined my brothers in the sky.

I can see the eagle
searching high along the mountain for a home.
Searching without finding
for she knows that every resting place is gone.
Wishing that the land were free
and searching for the peace I'll never see.
Resting in this lonely place
forever waiting here at Wounded Knee.

Passing time has changed the land,
but still I wander sadly in this place.

Tied here to this holy ground
by bonds so strong that time cannot erase.
Watching trees that slowly grow
from tears I cried for things I tried to save.
Waiting for the hunt again
and praying for the kind of life I crave.

A hundred springs I've waited
as I watch the evening sun desert the day.
Walking with the spirit
of my brothers waiting here beneath the clay.
Feeling that I died in shame
and knowing that my soul is never free.
And blood has washed my brothers heart
resting buried here at Wounded Knee.

******

THE ROUGH LIFE

It was dark there in the line shack
When Randy Jones and Booger Red
On a cold wet winter morning
Slowly stumbled out of bed.
The path down to the bunkhouse
Was two foot deep in snow
And tryin' to light wet kindlin' wood
Was sort of touch and go.

Dirty clothes and broken tack
Were piled up pretty high
The coal oil lamp was empty
And the water bucket dry.

Randy said, as he looked around
The cabin thus bestrewn,
"Do ya ever figure you and me
Wuz born forty years too soon?"

******

THE JOCKEY

The green-broke horse just stood there,
Takin' in the morning sun,
As Booger Red climbed on him
To go ridin' -- just for fun.

Red was gonna make him run,
Or just maybe make him buck,
So poked him with his gut hooks
And that's when the lightenin' struck.
That horse didn't pitch or buck,
He just took off like a shot,
And left ol' Red a'settin'
Like a thought he'd just forgot.

Red lost a stir'p the first step
And the next he lost his hat.
And then he went to sailin'
Like a circus acrobat.
He lay there in the yard dirt,
Wonderin' how this came about,
When he heard ol' Randy Jones
Come to taunt him with a shout.
"I seen what happened to ya'
so just take it in yer stride.
I allow this goes to prove
You spur faster'n you can ride."

****

THE RED CAP

The boss had bought 'em tickets
On an east bound Santa Fe,
To bring back some breedin' stock
He had bought in Iowa.
Reached the eastern town at eight,
Where lots of folks were millin'
Round the railroad station gate.

Booger turned to Jones and asked;
"Who's them guys with fancy caps?"
Randy said, "They carry luggage
Or yer saddle, and yer chaps."
Booger took a second look
And asked Randy to explain,
"They don't look so tough to me,
How'd they keep up with the train?"

******

HORSEBACK THEOLOGIAN

Randy jones and Booger Red
Ridin' through a dusty town
Where two churches, side by side,
Were slowly falling down.

Booger said, "Them there churches,
Uh standin' there like twins,
Used to be one congregation
And they ought to make amends."

"They got a theologic difference
And it really caused a split,
And when folks try to reason
It shore don't help a bit.

They agree on booze 'n gamblin'
And what it takes to be a saint.
But one church sez there ain't no hell
And t'other th' hell there ain't."

******

PROCRASTINATION

In an old brush arbor meeting,
On a sultry friday night,
A bible pounding preacher
Called out with all his might.

"Who wants to go to heaven?"
He called out to the crowd.
But no hand was raised in witness,
And every head was bowed.

Randy Jones and Booger Red
Were way back in the rear,
They squirmed down in their seats
As he called out loud and clear;

"Who wants to go to heaven,
Will nobody go with me?"
But there was no recognition
Of his loud salvation plea.

The preacher looked at Booger Red
And asked for some reply;
"Cowboy don't you want to go
To heaven when you die?"
"Why shore I do", said Booger Red,
To the preacher's great delight,
"But we all thought you wuz gettin' up
A load to go tonight."

******

Gail "GT" Burton,   Poet Reciter, Author, Story Teller
P. O. Box 1500
Benton, AR   72018-1500

Gail was born at Temple in Southwest Oklahoma, when the state was barely twenty years old, and has been a lifelong student of Western lore. Burton has a basket of love for the Old West, a bucket of information from years of study and observation, as well as a cup full of experience which has equipt him to write poems about cowboys and their trials and tribulations.

Burton is the author of "Cow Pies and Candel Lights", a collection of poems and an album of the same title. He participates in Cowboy Poetry Gatherings from Texas to Montanna, and since 1988 has been a featured poet in "The Tombstone Epitaph", The national newspaper of the Old West. You can see more about Gail at his web page www.gtburton.com.

50 YDS SOUTH

You may have heard those Okies are a whole different breed,
Or that they come from genetically altered seed.
Most likely they're descends of survivors, of the world's weirdest race,
And I don't mean a people, but an event that took place.

Man has designed some crazy stunts in search for thrills,
And invented strange games to test competitive skills.
But bungee jumping and ice hockey, pale like the moon to the sun,
When compared to the excitement of the Oklahoma Land Run.

100,000 line up along the South Kansas border,
A few U.S. Marshals, trying to keep some kind of order.
The needy and the greedy and all walks of humanity,
Ten seconds and 50 yds from instant insanity.

When cannon and rifle shots signaled the start,
The best laid plans, started falling apart,
It was go for bust, opportunity knocks,
Off in a cloud of dust and a shower of rocks.

A mass of horse and man, and leather and steel,
A moving blur like a giant pinwheel.
There was a yell and a curse, and screams and prayers,
Things went from hell to worse, dreams became nightmares.

A legacy for offspring, a place for your wife,
Was quickly reduced, to a race for your life.
If a picture is worth, a thousand words from the mouth,
This will speak volumes of what happened, 50 yds South.

******

BUNK HOUSE CAMPAIGN MANAGERS

It was a routine evening around the bunkhouse before the hands hit the sack,
      Billy Joe and Nathan were playing cards, and Frank was mending on
some tack.
Mort was looking at a Shepler's catalog, comparing prices of some shirts he had
      bought.
Old Alvin was laying on his bunk staring at the rafters, seemed to be
      deep in thought.
He said, "Boys I've cowboyed now for over sixty years,
      I remember most of the good horses I've rode, I've turned a lot of bulls
into steers."

"Now I'm not the kind to quit workin', don't plan to ever retire,
    but every morning when I mount up, that stirrup keeps gettin' higher."
"I've always kind'a had a hankerin' to wear a lawman's star,
    I'm thinkin' of runnin' for county sheriff, see if I can trade my horse
    for a car."
"Some may think I'm an old has-been, and reackon I am somewhat of a relic.
    but I think I could do a better job than the kid that's runnin', he seems
    like a lazy young smart aleck."
"While the county may not be overrun with crime,
    there's a little cattle rustlin' goes on from time to time."
"And I think I know most of the "midnight cowboys" and how they operate,
    and they know me and what I would and wouldn't tolerate."
"What do you think?" Is this just an old man's foolish thought?"
    "If I should do it, what kind of chance do you think I've got?"
Billy Joe and Nathan tossed in their cards, Frank laid a'side his junk.
    Mort put down his catalog and pulled their chairs around Alvin's bunk.
Frank said, "Politics now-days is rough and dirty, worse than rodeo hockey,
    'course the fastest horse don't always win the race, a lot depends on the
    jockey."
"Now if you really want to do it Alvin, us boys will help you all we can,
    but if you're going to mount a serious campaign, we got to lay us out
    a plan."
"Runnin' for office costs money, so we've got to raise some dough,
    and the fellow with all the money makin' ideas, is our friend here Billy
    Joe."
Billy Joe said, "Well we could have an old fashion barn dance, put on a Ranch
    Rodeo or two, then I got some more ideas for things that we could do."
"We could have a mountain oyster fry, get some cowboy poets to participate,
    everyone could have a ball, charge fifteen bucks a plate,"
Frank said, "Polling is an important part of a modern well run campaign."
    Mort said, "I've poled hogs in Arkansas when we were running short
    of grain."
"I put those pigs on a pole, held 'em up to eat acorns off the trees,
    any poling we need done, for me it would be a breeze."

Frank said, "And we would need a "Dirty Tricks " department,
    because you've got to harass and irritate."
"I think the one to head that up is our friend Nutty Nate."
"He's got a reputation amomg all the local folks,
    for all the crazy pranks he's pulled and all his stupid jokes."
Nathan said, "I would love to do it, I'd have no mercy on the bleepin' bleep,
    I would accuse him of everything from stealing horses on down to
    molesting sheep."
"I would start a rumor he had scruples, perhaps even a terminal case,
    that would cut into his support among those who make health an issue
    in the race."

"I would put out the word that he was a Heterosexual Homosapien,
    That would cost him votes
    especially from the Religious Right, they always separate the sheep from
    the goats."
Alvin said, "Boys I'm going to do it. it sounds like lots of fun,
    if I'd known politics was this exciting I wouldn't have waited so long
    to run."
Frank said, "And if the exit polling shows that to defeat we're going down,
    we'll just take what's left of the campaign fund and throw a party on
    the town."

******

DINING ALONG 166

The Buzzards roost there below the tree covered ridge,
By a bend in the river near the Old Arch Bridge.
They are gorged and content on this summer night,
As they rest and prepare for tomorrow's new flight.

This is paradise for them, with eveything they need,
A roost within yards of the place where they feed.
The hills and valleys hold a bountiful coffer,
To stock the banquet table, 166 has to offer.

Buzzards once needed patience waiting for something to die,
Endless hours of circling there in the sky.
But today they ascend only to make their selection,
From the vast menu, laid in every direction.

There is raccoon and skunk and coyote and deer,
And turtle and snake and some other smear.
And rabbit and squirrel and armadillo too,
It all looks so delicious from their vertical view.

And mouse and rat and toad and frog,
An old house cat and sometimes a dog.
Ground hog and badger and possym galore,
Throw in a few birds, who could ask for more.

We change with the times and adapt to the culture,
So he's really got it made, this modern day vulture.
Man's custom when he dines, is to give thanks to the Lord,
A grateful Buzzard might also say, "Thank you Henry Ford."

******

THE COWBOY AND THE BIKER

The High Plains of Kansas, at a roadside stop,
Where cowboys come for coffee and the local news they can swap.

A big ugly Biker rode up on a modified HOG,
In a side car was a monster of a dog.

The Biker stooped and squeezed through the normal size door,
And the building creaked when he walked across the floor.

A cowboy wearing a beat up felt hat,
Looked outside and said, "What kind of dog is that?"

The Biker said, "He's a quarter Great Dane, a quarter St. Bernard,
That makes big like me without packin' any lard."

He's a quarter Rottweiler, a quarter Pit Bull,
That makes him mean like me and four quarters makes him full."

"He was bred special just for me,
Matches my size and personality."

"But that's enough about all that,
I don't like small talk or idle chichat."

Now I'm fixin' to soak up a case or two of beer,
So you guys shut up or get on out of here."

Well another cowboy drove up, as gentle a fella as you'll ever meet,
There was a little dog riding beside him there in the pickup seat,

They got out and the big dog growled a sound like yoy never heard,
But the little dog stood his ground just waitin' for the word.

When the cowboy said, "Sic'em.", they came together like as one,
And it was over almost as soon as it had begun.

The big dog lay dying, gasping for his last breath,
The small dog had met an untimely death.

The cowboy stepped inside, cleared his throat of a frog.
Said, "Pardon me, who owned that big dog?"

The Biker said, "He's mine, stay away from him, he's bad,
And I don't like the way you phrased your question, what you mean by had?"

The cowboy said, "I'm afraid my dog has killed your dog, I hate it the worst way,
But like the old saying I guess, every dog has his day."

The Biker said, "Look old man, I don't like stupid jokes,
Especially when they come from broken down cowpokes."

The cowboy said, "No joke, just a simple fact,
I feel real bad that I let my dog attack."

The Biker said,"My dog could whip a lion or a tiger or a grizzly bear,
There is not a dog that could kill him on the earth anywhere."

"And when I ride out of here astride my hog,
Settin' tall beside me will be my dog."

The cowboy said, "I'll help you load him if you want, but like I said,
He won't be sittin' up because your dog is dead,"

The Biker said, "Soppose there was a dog that could do what you claim,
What breed would he be, just give me a name?"

The cowboy said, "Chihuahua, just a little house pet,
He was kind'a aggressive, I'd had him neutered by the vet."

"The chances of him killing your dog does seem somewhat remote,
But apparently the little fellow just got lodged in his throat."

******

Harold Carpenter, Poet/Reciter/Story Teller/Trick Rope Artist
311 S. Spruce
Sedan, KS   67361

Harold was born in Chautauqua County Kansas in 1930, during the depression and dust bowl era, on a farm where all the work was done by horse power and man power. All his early years were spent working farms and ranches. Rope spinning was picked up at an early age of about five or six, and has been a lifelong hobby. Harold has written poetry for over forty years and has performed at hundreds of events since he started reciting in 1992.

This was written the night before a group of folks, re-riding the Chishoms Trail, crossed the Oklahoma line into Kansas, where they were met by fourteen of Jesse Chisholm's direct descendents. It was really a privilege to be a part of the event.

GHOSTS OF CHISHOLMS TRAIL

A hardy bunch of cowboys, and a cowgirl name of "K"
Left the Texas border for Kansas one fine day
They rode through Oklahoma on a trail that Jesse Rode
With Jesus as their ramrod, their trail boss was our Lord.

They had no fear of danger, no thought of cold nor rain
The rivers they were crossing, no man had ever tamed
But like the ones before them they knew this must be done
For man must not foget, how the West was won.

Ride on Ghost Riders, can't you hear ol' Jesse wail?
We're ridin' right beside you, we're the Ghosts of Chisholms Trail.

They had'nt traveled very far when one cowpoke was down
Rusty'd caught a flyin' hoof, they said, "Go back to town."
But like cowboys before him, he's full of cowboy pride
O' Rusty "cowboy'd up", said, "I'll finish out this ride."

Along this trail of asphalt one rider rode ahead
To make sure that the trail was clear, find them board and bed
But one day in the distance, they saw a posse grow
They were chasin' their trail blazer! Pam thought the light said "GO".

Rise on, Trailblazer, the posse's on your tail
You've got to push them riders out across the Chisholm Trail.

Ol' Sky said, "Our ancestors fought varmits, storms, and stampedes
But the trail today is different, it's "man" we have to heed."
Ed led the prayer of thanks each night for life of horse and man
Impatient drivers came too close, they just didn't understand.

Dave said, "Children listen! Can't you hear their voices ring?
A'whistlin' to them dogies as they drove 'em cross the plains?"

Sky said, "To know your future, you've got to know your past,
Kids, learn of your ancestors, you're growing up too fast."

Ride on Ghost Riders, Can't you hear ol' Jesse wail?
We're ridin' right beside you, we're the Ghosts of Chisholm's Trail.

Late one night at Milford, they caught up with the crew
They'd started at Red River, but there were chores to do
A herd of Corriente takes lots of food and care
But Mike and Cindy finished fast, rode hard to catch 'em there.

Now friends this tales not ended for there's so much to hear
Like Chick from Illinois, and the Seawrights in the rear
Young John that they call "Mascot", and all those in between
To make this ride of history, it really took a team.

Ride on, ghost riders, can't you hear ol' Jesse wail?
We're ridin' right beside you, we're the Ghosts of Chisholm's Trail.

******

RODEO COWBOY

You came in the arena, tall and proud, ready to ride.
I watched you with a feeling that I knew I couldn't hide,
As you rode by I watched you, and I caught your eye with mine.
You winked, and gave me that now famliar sign.

I can still see your face as you held me so tight
And whispered, "I love you, won't you stay with me tonight?"
My heart said "Forever", but I knew that with the dawn
You'd be on that ol' pony, and gone.

Rodeo cowboy, where are you tonight?
Are you still lonely, do you still love those lights?
When the last bull's been ridden, and you're standing all alone?
Do you ever think of coming back home?

When you left I placed a ring in the bag you had packed
Engraved with "My love always", I knew you weren't comin' back
We spoke few words in parting, just "I love you good-bye."
Then I watched you as you rode on out of sight.

Now at night I still remember as I hold my pillow tight
And wonder where the rodeo has taken you tonight
And when the dream has ended, and you've taken your last ride
Will you come back, and ride here by my side?
2
Rodeo Cowboy, where are you tonight?
Are you still lonely, do you still love those lights?
When the last bull's been ridden, and you're standin' all alone
Do you ever think of coming back home?

A PLACE THEY CALL PAWNEE

Come along with me and you will see a place they call Pawnee
With a wild West Show, the best Rodeo, and the Buffalo run free.
So if you're tired of the rush and worry
I am sure you will agree that the folks are fine and you'll unwind
In a place they call Pawnee.

Well, a man named Bill rode up the hill 100 years ago
Met an Indian man of the Pawnee clan and he smiled and said, "Hello."
Said, "If you're tired of the rush and worry, stay out on this hill."
Then he sold him his land, and he joined the clan
And they called him "Pawnee Bill".

So grab your coat, don't forget your hat,
Bring your horse and saddle too.
Ride among the trees and I guarantee,
When you leave you'll be brand new.

So if you're tired of the rush and worry,
I'm sure you will agree,
That the folks are fine, and you'll unwind
In a place they call Pawnee.

******

COWBOY ANGEL

Another angel made Heaven today
A young man in his prime.
We don't understand it now, but I know
You'll show us why in time.

Thanks for sharing him with us, Lord
He left good memories behind
Of a wonderful brother, father and son
Of a husband strong and kind.

Mom remembers holding him as a babe;
He learned to work from his father
He learned to be gentle, loving little sis,
Learned to gunfight with his brothers.

These family ways learned in his youth
Carried him through his short life

As he worked, loved and cared for the children You gave,
And cherished his beautiful wife.

So, tell him we love 'im and miss him, Lord.
Life won't be the same,
But he taught us a lot in his short time here
And we're sure glad that he came.

******

I KNEW AN ANGEL STRAIGHT-ON

He was a soft spoken man with an outspoken love
A smile that warmed up a room
Eyes that saw God's creatures
As flowers needing nurturd to bloom.

So he walked among us, God's Angel of Light
With a spirit of meekness and joy
Encouraging, helping, lifting us up
Reaching out to each girl and boy.

Such love is seldom seen
Always thinking of others
Looking for ways to teach us of God
Accepting each one as a brother.

He loved horses and wagon trains
Said they were "addictive"
Couldn't wait for the next one, he said
"Now that's the way to live.

He was a trader, didn't you know?
He'd take an old wagon in trade
Then make it fit for travel and such
Just like in it's youthful days.

God decided that he'd done his work
And called him to come home
But I'll always remember and thank you,
God above God above
For I knew an angel straight-on.

I DON'T WANTA FIGHT THAT BULL

I came out west ten years ago
Lookin' for a place to belong.
Next thing I knew there was a rodeo
Someone said, "Would you sing us a song?"

It wasn't long before my heart was planted
Deep in that Oklahoma dirt.
I said, "I wanta be part of the Rodeo
But Lord, I DON'T WANTA GET HURT!!!!!"

So Mr. Jestes won't you let me join,
I know you've got some pull
I wanna be a clown and make 'em laugh
BUT I DON"T WANTA RIDE THAT BULL!!!!

I'd be singin' songs , and tellin' jokes
Riding a long eared mule.
I wanna see them smiles, an' hear 'em laugh
BUT CAN SOMEBODY ELSE FIGHT THAT BULL???
'Cause I'm just a city girl!

Mae Lilly was a city girl too,
but she soon learned to shoot an' ride.
It wasn't long before Pawnee Bill
Had her ridin' by his side.

Well Mr. Jestes, I'm a city girl too
But I found me a big ol' mule.
I'll sing my mule and sing, an' make 'em laugh
BUT I STILL DON"T WANTA FIGHT THAT BULL!!!!

****

GRANDMA'S COWBOY

The cowboy climbs on the big black horse.
He can feel him quiver with rage.
This one called "Fury" no cowboy's rode
But today that's gonna change.

He checks the riggin', nods to the stands
   As if to say "Don't worry.
I'm a cowboy, and today's the day
   I'll ride this horse called "Fury."

He gives the signal, the gate opens wide,
   Fury bursts from the chute with a scream
Twistin', snortin', sunfishin' high
   In his eye's a menacing gleam.

The cowboy spurs him, his hand held high
   Ol' Fury responds with a leap.
The cowboy's holdin' his own on this bronc
   But that buckle ain't gonna come cheap.

For the hate-crazed bronc is determined to buck
   Another rodeo cowboy off
But this cowboy's ridin' for all he's worth.
   He'll show the bronc he ain't soft.

Then the sound every cowboy loves to hear
   The bell says eight seconds is passed.
The cowboy jumps off, takes a bow to the crowd
   Then he wakes from his dream at last.

He lies there in bed, a smile on his face.
   He'll make that ride someday.
Until then he'll dream of this ride every night
   And ride Fury each day in his play.

Then Grandma's cowboy climbs out of bed
   Don's his boots and jeans.
They'll go to the rodeo, he'll ride the sheep
   And ride the broncs in his dreams.

                    ******

COMIN' HOME FOR CHRISTMAS

She puts up the Christmas tree, and wraps the gifts with care.
Her heart is beating faster, she bows her head in prayer
He's coming home from somewhere, he's on the road she knows.
It seems like such a long one, this road called Rodeo.

Comin' home for Christmas, it's the best time of the year.
Jingle bells and Santa Claus can fill a heart with cheer
Rodeos call cowboys out on the trail all alone
But when Christmas comes around, he'll head for hearth and home.

He fills his tank with gas once more, and checks the trailer hitch.
Ol' Henry seems to sense they're close, his ears begin to twitch.
"Ol' boy," he says, "It won't be long, can't you feel it in the air?
Fresh hay for you, warm bed for me, and the families waitin' there."

Comin' home for Christmas, it's the best time of the year.
Jingle bells and Santa Claus can fill a heart with cheer.
Rodeos call cowboys out on the trail all alone
But when Christmas comes around, he heads for hearth and home.

As he pulls in the front gate, his eyes fill up with tears.
His little boy, ropin' imaginary cattle, usin' dad's old gear,
Through the window then he sees her, his wife who waits for him
And for this Christmas Season, the Rodeo's lure grows dim.

Comin' home for Christmas, it's the best time of the year
Jingle bell and Santa Claus can fill a heart with cheer
Rodeos call cowboys out on the trail all alone
But when Christmas comes around, he'll head for hearth and home.

******

RODEO YOU'RE A WOMAN

The lights are all turned out, the crowd has all gone home.
Out in the arena a cowboy stands alone
He's thinkin' of his ride tonight, 8 seconds he rode high.
The crowd lets out a mighty roar,
The cowboy smiles and sighs.

Somewhere in Oklahoma a woman sits at home.
She's thinkin' of her cowboy, wishin' he would phone.
She wonders where he is tonight, - did he miss his ride?
Or is he lyin' injured?
Her heart aches, and she sighs,

Rodeo you're a woman. You claim a cowboy's heart
But you're as cold as stone

He'll leave his home and family to join your trail of dreams
And when his body's broken, you'll leave him there alone.

An ol' cowboy stands watchin', the young men rope the steers.
His mind roams back in time to his younger years.
He'd roped and rode the best of 'em
He'd made the crowd go wild
He touches his prize buckle, and the old cowboy sighs.

******

Peggy Coleman,   Poet Reciter, Musician/Singer, Humorist
P. O. Box 122
Pawnee, OK   74058

Peggy is a musician, singer, song writer and humorist. She plays the guitar and is a fine singer of western, country, and gospel music. Peggy is a delightful performer, and is always very well received at every performance. Peggy is also a comedian with her hilarious character "Lucy" routine. She also presents a very delightful puppet show for children.

Peggy has performed at the Cowboy Hall of fame, and other festive events in other Western states.

DON'S CHUCKWAGON MENUS

SPIT SIRLOIN

One 12 lb. sirloin aged well with plenty of fat.
Put on adjustable spit and turn often to brown evenly.
Baste with butter as desired.
Cook for 8 to 8 1/2 hours or to desired doneness.

******

BREAD PAN APPLE CRISP

12 apples, peeled and sliced
1 1/2 to 2 cups sugar, depending on tartness of apples
2 t cinnamon
2 T butter topping
1 C flour
1 1/2 C oats
1/2 C sugar
1 C brown sugar
1/4 C butter

Stir together and spread over apples.
Cook for 20 to 25 minutes or 'til done.

******

COWBOY SLAW

3 heads of cabbage
4 large carrots
Shred cabbage and carrots. Mix.

Dressing:
>   3 C Miracle Whip
>   1/2 C sugar
>   1/2 C milk
>   1/4 C ranch dressing
>   1/2 t celery seed

1 medium carrot
1 small pepper

dash salt
dash pepper

Mix dressing ingredients.
Add dressing just before serving.

******

UP ON THE L & M

Now I's up on the L&M a few years back
Helping with the gather off the North flat.
We started early that morn
Fightin' the bushes, brush and thorns
Gathered and bunched for the bigger part of the day
And thought with a little luck
We'd be back at the home ranch by chuck.
As fate would have it things did go our way
Until the next day
When I was a separating those momma cows from their calves
And sometimes that's not so easy
When this 1300 pound Charolis heifer came running by like a rocket
Reached out and touched me right on the hip socket.
Dropped me there in the spot and I couldn't get up
So a couple hands came and picked me up and took me to the truck
Took me into the hospital, doc checked it all out
Said I'd only cracked that hip, but I'd be laid for several days.
As I pondered on my past fate
I decided that
When I'm up on the L&M
Helping with the gather
I dang sure ain't gonna leave my saddle.

******

GOIN' TO TOWN

Come along late September
'fore the winter snows fly
Pappy and I would hitch the team to the wagon
So we could go to town and get supplies
Now it was nearly 50 miles to town
That is as the way the crow flies.

And it took several days
But Pappy would always make sure we had a place to stay
Now we would sleep in the next morn,
'Cause we didn't have chores to do
And when we would get up Mother would get out her list
to make sure of things she wouldn't miss.
Pappy would have his too,
And us kids we were sure relishing this idea,
cause we would get to play with kids we hadn't seen in months.
And Pappy would make sure that there was something to do that night,
So him and mom would have some fun too.
An' he'd be up early the next morn, and have the team all hitched,
So we could head back home.
Now us kids we would be sleeping a lot, because we had been up
late the night before,
And when we got all rested we'd get to talking 'bout all the
fun we'd had
people we'd seen and how's we were looking forward to next spring
So would could do it all over again.

******

A TRIBUTE TO MY WIFE

Now there is a girl that I know
that I truly love so
And as each new day is born
she wakes me to greet the morn
she kisses me and sends me on my way
and is always glad to greet me
at the end of the day
She follows each trail I ride
and hopes that I see the other side
She's my friend and she's my lover
And for sure, there will never be another.

******

Don Collop,　　　　　　　Poet, Reciter, Chuck Wagon Owner/Cook
10419 Andrain Rd. 379
Mexico, Mo. 65265

Don is a Charter Major Member and one of the founders of the Missouri Cowboy Poets Association, and a member of the Board of Directors. He is also the current MCPA President for the two year term, July 2000 through June 2001. Don was born and raised in the farming community of Kirksville, Missouri. He followed the rodeo circuit in California during the 1970's. He and his wife Evelyn presently reside on their ranch in Mexico, Missouri. Don is a very colorful character who recites his own and the traditional favorites of the old timers. His hobby is teaching youngsters in hunter safety programs. He has a cassett tape entitled, "The Way It Was", and has a second one in process.

OLD COWBOYS IN TENNIS SHOES

Most old cowboys I know wear tennis shoes.
They cannot pop their whips
The way they used to do.
They walk with canes;
They creep with metal walkers.
They've bummed up knees
And banged up fingers
From hammering on things with gnarled fists.

They need new knees and hips
And carpal tunneled hands
Because they ache and swell
From bucking broncs and bales of hay
And battering years of cows and life.
Brutal work has stiffened hands,
Being hit by butted gate,
Smashing muscles and bones.

Sock roping a big toe
And easing the sock upon their feet,
They can't bend over to pull on their boots,
But if they get them on,
They can hardly take them off.
So, their boots and hats,
They gather dust and fuzz.
"But," they say, "I'll keep'em 'til I die."

Old cowboys view the world with gray film eyes.
But when talk turns to cattle prices
And weather patterns,
Backs straighten; eyes clear.

They quietly laugh at scrambling up
A bull wire fence to escape
The charges of pure bred cows
That are unpredictable as bulls penned,
Chafing for breeding season,
Bulls that have forgot the butting order,
Fighting for days until
Old Big Balls dominates again,
A domination that takes longer
With each passing year.

Young bulls seem docile under strain.
Sometimes they turn to charge him

Who carries the protein cubes.
Without warning, a ton of bullish
Unpredictability flares nostrils
And charges with lowered head
As if bidding time to dominate.

With an alertness that was
Learned so young and trained so deep
That it seems genetic,
The boy walked with the bulls.
He showed no fear though quaking inside
Because all this bluff might not work.
He was ready to drop the sack
And climb the closest fence or hay rack.

These docile old cowboys
Forget their aches and pains
To debate the price of stockers in '41.
They drop the winter of their years,
And animate about the drought of '52.

Those were long rainless months of hanging on,
Few cows, no grass, no ponds.
Month after month,
They hauled water for the few cows kept,
City water on a flat bed truck,
A quarter a thousand gallons
Poured into Butler tanks.
This reminds us of
The eternal ebb and flow of flood and drought.

They waited for the weather break.
Some paid for seeding clouds;
Some hired fading old Comanches
To perform rain dances never done
When they were Lords of the Plains.

They exaggerate the rains,
How fast the grass renewed.
They tell ribald jokes of pissin' dust
Until the rains returned again.

In their heads, not diminished or forgotten,
These old tennis shod survivors
Carry years of high powered bulls
Bred to sister Middle Pasture cows
That dropped high priced calves.

These old bullish boys sometimes
Know the pride their off spring have for
Sire and Dam who can tell at a glance
The genealogy of three year old cows.
"Your dad's the best damned
Cowman in the county,"
Spoken as if county encompassed the world.

They've lived their simple lives of the poor,
But they are rich in soul and mind.
Their feet rooted in good grass and soil,
They're like mesquites,
Without the beauty of pines or elms
Or spreading chestnut trees.

Plain, ordinary mesquites,
Majestic, gnarled survival,
Have adapted to drought and wind.
They have endurance and strength easily overlooked
By those foolish for glitsy fashion
Or air brushed perfection.
Like mesquites,
They don't just survive.
They multiply.
Times pass.
Customs change.
Men die.

But this old species
With creeky knees and aching hips
Pass their boots and genes to grand kids,
Who often hardly know heifer from bull,
But they will know in time to survive.
These return to their roots;
They form a stubborn few
Who will keep a new Old West alive.

******

RANGE FIRE

The racing fires began because
They burned the prickly pears unwatched
Whipped by southern winds,
And restarted by rolling cow chip embers,
Which kept a generation of pioneers
Alive in bitter winters.

The flames devoured miles of grass and fence.
The bunk house is now an empty spot
Where grass will grow again.
An almost rainless prairie creeps back;
Because mesquite grass remains a constant.

The stucco house escaped the fire.
Once the hub of an active ranch,
It was built over a now dry cistern,
That became a haven for rattlesnakes,
Rumbling spring and fall like seasonal storms,
When boots boomed on hardwood floors.

The house still stands,
An aging derelict,
Needing a bath and shave,
Mutely staring into space,
Wondering where life and time have gone,
Looking seedier as years fly by.

The stench of burning flesh is gone now
From a silent, empty kitchen.
The outer skin on the boy's leg
Had rolled down with his Levis,
Caused by the thoughtless
Click of a Zippo lid and
A stupefying spin of the flint wheel.

Sudden shock!
A treacherous lazy blue flame
Played around the mouth
Of the gas tank opening.

One adrenalin kick knocked the nozzle out,
Pouring liquid fire onto rocky ground.
With mindless fear of razing ranch,
The older boy had capped
The fascinating flickering,
A snake's tongue dangerously darting.

These soft and gentle looking
Flames were smothered
In one exciting, frightening,
Century long moment.
The brief relief was
Shattered by a scream.

Searing fire on the boy's ignited leg
Was finally snuffed out
With tow sack slaps.

In early morning memory just before dawn,
The dreamt smell of burnt flesh and gas
Begins another bitter day.
I still can hear the silent wail,
That destroyed layers of innocence.

The mad dash over country roads to town
Matched the meteoric passage of time.
A young tree was almost grafted new.
Like others which swept across fence lines,
This fire burned mostly grass and wood,
But it left intact childhood body and soul.

******

A MAN HAS GOT HIS PRIDE

Bill walked away from the job he liked best,
The only job he ever really wanted.
He walked away holding his head up high
And standing really tall.

He knew in life you often can't have it all.
He had regrets.
He felt bad for what he had to do.
This he would readily admit,
But a man has got his pride.

The foreman had died in early fall,
Leaving Bill as the top hand on the ranch;
For many years Bill had ridden for the brand.
The old Boss Man rode up in a big fancy rig.
A real shrewd businessman he was.
Every angle he knew how to take.

About who the next foreman would be,
He had already made up his mind.
But the dollar sign
Sometimes casts a long shadow
Over the judgment of this kind of man.

He knew young guys lived longer than older men do.
So, he offered the job to the foreman's son.

With sadness in his eyes, Jim looked at Bill.
This job, he said to the Boss Man, was my dad's.
But he left boots too big for me to fill.

Mr. C., you've asked the wrong man
To head up your spread.
Bill has been like a father to me,
Even when mine was alive.
Big Jim refused the job, and then he took a ride.
One thing he knew for damned certain.
Old cowboys have got their pride.

The Old Man wavered for only a moment before he said,
Bill, you've always been a faithful hired hand;
So, the job is yours if you'll just give me the nod.
And over my ranch, you'll become my new ram rod.

For a minute Bill looked down at his boots
As if thinking about what he would say.
Then he stared straight into the eyes
Of The Man who for years had signed his paycheck.
"Mr. C., for all these many years,
I have cared for all of your stock;
Every white faced cow I know by sight,
And I've doctored most of them back to health.
I've searched for and checked on
Every cow that has dropped a calf.

The fences are all up because I do my job right.
The posts are solid, and the barbed wire is tight.
The water gaps are all back in place,
No longer pushed loose by floating drift.
Just this morning I made sure of that.
We got three hard inches of rain last night.

I've really liked ridin' for your spread,
And I would have run things real good.
As foreman, I would have kept
This ranch in the black.
As for Jim, I love him like a son,
Even more now than I did just an hour ago.

All of my life I've paid my debts,
And all of my life I've paid my dues.
On important things I won't be driven,
And on some things I can't be led.
So under these conditions, I'm sorry to say
There's absolutely no way I can stay.
Because a man has got his pride.

Bill walked away with a stone in his gut.
He knew that moving to town would change
His life in ways very profound,
But he'd raised his kids to do what was right.
They'd know this here walk was not done out of spite.

Bill stocked food in a grocery store.
He pumped gasoline in a filling station.
To the farms and to the ranches,
He delivered fuel in a red Texaco truck.

Years later Bill would say to his son,
I've watched you grow up to be a man,
And I think you'll make the right choices.
But there's one thing
I really want you to understand.

You know I finish whatever I start.
I liked that job better than any I ever had,
But on that fateful and catastrophic day,
I had no choice but to walk away
Because a man has got his pride.

On most days since I've hauled gas to the ranches.
This shore ain't my idea of a good job,
But I still get to see the cows on the hillside,
And I still get to see the lush green grass in the valleys.
I still get to see the crimson sunsets on the rollin' prairie.
Every day I breathe the air that is fresh,
And the open road makes me feel what sets me free.

There are some things more important in life
Than having a good horse between my knees.
Every minute for the rest of my life,
I can look any man straight in the eye.

Even if the job is diggin' ditches,
Even if town work means dull and tedious tasks,

No job can ever mean more to a cowboy
Than standing tall and holding his head up high.

Sometimes I feel really sad,
But I think clearly pretty damned quick.
You see, being a cowboy is a frame of mind,
And a cowman has got his pride.

You don't have to have fancy titles
Or a general's medals on your chest
Or have your very own page in history
To prove you have great renown.
For me being true to the Code of the West
I'll have plenty of stars in my crown.

I always try to take life in stride.
As you surely must know by now
But, don't you never never ever forget
You don't have to bow down to nobody
Because a man has got his pride.

******

AN OLD COWBOY CROSSED OVER THE BAR

The old cowboy crossed over the Bar,
But before he did, he had made
The promise of his life.
He pledged to care for his loving mate,
For almost sixty years, his faithful wife.

A soft and gentle haze
Had settled slowly over her;
For only a very brief moment,
Did she comprehend what he had said.

He promised. He promised
That he would take care of her,
For as long as he did live.
"Doctor you've got to make me well;
I made a promise that I must keep,"
Said this tough old cowboy,
As he struggled to hang onto
What little strength that he had left.

A promise is a promise,
A sacred trust not to be broken.
So he held on,
Enduring pain, month after painful month.
He grew increasingly frail,
And then he became much more frail
Until Death released him
From the promise that he had made so true,
Keeping his wife at home much longer
Than he really was able to do.

Three long days after his burial,
Holding hands, my wife and I
Walked to the banks of the Brazos,
Just steps away from the home of
The old cowboy in tennis shoes.

Near the bottom of the slope,
Nine wild turkeys grazed
As peaceful as the dusky breeze.
They were alert at once as we neared the edge;
Nine wild turkeys, so awkward upon the ground,
They rose so very majestically in flight
And flew westward over the Bar.

Once they had crossed the wide shallow river,
Three times three wild turkeys
Glided down into the cedar breaks
That grew beyond the salty stream.
They were three times the Resurrection
For this old faithful cowboy.

On that very same day we visited the grave,
Covered with the flowers of love.
His wife, my wife, my daughter and me,
We looked at the striking paradox,
Beautiful fresh cut flowers
On the desolate grave,
As the dusk began to settle in
And the windless night drew nigh.

Something moved from
Flower to flower.
An insect at first we thought.
But no!

It was a hummingbird
That was much too early in the season.
It gathered nectar from the dead.

We were silent in the mystic silence.
We held our breath as we watched.
As suddenly as it had appeared,
It rose above the tomb
And flashed away toward the sun
That faded in the west.

Others must now tend to the stock,
But the cattle that the old cowboy drives
Are not the demon herds
Of the Sons of the Pioneers.

Mortal life is much too short,
But, oh, thank God!
Life now is eternally long
For the old Cowboy who has just
Crossed over the Bar.

******

HENYAN GHOSTS

Fifty years have past.
Oh, God! What changes creep upon us.
Weeds are five feet tall
Around a house that once had been a home.

Sudden, sharp memories!!
Two quarts of rattles were cut off each year.
I have the clear image of Lady,
Lying stiff, her head swollen.

My father had spent our last dollar
To buy me a Boston terrier pup
Before I walked my first steps.
Lady was the tough survivor
Of earlier rattler venom.

Lady woke us from our sleep early in the night
Because she barked her highest pitch.
. An open door revealed a six foot diamond back
Coiled on the back stone step.

My dog attacked;
She yelped with the strike,
And then she attacked again.
A second yelp!
My father smashed the serpent's head.
Before Lady could attack another time.
The past had repeated itself.

Two years before this dreadful night,
A smaller rattlesnake had crawled too close;
And Lady was struck protecting her litter of pups.
Then, I felt a four year old's fright
At the sight of Lady's grotesque head.
I was scared by her venom sickness heaves.

This time, however, would be her final fight.
Through our troubled sleep
We heard her painful moaning
Into the early morning hours.
Lady went gently into that moonlit night.

An old saw says,
"If the snake bite's on the head,
The dog won't die."
Bull!!
Next to the sturdy field rock barn,
We found her dead
Underneath the loading chute.

My Dad had wept hard heavy tears.
At my young and guileless age,
I could not understand.
A lone mesquite now marks her spot.

The house is now as dead as my Lady.
I can hear a hundred rattler ghosts
Slithering alongside of
This tall, two story stone house.

It is as silent as the Henyans,
A family of stone mason ranchers,
Who built this home.
I hear a rattler spirit inside the house.
Father and son had struck
Until the snake was dead.

Now the house is as still as Midnight,
Lady's contemporary.
The cat had stalked the snake beside the well;
Midnight's head was lowered,
Body suspended in mid stride.
His tail made its constant, hypnotic motion.
This was the primordial crouch against
Timeless time's enemy.

The snake was coiled;
Its head, the deadly triangle, was raised.
Staring its non-blinking glare,
It must have sensed a furry death
But could not loose the spell.

I broke the natural magic;
Afraid for my cat,
I crushed the snake's head with a rock,
Interrupting nature with a human act
As ancient as this feline attack.
Rhythms as old as time,
The snake's long length had writhed for hours
Like a loser caught in fate's grip.

Near where Lady died,
The once clean pens
Are filled with mesquites.
The posts have loosened in the rocky ground.
Carelessly left unlatched,
The gate now droops
And swings at a breeze's whim.
It is battered and bent by time and wind.

The barn is much less impacted by time,
Except for the flapping, rusting tin roof,
Revealing corrosion caused
By infrequent, but relentless, blowing rain.

Even after living and working the best we can,
We sometimes know the mark we make in life
Is little more significant than
The hole left in water when our hand's removed.
Wind tears blur my view and propel my mind's eye
To see the innocence of my youth.

******

COLD MORNING SADDLING

In the predawn hours feeling all alone,
He had to check the water gaps.
At ten above on this sleeting morn
The boy was chilled zero to the bone.

Through his chattering teeth, he grumbled
"The coldest spot of any place on earth,
Is astride the most maddening horse alive."
He breathed out a frozen groan half mumbled.

He sensed the horse was about to fight.
Little Joe, you fat, oat fed,
Pre dog food and glue son of a buck breathe out!
Or your eyes'll bug when I jerk the cinch up tight.

You've got that smug glint in your eye
Just before you break into your freezing morning
Stiff legged,
Crow hoppin',
Bone jarrin',
Teeth chippin',
Four short jumps
That makes me think I'm gonna die.

You devil bred cayuse,
You dumped me once to the frozen ground.
Because you puffed your belly out,
I foolishly left the cinch too loose.

I'll lead you through the open gate.
I'll ease my foot into the stirrup,
Quickly I will stomp down my foot.
And yank up the cinch before it's too late.

Try to feel your frosty morning oats now
You mousy buckskin sneaky nag.
I'll wrap the reins so tight around the horn
You cain't take your usual morning bow.

******

SPURS CAN MAKE THE MAN

Randal and Yellow Jacket each time
Wheeled and turned;
They spun on a dime
And gave back change.

Randal swayed
And matched the horse's every move.
They were an unbeatable team.
Everyone around could tell
That horse and rider
Had never worked so well.
This year pink eye
Had been a plague.
So, Yellow Jacket spun and chased,
Never letting a cow get by.

The cowboys knew just what to do.
Each sick eyed, white faced cow
No matter the move they might try
Was sent running into the chute.
They doctored them all,
Painting around each infected eye.
A circle with black Sixty-two.

In his light-gray Stetson hat,
And in his spit polished boots,
The Boss Man in his Cadillac sat.
These herefords were the champion
Blue-ribbon prizes of his life.

The warm spring day
Thawed the Old Man's frosty soul.
The Old Man grabbed up
Randal's brand new cattle prod,
A tool that could drive the cattle wild.

The two boys watched with anticipated glee.
They knew Randal's self control would be tried
Right before their very eyes.
They couldn't wait for what they were to see.

The Old Man jabbed the cattle prod
To a prize registered Hereford cow
And crashed her down the line.
Every cow almost knocked the header loose.

Now, Randal was a straight forward sort,
An independent cuss
Who could charm or agitate
In less than a minute's time.

He was a top foreman,
Very protective of the
Herd of Hereford cows
Under his watchful care.

The horse had worked up a lather,
Like the man on top of him.
He glowered down at the Boss Man.
Who had scared another Hereford cow for life.

He sensed his foreman's growing irritation.
The Old Man nervously thought out loud that
The horse was really doing fine,
Hoping to extract himself from this situation.

Randal exhaled in a long whistling sigh,
Thinking what's a man to do.
By gad!
If you were hemmed in between my spurs,
You'd work good, too.

******

I USED TO BE A COWBOY BLUES

I walk alone in city shoes.
Trudging along these filthy streets,
I don't feel like a cowboy anymore.
This makes me want to run in full retreat.
Instead, I sing I once was a cowboy blues.

Now, I read a different stock report.
No longer do I feed the fighting bulls,
Penned away from their herds of cows.

This memory constantly at me pulls.
I'm battered by bearish markets and court retorts.
For moving away, I've paid my dues.
No longer each morning can I hear
A gentler, kinder Tube Rose news.
Now, I hardly know what I held dear.
My heart aches with I used to be a cowboy blues.

The Sons of the Pioneers have sung my life.
For now I'm chased by vicious, demon herds,
My mind seems ready to explode.
In thickets of bricks I hear discouraging words
Where gangs stir up inner city strife.

My soft hands work dull and deadening jobs.
I sit all day in rolling chairs.
Longing for the plains, my heart throbs.
My life's consumed by city cares;
An indifferent blues is chanted by urban mobs.

I no longer look over rolling plains.
Because I've moved from coast to coast,
And I'm compelled to travel again,
I'm always far from where I love the most.
All around I see pain on pain.

No longer any horses do I ride.
I can't sit the saddle with legs so straight,
I've lost the time to reach my stride.
On my frayed nerves city noises grate.
So little is left for me to feel much pride.

Ole Garth's song is mighty true.
Cowboys didn't used to wear designer shirts;
Back then we wore Levi's, not 501's, not 502's.
And cowgirls didn't dance in mini skirts.
I hum I once was a cowboy blues.

My world is far from the mesquite tree.
I ache to wear boots, not spit polished shoes.
But as long as I have memories, though they depart,
For as long as my mind roams free,
I will continue to be a cowboy at heart.
I'll always sing I want again to be a cowboy blues.

******

BLACK DOGS

The small and wiry, hawk nosed man was old and thin.
He hunched down low in the car seat,
Looking really frail.
Tight lipped and squint eyed,
His hat, pulled down low to shade his face,
He stared straight down the highway,
Never saying a word.

His boisterous and happy wife from a loud family of
Ozark practical jokers had died young
After the death of their fourteen year old daughter.

His wife was all that he was not
But what he really wished to be.
After her death, he had shrunk into himself,
Slipping back into his normal dark moodiness.
For him much of life then dried up on the vine.

As they drove down the road,
He saw a silo on a farm.
It reminded him of the past.
So, he began to talk;
He talked about the woes
Of the Great Depression years,
When nobody had money for anything.

He said that government projects
Had kept poor folks alive,
Whether they built the Hoover Dam
Or built stone fences around the city parks
Which stand like mute monuments
To times gone bad
Which then had dropped from bad to worst.

He talked about Bonnie and Clyde,
Who were two bit crooks turned into heroes
By people who were down and out.
Rumor had they robbed from those who robbed the poor,
For banks foreclosed on ranch and farm and home.

Quietly laughing underneath his breath,
He quickly warmed to
His story of a left handed bet
Made during those terrible times,
When he and oldest son worked side by side.

The project foreman for grain elevator repairs
Was angered because farmers and
Cowboys had turned into carpenters,
As they slaved to make a wealthy man richer.

The foreman had pitched a fit about bumpkin bungling,
Swearing to pay $5.00
To any sod bustin' son of a bitch
Who could saw a straight line.
This was money that took a week to earn --
If a man could find a job.

"With the wrong hand I won that bet,"
Chuckling out loud at left handed contempt
Suffered usually in silence.
"I only refused the money once.
He respected me after that.
I was the only man who dared
Or was fool enough to take the saw in hand."

"Look at that dead dog beside the road,"
Deadpanned his granddaughter.
"Helen, do you think we could stop for a beer?"
Asked as if the sight of the big dead black dog
Reminded him of mortality,
And he would savor one more beer
Before he left this vale of tears.
He was a small beer man,
Maybe one or two beers a month at most.

Miles further down the road,
His beer was only half finished.
He was a real slow sipper.
He saw the scattered remains
Of a truck tire run flat.
Looking slyly at his granddaughter he said,
"Whoopee! Look at all them dead dogs."

She was surprised by the humor
Of a man who seldom made a joke.
"Grandad, no more beer for you."

******

DARK MAGIC

Dark fertile plowed ground
Hammered the depths of my senses.
Without warning the Kansas scene
Exploded in my consciousness.

Mulched wheat straw disked
Into damp, black soil
Is memory's elixir,
A fragrance never forgotten.

Once I drove through the Kansas plains
By a harvest moon.
No wind blew, but I knew that
One of God's tenants,
Unknown, unseen by me,
Had stirred Dark Magic.

The tilth was right.
The sweet smell of warm,
Moist humus made by
Wheat straw plowed under,
Beckoned to my soul.

For this flat land
I felt a kinship
Stronger than blood.
Rejuvenating!
Intoxicating!

Instinctively I slowed,
Almost fearing to stop
Lest some ancient, fantastic force
Be unleashed in some
Unknown, mysterious way,
Either to harm or help.

I felt this same exilaration
On my first airplane ride.
When I was seven years old,
A Piper Cub had landed on wheat stubble
In a three hundred acre cut.

Two by two we took turns in this aerial ark.
We soared like Isaiah's eagle,
Viewing fence lines perfectly drawn
As if by the divine Architect.

Holding my breath,
I felt that Great Heart beat
Above the drone of the plane.
Nothing was between me and eternity
But a barbed wire fence,
Strung in mini scale.

I saw the tiny sheaves
That I had drug for adult arms
To stack into sturdy shocks
That would withstand the daily winds.

Random shocks of bundled sheaves
Became straight lines.
Horizontal, perpendicular, diagonal.
Below toy white faced cattle
Grazed, all the cows
Facing the same direction
As if a child had been very observant.

Tiny combines wheeled along,
Reels whirling and clouds of dust flying.
Toy trucks lurched to catch
Dry bits of golden manna,
A visible sign of God's bountiful promise.

High above, I saw them like ants at work,
Scurring about slaving for the
Instinctive urge to produce.
They readied for the cold months,
A preparatory time
For the cycle to begin once more.

The sprouted germ had
Become germ again,
This is the generative force of eternity,
Compelling season to follow season.

My spirit had soared,
Never to be the same again.
My arms virtually became wings.
I was just old enough to comprehend;
I could almost taste
This untamed, unnamed power.

The perspective in miniature
That I had just experienced
Re-adjusted itself
As the plane lowered to land.

At the age of twelve
On an "M" Farmall,
This boy completed his own cycle,
Stirring his own Dark Magic
That forever remained a part
Of his deepest soul.

Years later on that
Dark Magic Kansas night,
This boy closed adult eyes
To re-experience the exuberance
Of innocence, not lost, but reshaped.

In a moment, memory and
Spirit had given wings
To imagination, the same that
Compelled mankind in the past
To leap from cliffs with gossamer wings,
To shatter on intoxicated ambition.
But the Wright brothers' dream endured
Until success at Kitty Hawk.

Western pioneers, their feet planted
In good grass and soil,
Dreamed of fertile successes.
This Dark Magic
Sustained those persistent
Wilbers and Orvilles of the Plains.

******

Jimmy Couch,   Poet/Reciter
2709 Vermont
Joplin, MO   64804

Jimmy Couch lives in Joplin, Missouri, and has taught in the English Department at Missouri Southern State College since 1970. He was born in Baylor County, Texas, and until young adulthood, lived on a ranch where he helped with all of the ranch jobs: working cattle, bucking hay bales, and harvesting wheat and oats. Jimmy learned responsibility at a young age, feeding out and showing 4-H Club steers for ten years. Farming and ranching have always been the basis for his work and religious ethic, developing his reverence for agrarian life. Writing about rural life and its people gives a keen sense of reality to Jimmy's poetry. With his poetry, he works to contribute to a Western revival that is evident in current cowboy poetry.

HORSES IN THE WIND

Horses in the wind, shake heads and bound,
their noses and their ears sense wiffle sounds.
They twist and turn, beauties with flowing manes
who dance ballets in space to winds refrains,
then snort fierce gusto as they come unwound.

Like Pegasus the flying horse they soar
across the fields, they cantor, spirits roar,
they pace, then whirl two axial spins again,
                    horses in the wind.

Their feet with metric motion tap the ground.
They gallop as if chased by tracking hounds,
equine allegro--on only natures rein,
They are so free, their exertion without pain.
as they trot around the barn, then back around,
                    horses in the wind.

******

WINTER COWBOY POETS PASSE

Cowboy poets come in from the cold January storm
...dry out your clothes by the fire,
stand over here where it's warm.

Unpack your bag of rhymes and cheer
Stew is cookin', taters, and meat from a steer
Hot brown bisquits for soppin' or buttered with honey
Hummmm.....quick lick your fingers, it's good and runny.

That's how it is at this Cowboy Poet meetin'
Soon as you've eatin'...it's your turn for speakin'.

******

Jennie Cummings   Poet/Producer
P. O. Box 1022
Mountain View, MO   65548

Jennie Cummings is the sole Honorary Life Member of the MCPA. She is head of the Mountain View Arts Council, and is the producer of the Missouri Cowboy Poets Association Annual Gathering at Mountain View. Jennie is also the delegate MCPA contact with the Missouri Arts Council, as well.

WAITING FOR THE PEAR TO FALL

Like a silent the sentinel on a lonely hill,
The gnarled old pear tree stood.
Having endured the test of wind and time
Its fruit was true and good.
And on any given night,
A number of pears will fall.
Till the grazing herd makes their rounds next day
And consumes them one and all.

One kind of poor and timid old cow
Hangs back from the rest.
She avoids the pecking order established
By younger, stronger cows I guess.
But when the rest of the herd is through feasting
And moves on she remains.
With uncommon diligence and patience,
She stands there and she waits.

How long her patience must endure,
No one can ever tell.
She knows that sooner or later,
Mr. Newton's law must be upheld.
And like a soldier at attention,
She stands there straight and tall.
Her eyes intent upon that tree,
Waiting for her pear to fall.

The forces of wind and gravity
Will finally do their trick.
When a juicy pear lands with a thud,
She pounces on it quick.
Her diligence has paid off,
She's won her reward without a fight.
You can almost see a twinkle in her eye
As she relishes every bite.

How we all could take a lesson from that old cow,
On the virtues of patience and faith.
And believe that good things will really come,
If we only patiently wait.
And trust in our Creator,
Who promises to provide us with all.
And know that if we just have faith,
Some day our pear will fall.

THAT AIN'T MY COW

My partner in that cattle business and I
Were cutting and sorting one day.
When he notices this poor old gaunt looking cow,
Limping along and making her way.

" Just look at that old bag of bones!
Why, she ain't worth a bullet to shoot her.
You're just wasting hay on that old crip,
I can't believe you ain't moved her.

"You're plumb silly to keep such a critter,"
He chastised me with a shout.
"Just look at her mangy, scarred-up hide,
With every rib a-poking out."

Why you keep these old gummers,
Is something I'll never know.
She'll be coyote and buzzard bait,
The first day it comes snow."

"You ought to take her off to market today,
Though she surely won't bring you much.
Ain't fit for butchering, she can't raise a calf,
Might use her for dog food and such."

Well, you'd have thought that old cow was personally responsible,
For all the ills of the world.
And I listened in contemplative silence,
As one verbal tirade after another was hurled.

"You're absolutely right," I agreed.
"That cow should have been sold long ago.
With her one bad eye, and busted up hoof,
It's a wonder she can even go."

"Yes, I must agree with your assessment
Of this pathetic creature for sure;
Just one point of clarification though,
That ain't my cow, - she's yours."

******

LITTLE GUYS

We don't have twenty hired hands
Gathering strays from all the breaks.
Just me and my horse, and a few closed gates,
Are usually all it takes.

And our spread's not measured in sections,
But in mere acres I'm afraid.
It's not the King Ranch or the Padlock,
But we're proud of it just the same.

Our herd doesn't number in the thousands,
Double-digits will have to do.
And they're not all registered pure breds,
We do have a mongrel or two.

My old mare's no national champion
No futurities has she won.
But she rides the fence and moves the cows,
And always gets the job done.

Some days we spend in the saddle;
Others in the tractor seat.
There's hay to be mowed, and raked, and baled,
For our cattle have to eat.

We have to fix our own fences,
And pitch hay in the summer's heat.
And work a job in town to boot,
Just to make ends meet.

We've pulled calves in icy blizzards,
When it was over twenty below.
And watched our taxes keep going up,
While cattle prices stayed low.

So, no, we're not big ranchers,
Or big farmers by any means.
We're just little guys, trying to get by,
And realize our dreams.

******

THE STEWARD OF THE LAND

He doesn't plant from fence row to fence row,
Like some of his neighbors do.
He leaves a little cover there,
For the quail, and the rabbits too.

He fertilizes his pastures each Spring
And limes them in the fall.
He knows you can't keep taking,
And never give back at all.

Though he has a tractor and equipment,
He's been known to bend the rules.
And he works his garden every Spring,
With a team of big, Missouri mules.

His cattle still graze green paddocks.
You won't see them cramped in little pens.
He still gets his milk from a Guernsey,
And eggs from his laying hens.

He does a lot of things the old fashioned way,
And others may not understand.
He may not be a modern day farmer,
But he's a steward of the land.

******

WHEELCHAIR COWBOY

I was in our local farm and ranch store,
Just browsing through the aisles.
When I happened across this feller in a wheelchair,
He greeted me with a smile.

We were both there looking at farrier's tools,
Nippers, and rasps, and such.
And I listened as he talked to me;
That day I learned so much.

It had been years since the accident,
That had claimed his ability to walk.
But it hadn't diminished his spirits,
His love for people , or talk.

A pair of house shoes now took the place,
Of cowboy boots on his feet.
But the weathered hat pulled low on his face,
Said here was a man who wouldn't be beat.

The lines on his face, and his callused hands,
Said "Cowboy" in every way.
And I couldn't help feeling a sense of awe,
As I listened to him that day.

He told me about the contraption,
He'd contrived of pulleys and ropes.
How he used it to hoist himself horseback.
He spoke of his dreams and his hopes.

Of how he had managed to keep his little spread going,
After all these difficult years.
He still had his horses and a few head of cows;
They were well worth the sweat, and the tears.

As we parted that day, he shook my hand,
With a grip that was strong and sure.
And I left a little better having met him;
The Wheelchair Cowboy, may his spirit endure.

******

DON'T SEE BUT ONE

The rancher stopped at the station,
His gooseneck trailer in tow.
Then went inside to pay for his gas,
And maybe get a fresh cup of joe.

His jacket was frazzled and faded;
The pockets all pooched out with hay.
His hat was pulled low against the cold wind;
It was sweat stained and had seen better days.

His boots were lace-up packers,
Down-at-the-heel, worn, and scuffed.
Still bearing evidence of where he had been,
A layer of manure and muck.

Inside he met another fellow;
They greeted with a nod and a smile.

This guy was wearing a hat and boots too,
Though of quite different style.

His feather-topped hat was perfectly creased,
Like the day it had come off the shelf.
A buckle as big as a dinner plate,
Was centered on his concho-lined belt.

His boots were those pointy-toed roach killers,
With loud metal taps on the heels.
The leather was scaly and shiny,
Could have been shark, or maybe an eel.

It was then that a youngster of four or five,
Spied the two gentlemen in boots and hats.
He pointed and tugged at his Daddy's sleeve.
Said, "Look at the cowboys, Dad!"

His father stared for a moment.
Then he said, "You must be mistaken, son.
For try as I might, and hard as I look,
I'm afraid I don't see but one."

******

I'VE BEEN A RANCHER

I've been a rancher
Most of my life.
I've known my share
Of worry and strife.

But it's been a good living,
And one you can't beat.
And I've done what I had to
To make ends meet.

I've hired out to neighbors;
Both those who farm and ranch.
Took work when I could find it
Seldom passed up the chance.

I've mowed cemeteries;
Cut brush along the road.
Come harvest time
I've hauled grain by the load.

I've worked as a nurse,
And an EMT.
I've been a soldier,
And served my country.

I've even sold vegetables,
And tilled the soil.
(Don't say it too loudly.......
My cowboy friends might boil me in oil.)

And no, I'm not a big or wealthy rancher,
And probably never will be.
But I thank God for my blessings,
And this life He's given me.

******

COWBOY SONNET

Fact is I'm a cowboy poet.
My rhymes are the simple sort.
And for those of you who don't know it,
I'll give you a little report.
My words aren't fancy or flowing,
Eloquence is much to be desired.
On the finer points of verse I'm unknowing;
On the forge of life my words are fired.

With tales of barbed-wire and bovine adornings,
And thousands of bales to be bucked.
Of cold-backed horses on Winter mornings,
And landing face down in the muck.
But I'm sure Mr. Shakespear would have bees in his bonnet,
Were he forced to endure a cowboy sonnet.

******

TO RIDE A HORSE NAMED SATAN

My nephew from the city was visiting,
Said he'd like to go for a ride.
So I caught up and saddled a horse for him,
And as I pulled the cinch up tight,

Said I've been trying to break old Satan here,
For nigh on six months now.

You just climb right up there, boy
And take him for a round.

Well his eyes got wide and his face got white.
There was no longer any cause for revel.
It was plain to be seen, he wasn't too keen,
On the thought of riding a horse named after the Devil.

About then my conscience got the better of me,
I felt a deserved twinge of shame.
This is a good and gentle horse I told him,
And KC is his real name.

Well since that day I've often pondered,
The times I found myself hesitating.
Whenever I was faced with the prospect,
Of riding a horse named Satan.

I don't necessarily mean a real horse,
Some bucking, snorting Diablo.
With venom in his eye and hate for man,
The draw of some hellish rodeo.

No, I'm talking about the stumbling blocks,
That we encounter most every day.
The wanes that crash against us,
As we sail life's stormy sea.

And how many times we're often faced,
With such a situation.
When we must conquer our fear and put it aside,
And climb on board a horse named Satan.

'Cause you know the Lord has told us,
We can do all things through Him.
Who strengthens us in our time of need,
When our courage is waning thin.

With God as our refuge and our strength,
There's just no cause for debatin'
For we'll pass the test when we're called upon,
To ride a horse named Satan.

******

Richard Dunlap.   Poet/Reciter/Singer/Musician
3427 S. 240th Rd.
Louisburg, Mo. 65685

Richard is a Major Charter member of the MCPA, He was was the first president, and one of the founders of the MCPA. He was raised on a livestock farm, and has been working cattle most of his life. He now runs a cow-calf operation in Polk County. He has performed at Cowboy Poetry Gatherings in five states. He is currently working on his third book of poems, which chronicles the "little guy", the family farmer and rancher, who is constantly struggling to make ends meet. Richard is a song writer as well as a poet. He plays a twelve string guitar and sings his own, as well as the old traditional songs. Richard is also a member of the Springfirld chapter of "Cowboys For Christ."

SORE FEET

We'd been working cattle all day long,
And all of us were beat.
The boss said he was going home
To soak his aching feet.

We'd penned a heifer, due to calve,
Would check her later on,
After we'd had dinner,
And our company all had gone.

Well, our company knew cowboys,
Knew their day is never done,
So we all went to the barn
To see if labor had begun.

The boss was driving up just then,
He didn't see us there.
He went to leap out of the truck,
His foot paused in mid-air.

For it came to his attention
That he wasn't there alone.
He looked very embarrassed,
He had thought we'd all be home.

He'd gone home, cleaned up, had dinner,
But that heifer stayed in mind,
Thought he'd best return to check her,
She could calve now anytime.

As he stepped out of the truck,
He was a picture from the West,
He only lacked a sheriff's badge
To pin upon his chest.

The jeans he wore were Levi's
In the classic cowboy cut,
And his shirt, like other cowboys,
Had those snaps all down the front.

A Western belt, hand-tooled,
 Bore his name across the back,
And his face was tanned to leather
 Beneath a Stetson hat.

What then marred the picture,
 Had us trying to hide grins,
And the boss looking so flustered,
 Agitated, and chagrined?

With just one more item
 His ensemble was complete
Wore his wife's pink satin houseshoes
 On his tired and aching feet.

******

CATTLE WORKING

Horses snorting softly
 Send a warning to the cows,
That round-up day's beginning,
 And they're being gathered now.

The Texas dawn's still cool
 As old Sol begins his rise.
The scene that was in shadows
 Comes alive before our eyes.

Conversation has been muted,
 The hour far too new.
Upon the morning stillness
 Not a voice cared to intrude.

But now among the muffled thud
 Of hoofbeats in the dust,
Noises native to the day
 Into the air are thrust.

Orders being issued,
 Riders fanning out in pairs,
Start gathering and bunching up,
 Some hold the herd there.

Around the herd loping,
 Other riders hit the brush,
To search for hidden cattle
 That were missed in the first rush.

'Midst raucous shouts and whistles,
 Slowly on the herd moves mute
To working pens where against their will,
 They'll be put through the chute.

Calves from cows are parted,
 With loud voices they protest.
None has the slightest inkling
 As to what will happen next.

With skill from years of practice,
 Each calf is so quickly done,
Ear-marked, shots, cut, and branded,
 Then back to his mama run.

As the day progresses,
 Cowboys joke and sweat and cuss,
The work flowing ceaselessly,
 Despite hot sun and dust.

When finally the work is done,
 The herd put out to graze,
Weary teams of man and horse
 Back to headquarters laze.

******

HOT IN TEXAS

That day was hot in Texas,
 Tempers flared to match the day,
When that bunch of steers we'd gathered,
 Broke, and tried to run away.

There were seven of us riding,
 None of us in the right spot,
Except for my husband,
 Who found cause to chew me out.

He threw a curse word to the wind,
 I caught it on the breeze
And hollered back at him,
 "Don't you dare to cuss at me!"

He slid his horse to sudden stop,
 I pulled mine to a whoa,
And we had us a discussion,
 Horses standing nose to nose.

A couple cowboys heard us,
 And rode up to watch the show.
The others noticed something up;
 Soon all had drawn in close.

The cattle were forgotten
 In the midst of our exchange,
Entertainment's free but far between
 Way out there on the range.

But those Brahma steers had seen their chance,
 Hit the timber in a rush,
When we finally pulled our hands up,
All'd escaped into the brush

We left them there that day,
 Let temperature and tempers cool,
Can't swear we ever found them all,
 Could still be one or two,

Hidden 'mongst those mesquite thickets,
 Thanking lucky stars and us,
For that diversion we created, and
 Laughing at us from the brush.

******

GROUND TIED

Mane flying, stirrups flapping,
 Buck came pounding down the road.
He jumped the cattle guard with ease,
 No rider was aboard.

As he raced off to the barn,
 We raced off to the truck
Fearing the worst for Jim,
 The rider of old buck.

And our fears were compounded
 When the boss we did meet.
He said that Jim had left
 With a rifle, case he'd see

That pack of stray dogs that'd
 Been killing calves and sheep.
But Jim was new to cowboying;
 Buck had an ornery streak.

No one before had fired a gun
 Between old Buck's ears,
And the though of what could happen
 Only added to our fears.

We could picture Jim lying there,
 A broken, bloody mess,
And almost certain of the worst
 His where'bouts tried to guess.

As we turned into the pasture
 That Buck'd tracks had led us to,
We spotted Jim walking
 And his injuries seemed few.

We asked what had happened.
 Said we thought that he'd been thrown,
He replied that he'd dismounted
 Dropped his reins, and Buck had flown,

Back towards the barn, left him a-foot,
 Showed no hint of remorse.
That unfaithful, untrustworthy,
 Just plain cantankerous horse!

He was glad we came to find him,
 Though a cowboy just a while,
He's learned to detest walking,
 Every yard seemed like a mile.

Relieved to find Jim safe and sound,
 We took him back, Of course,
He was in for lots of ribbing
 About ground-tying his horse.

******

THE LIGHT IN THE WINDOW

We've been riding, checking cattle,
 Now the hour has grown late,
Darkness is descending fast,
 And landmarks getting faint.

Shadows in the breezes sway,
 Blend cattle, trees and brush.
The evening star is shining down
 Upon the twilight hush.

I've no need to guide my horse,
 He knows the way as well as I.
In the distance, 'cross the miles,
 From a window, shines a light.

It promises a welcome warmth
 Despite the valley's chill.
My horse's pace has quickened.
 He seems to sense my will.

Saddles creak in rhythm
 With the clop-clop of shod hooves.
Coyotes begin howling
 As we pass a stretch of woods.

Towards home we ride, towards light and warmth,
 Across the dark prairie,
Bodies tired, but hearts content
 In quiet comaraderie.

******

A BAD DAY

A neighbor called one morning,
  Said our fence was on the ground,
And somewhere 'mongst his weeds and brush,
  Our yearlings could be found.

I saddled my colt, Lucky,
  Don saddled up his mare,
And we rode across the pastures
  That divided us from there.

He hadn't lied about the brush,
  We looked for quite a spell,
Then found our strays along a draw,
  Thought things were going well.

Lucky's eyes were on the cattle,
  One ear turned upon them too,
Head down, he was all business,
  Till that weed hung on my boot.

Of course it was a thistle,
  And it snapped him in the flank,
With a grunt, he bounded skyward,
  While my heart and stomach sank.

He soared so high, my ears popped,
  But then, to my surprise,
As his front end started downward,
  His hind end was on the rise.

I flew out of the saddle,
  Over horn and pommel rose,
In very present danger
  Of crash landing on my nose,

For I came to rest on Lucky's neck,
  My head was hanging down,
If I didn't change direction,
  I would end up on the ground.

I summoned every resource,
  Willed each muscle to hold tight,
Used every ounce of strength I had,
  To push myself upright.

Now, there I sat on my horse's neck,
 The horn behind my back,
My reins were dragging in the dirt,
 Soon realized their lack,

For Lucky went to spinning,
 Couldn't figure what the heck,
In the whole year I'd been riding him,
 I never rode his neck.

His eyes were large as saucers,
 Though not quite as large as mine,
And I couldn't stop this dervish,
 Whirling faster all the time.

'Bout the nineteenth revolution,
 Saw no help was on the way,
Don was doubled over laughing,
 We had clearly made his day.

I hollered, "Help Me. Help Me,"
 Don responded with a "whoa,"
And Lucky stopped immediately,
 Why hadn't I said so?

I thought the worst was over,
 And slid slowly off my perch,
But only added fodder
 To refuel my husband's mirth.

I was in another pickle,
 Just as bad, or maybe worse,
My right heel hung 'neath the saddle horn,
 As my left toes touched the dirt.

I wasn't then a dancer,
 And I'm still not one today,
But those splits would be the envy
 Of a student of ballet.

Again, I had to call for help,
 My hero came to aid,
No attempt to hide his laughter,
 As he freed my captive leg.

If you ever meet my husband,
 I am sure you'll hear this tale.
Even twenty-some years later,
 It has never become stale.

And with each and every telling,
 It's enhanced in the recall,
If I had to do over,
 I'd prefer to take the fall.

******

DOUBLE UP-SET

Possum was no part a cow-dog,
 Though a mix of several breeds,
And she's never helped with cattle,
 Running rabbits was her speed.

Though she'd never helped, she'd never hurt,
 We never felt a qualm,
Whenever we went horseback,
 Good old Possum tagged along.

We rode out to hunt a heifer
 Who'd gone AWOL from the herd,
As usual Possum ran beside,
 For rabbits on alert.

We found the cow and rabbit
 at Exactly the same time.
The rabbit jumped to get away,
 Ran into Possum's side.

Her trajectory and impact
 Were just right to save his meat,
When he crashed into Possum,
 He knocked her off her feet.

Then, was gone before she got up,
 Left her looking all confused,
That rabbit didn't play fair,
 He had gone and changed the rules.

Don't know what that dog was thinking
 As she got up off the ground,

But she took after the heifer,
 To far pastures they were bound.

Never barking, never biting,
 On that heifer's heels she stayed,
'Cross two pastures, through three fences,
 Kept her going the wrong way.

We got close enough to throw a loop
 Around the heifer's neck.
She seemed almost relieved
 As we started on the trek.

To the pasture where she'd come from,
 She led docile as a pet,
And Possum trailed along beside,
 Not done cow-dogging yet.

The rope was dragging in the dirt,
 'Tween horse and cow was slack.
Possum got caught in the rope
 And flipped upon her back.

With that jolt, regained her senses,
 Never cow-dogged after that,
But then again, no other rabbit
 Ever knocked her flat.

******

NEEDLED

We arrived down in Texas
 In a wave of April heat,
Found instead of milk and honey,
 Cactus, locust, and mesquite.

By August, ponds had dried up,
 Brahma-cross cows, lean and lank,
We were moving to fresh pastures,
 Where they'd drink from steel tanks.

We gathered up one bunch of cows,
 The tally was two shy.
My husband, Don, and I rode out,
 To find them 'fore they died.

We rode together, side-side,
  Across that Texas spread,
Upon his head a Stetson hat,
  No hat upon my head.

I'd listened to his lectures
  On the need to wear a hat,
But disdained such head apparel,
  For it crushed my hair-do flat.

Plus, it took a special talent,
  And I didn't have the knack,
To ride through brush and out again,
  With head-gear still intact.

Riding thus, we found the cows,
  A wild and roguey pair,
With no bent or inclination,
  To be driven anywhere.

We out-flanked them, got them moving,
  Towards the gate that we'd left down,
One obliged, went through the gate,
  The other, ducked around.

She was heading for the timber,
  Don hollered out to me,
"Turn her back!" He'd watch the gate.
  She beat me to the trees.

Then Don did get excited,
  Knew I'd let that cow escape
Went to shouting inspiration
  From his post there in the gate.

While he ordered, "Watch her, Watch her,"
  I forgot to look to see
If my horse and me together,
  Could get safely through the trees.

Of a sudden, something struck me,
  Felt a sting above my brow,
Found two locust thorns embedded,
  But I didn't lose the cow.

Apprised Don of what had happened,
 He responded "Bring the cow,
I'll take the thorns out later,
 But we've got to pen her now."

I caught that roving bovine,
 Turned her, put her through the gate,
Don pulled out his picket knife,
 I rode to meet my fate.

One thorn he dug out quickly,
 The other wouldn't come,
He'd remove it with a needle,
 When our working day was done.

To his litany of "I Told You So's,"
 I mounted, thinking that,
I'd have spared myself much torment,
 If I'd only worn a hat.

******

THE BIG BLACK BULL

The big black bull, as the way of bulls,
 Was not where he belonged,
So, Gary, Don, and I rode out,
 To remedy the wrong.

We found him with no problem,
 He was grazing with the herd,
But it seems that he had bonded,
 And he couldn't be disturbed.

We whooped, kiyied, and hollered,
 Finally got him all alone,
But he lit off for the timber,
 Had no hankering to go home.

Gary loosed his rope and shook it,
 His jaw was set and firm,
Said he'd bring that old bull back,
 If we'd wait for his return.

So we waited in the open,
 Heard some noises, and we thought
They'd both be coming shortly,
 Had no doubt the bull was caught.

Then Gary rode out of the woods,
 His rope again was coiled,
No bull upon the end ot it,
 His clothes were kind of soiled.

As he slowly jogged back to ue,
 His face was all a-flush.
He asked if we had seen
 What had happened in the brush.

Ah, now our interest was aroused,
 But, no, we hadn't seen,
He'd gone too far to turn back now,
 He had to spill the beans.

He said he'd raised his arm to rope,
 His loop was open wide,
And hung upon a cedar branch
 As he had galloped by.

Before he knew what happened,
 He was lying on his back,
Jerked out of the saddle,
 When his rope ran out of slack.

He sure was glad his horse had stopped,
 He hadn't lost his mount,
But the bull was in the timber,
 Though we'd better drive him out.

******

DAY HELP

The foreman had misgivings
 'Bout putting Louie on Ol' Red,
But Louis pushed those doubts aside,
 "I'm not afraid," he said,

"For when I was about fourteen,
 I rode a horse, you see,
And like a bike, you don't forget,
 Just give the reins to me."

He stepped into the stirrup,
 Which was higher than he thought,
And pulled himself up with the horn,
His muscles getting taut.

As he flopped down in the saddle,
 Ol' Red's eyes flew open wide,
He left there running open,
 Taking Louie for a ride.

A cow bolted from the herd,
 And Ol' Red's instincts kicked in,
He raced to turn that cow around,
 Poor Lou was looking grim.

His hands were frozen to the horn,
 His reins were hanging slack,
The foreman sped to Louie's aid,
 'Fore Red turned that cow back.

He called to Red to "Whoa now,"
 Red came quickly to a stop,
Lou pried his hands loosed from the horn,
 And from the saddle dropped

He left Red to the foreman's care,
 He'd walk back to the lot,
Said "I thought that I remembered,
 But I guess that I forgot."

******

Carol Ellis,   Poet/Reciter
16581 Freedom Rd
Willow Springs, MO   65793

Carol Ellis, and her husband Don, worked together running cattle ranches in Oklahoma and Texas before settling down on their own ranch in Texas County Missouri in 1984. They now ranch their own stock, and Carol performs at gatherings, and civic events reciting her original poetry.

THE COWBOY AND THE LADY

He wasn't a very pretty sight,
Standing there by the side of the road.
A cowboy without a horse, just didn't look right,
With only a saddle to be rode.

But Ole' Cookie had "cut him loose"
On his way back to the ranch.
Without a pony, he wasn't much use,
And he thought he might stand a chance,
To catch a stage coach into town,
For a hair cut, a bath, and a shave.
The end of spring round-up had just come around,
And he had two weeks worth of grit, and grime,
And his hair just would not behave.

He'd used a company horse for the round-up,
Then he turned him in when he was through.
It seemed like he hadn't seen soap and water since he was a pup,
And burnt hair and hide, was all the smells that he knew.

Well the stage coach came along, and he flaged it down,
Threw his saddle on top,
And climbed inside headed for town.

He sat down on the seat
And just settled in well,
When a voice said, "No need to be discrete,
What is that horrible smell?!"

Across the coach, in the opposite seat,
Sat a lady of the upper crust,
Dressed all in frills, so nice and neat,
And wrinkling her nose up, at him in disgust.

The cowboy knew what she was talking about,
Bt he just looked at her and grinned,
Then said, " Mam'm, there's no need to shout,
Maybe one of the horses broke wind."

Oh! This was more than she could stand,
And a cold, hard stare resulted.
Then she said, "I'll have you know, young man,
I didn't get on here to be insulted."

He hid his grin under his old hat's brim,
Then he said, when he was able to talk,
"I didn't either, Ma'm, and if he does it again,
We'll both get out and walk.

******

BUB'S BULL RIDE

In Oklahoma, in '51, at least in our little corner of the state,
We had "Open Range".
And to some of us it worked out really simple and great.

Now open range simply means you can let your livestock roam,
As far as they want, without restraint,
If you don't have much pasture at home.

So you "earmarked" your hogs, with your registered mark,
And branded your horses and cows.
Then you rounded them up in the spring and the fall,
For the offspring of your heifers and sows.

These "outside" animals, or so they are called,
"Bunched up in herds of their own kind,
And roamed around from place to place,
Eating what grass they could find.

I have three tales, or stories, or yarns, that I rell of these times,
At least three.
This one I tell, I can vouch is the truth,
I know, for it happened to me.

A herd of these "cows" were cooling their hocks,
In the shade of great-grandpa's old barn.
Some lying down, chewing their quids,
Some switching their tails at the swarm.

A bunch of us boys were hangin' around,
Trying to think of something to do.
The school year was over, and summer was here,
With it's sunshine and skies of bright blue.

Of course there was me, and my big brother Russ,
And our cousins, Junior and Tub,
And one other kid, I don't remember his name,
SO I reckon I'll just call him Bub.

Someone spoke up, I think it was ol' Russ,
And said, "Let's have us a show.
Let's catch that young bull, and take us a ride,
And have us a rodeo."

Sure 'nuff in the ranks of the herd,
Was a little ole knotheaded bull.
He was rangy and mean, a real buckin' machine,
And with oneryness he was plumb full.

Well, we needed a rope to capture our prize,
Most any rope would have been swell.
But we located one, just the right size,
On the bucket of Aunt Mandy's well.

Next we needed a handle tp hang on to
While upon the bull's back we rode.
Something to wrap around the bull's girth,
To make sure we didn't get throwed.

There on the wall of great-grandpaw's old barn
Hung a buttline, plain as could be,
Coiled up like a snake, hangin' there in the dust,
On the fork of a harness tree.

Now anyone who has driven a wagon team
Knows what a buttline is
But if you don't know, I'll try to explain,
If you don't get in a fizz.

The check lines are ribbons of leather,
That reach from the drivers mitts,
All the way down the outside of each horse,
And snaps to the bridle bits.

Each line has a buttline attached to it,
It's leather too of course,
And it snaps to the inside bit,
In the mouth of the opposite horse.

This steering system, I think, is the best I ever saw,
When you pull on the "gee" line,
Both horses turn right
And left, when you pull on the "haw".

The buttline we found was sorta frayed one end,
Where the rivits had been tore out.
But it was long enough for the job,
And the leather was still pretty stout.

Well a couple of us rode that little ol' bull,
And he gave us a pretty good ride,
But "Bub" said. "Whoa" when it came his turn.
"I'm afraid this will hurt my pride.

That bull ain't buckin' hard enough
To be worthy my time
Let's pep him up 'cause when I get on,
I want my ride to be prime."

Well we took that rope that we had on the horns,
And slipped it around his neck,
Then he pulled a half hitch up on the ol' bulls nose
For better control, by heck.

Then we snubbed him up close, to the side of the barn,
And we all held him there, real tight.
While Bub did his thing to that little ol' bull
And man was it ever a fright.

Bub caught hold of that little leather sack,
That makes a bul a bull,
And slipped it out between the hind legs and back,
Of that little ol' animul.

Then he took the buttline that we had found,
And commenced to lash that bag.
Bub peeled the hide a time or two,
And the bull began to sag.

He then began to beller and bawl,
And he raised an awful stink.
His eyes rolled back, he was hurt and mad,
And a little bit scared, I think.

Bub wrapped that line around the bull,
And got on, ready to ride.
He looked like a "pro" with one hand in the air,
And "Turn him loose.", he cried.

That little bull was still awful mad,
And I'm sure still feelin' the pain.
He went up in the air, and spun plum around,
Before comin' to earth again.

Bub lasted about three of these jumps,
Before he finished his ride.
Then he fell in a heap on the ground,
With dust, the dung, and his pride.

Now this little bull was equipped with some horns on his crown,
Not very big, but they sure were pointy,
And he caught ol' Bub as he was spinnin' around,
And grazed him across the belly.

Ol' Bub squalled like a scalded dog,
And hollered, "Oh my Lord!
Get this animal away from me,
And take me home, I've been gored!!"

Well I've lost track of ol' Bub these many long years,
But I'll bet, as sure as you're born,
That he will tell you, "If you mess with the bull,
You're liable to feel the horn!!"

******

THE JUMP

As far back as anyone could recall,
It was called Comindeer's Store.
This little old building that seemed ready to fall,
Back East of the river, 'bout a mile, less or more.

By the time I came and saw it,
The old building still stood.
But a post office had been added to it,
And they'd changed its name for good.

Chewy Oklahoma,
That's what they call it now.
Turkey farms provide an aroma,
But, they still have a few old cows.

The Skelly Oil Company built the school,
And operated a ranch near by,
To teach the kids the Golden Rule,
How to keep tally, and to add, subtract, and multiply.

About five of the boys who lived close to the store,
Got busy one summer's day.
It took about a month or more,
To make this place to play.

They dug their holes, and strung their fence,
With a chute and a pen at one end.
To hold the calves; It really made sense,
If you have the time to spend.

Then on weekends, usually Sunday after noon,
They would practice their ropin' skills.
They kept this up, and pretty soon,
There was an audiance to watch the thrills.

There was Memphis, Tulsa, and Curly;
Lester and Little Bill.
They'd usually get started pretty early,
And would go till they got their fill.

I was just a barefoot boy of ten,
But I wouldn't ever be late.
They'd let me work the holdin' pen,
And kick the calves out of the gate.

I had to walk 'bout three miles,
And wade the river to boot.
But sometimes, midst all their smiles,
They'd let me ride a calf out of the chute.

Now these boys were proud of their skills,
And proud of their horses too.
They liked to make bets with each other,
And brag 'bout what their ponies could do.

Now in the audience that gathered in the stand
To watch them rope and ride,
There were always a few girls on hand
To see their "showman side".

Them boys liked to show their stuff,
Mainly for the female folks.
It didn't matter if things got a little bit rough,
After all they were just ornery ole' cowpokes.

One day as they performed for the ladies fair,
While in the midst of a ropin' slump.
Little Bill started braggin' about his little mare;
And how well she could jump.

The fence around the holdin' pen
Was about four feet high.
Bill said she could, while carrin' him,
Clear the fence, "on the fly".

Well they made their bets, as they usually did,
Some for, and some against.
So Bill and his mare made their bid,
To jump over that little ol' fence.

They loped down the lane, to the bottom of the slope,
Then turned around and headed for the fence.
Bill "kicked her out" from a trot to a lope,
Then a run, he should have had more sense.

He crouched low in the saddle, then stood as he lifted the reins,
A sign for her to jump over,
But she pulled up short, (she probably had more brains)
And Little Bill wound up in the clover.

He did a beautiful flip, from the back of his horse.
That I'm sure caused some pains.
He made it across the fence of course,
Flat on his back, at the end of the bridle reins.

He laid there a minute, after his fall,
To sooth his wounded pride.
His buddies had no sympathy at all,
Not after the way he finished his ride.

He smiled through clenched teeth, least he tried,
As his friends began to scoff.
Then he said, "Boys, when I ride, I ride,
But when I stop, I get off!!"

D. J. Fry   Poet/Musician/Singer/Story Teller
662 N. Hwy "MM"
Oronogo, MO   64855

D.J. Fry is a Major Member of the Missouai Cowboy Poets Association. D. J. is a poet and musician. He was born in a small sawmill shack made of logs cut by the mill, which was owned and operated by his family in Robinson Arkansas. Later they lived on and worked a ranch in Northeasten Oklahoma. During this period he collected family stories and he still writes poetry, and enjoys entertaining at various civic events.

115

MCPA ANTHOLOGY

Lucky Glasscock

Back in my day, we didn't have stock trailers and trucks to take the cattle to market. We would just gather up the critters, and trail drive 'em to the stock yards. Camp Cooky would bring the chuck wagon along because we would usually have to stay over night before we would load the cows.

Almost without exception as we sat around the campfire drinking black coffee, strong enough to float a horse-shoe, some city boys would come around talking about how they wanted to be a cowboy. This is the way one old waddie answered a town-boy who wanted to be a cowboy.

SO YOU WANT TO BE A COWBOY

So, you want to be cowboy,
Well kid, come and hunker down-,
By the fire, while I tell you,
Why you would be better off in town.
Cowboying is hard work boy,
And it's dangerous as can be-,
If you think I'm just funning,
Take a closer look at me.

See these hands, how they're covered with scars?
From wrist to finger tips,
From stretching bob-wire,
Or from branding irons that slipped.
And the fingers, yep, three gone,
They got caught between the rope and horn;
When you throw a dally and catch a finger,
It's gone just as sure as you're born.

This black patch over my left eye,
Well, it's there to cover up a hole-,
Left when a tree branch took my eye,
And it helps keep out the cold.
You know my old hips and knees,
They've been busted so many times-,
That now I can hardly walk,
And I used to dance real fine.

You can see what cowboying done to me,
Son, It'll do the same to you;
So stay right here in town boy,
You'll live longer if you do.

Cowboying has plumb ruined my body,
And it's made me old before my time-,
I'll bet that you think I'm over sixty,
But hell, I just turned twenty-nine.

******

THE FIGHT

Way down in the Oklahoma hills,
The land of oak and black-jack trees,
There was a heck of a fight on a Saturday night,
Between Curly Bob and me.
It was out at the old red barn.
Just outside of Kiowa town;
The place was pretty crowded,
Because people came from miles around.

Now the cause of this here combat,
Was a girl named Cindy Lee,
She came to the dance with Curly Bob,
But she wanted to dance with me.
Now Curly Bob was an old cowboy,
Just twelve years shy of forty,
While I was a wild and woolly kid,
Who thought he was immortal.

Now old Bob kept his cool,
For the first three dances or four,
Then he came walking straight at me
Across that hard-wood floor.
He said, "Boy, I went and picked her up,
And I paid her entrance fee.
Now don't you think it's nothin' but right,
That she should dance with me?"

Now to me he was an old man,
And Cindy was sweet and trim;
So I decided I'll let her decide.
And old Bob got mighty grim.
He reached out and grabbed my arm,
And he held on to me real tight;
He marched me out that old red barn,
And he said, "you and me is gonna fight."

A bunch of waddies followed us out,
And before they would turn us loose;
They made sure we both were fortified,
With a slug of moon-shine juice.
Now Curly Bob he started it off,
And he caught me with a right.
I saw the stars and planets too,
And even the northern lights.

Then I got in a lucky punch.
Caught him flush on the nose;
His bright white shirt turned mighty red,
As the blood began to flow.
Well he was gettin' the best of me,
And my gut was kind'a cold.
I was beginning to see that twenty-eight,
Was not so dog gone old.

Then someone yelled, "Hey look at that.",
And we both turned to see;
And there was pretty Cindy,
Riding off with Buck Mcgree.
Now Bob and me learned a lesson that night,
It was don't fight over a woman of course;
And that the only time a cowboy should fight,
Is if somebody insults his horse.

******

GIRL ON THE CIRCLE BAR RANCH

It's lonesome out here in west Texas,
Where I'm riding fence on the Tumbling T.
Ain't nothing out here, but cactus and deer;
Horney toads, two horses, and me.
I ride ten miles of east fence one day,
Next day it's ten miles to the west.
Every day I change out my horses,
And let the other one have a good rest.

Each month they bring out my supplies,
Mail, flour, bacon and beans;
But this time they forgot the books and papers,
So I'm sitting here reading a can of sardines.

Yeah, there's a letter that I haven't opened,
I will, after I have a bourbon and branch.
I need whiskey to give me some courage,
'Cause it's from the girl on the Circle Bar Ranch.

Her dad is a big time rancher,
And she's pretty as a foal in the spring:
Me? I'm just a ragged underpaid cowboy,
Without even the money to buy her a ring.
She says that her dad will make me foreman,
And later we'll have a chance to buy in,
But I can't take money from a woman.
That's the way I always been.

Now I've had my bourbon and branch water,
In fact I've had two or three;
So I guess I'll just open up her letter,
I hope she's not saying good-bye to me.
I swear before heaven I love her,
But I couldn't give her any kind of life;
How could she go from being a rich rancher's daughter,
To just being a poor cowboy's wife?

In the envelope there's just one sheet of paper,
As I open it, hot tears fill my eyes;
For I think that I'm loosing my one love,
But the short note contains a surprise.

She wrote, "I've prayed for your returning,
But it looks like you're not coming back;
So if you won't come to me, then I'll come to you,
And live there in that line rider's shack."

She said, "I love you without reservation,
And I'll come to you, no matter how far;
So if you won't come back to Missouri,
I'll come to wherever you are."
I've got to go, it's my very last chance;
Soon I'll be on my way to Missouri,
And the girl on the Circle Bar Ranch.

******

Lucky Glasscock

A COWBOY LOOKS AT CHRISTMAS

Old Hoss' I been a sittin' here figgerin',
And if, I figgered right-,
It's the twenty fourth of December,
This here is Christmas Eve night.
We ain't decorated this old line shack.
And we don't have no fancy lights;
And of course we ain't got no tree,
'Cause out here there ain't a tree in sight.

I don't think the Lord will mind,
That there's no gee-haws hangin' 'round,
And we ain't doin' all the things,
That they're doin' down in town.
They're rushin' round and buyin' things,
And makin' the merchants fat;
And I don't think the good Lord meant
For his birthday to turn into that.

It seems to me that we've lost sight
Of what Christmas was meant to be.
It ain't about no Christmas sales,
Or tinsel on a tree.
It's about the blessed Son of God,
Sent to take our sins a way,
And I wonder what would happen,
If instead of then, He was born today.

If Joseph and Mary went to a motel,
In some modern day town;
With no ID or credit cards,
They surley would be turned down.
They would probably have to find a farmers barn,
Somewhere out of the way-,
And there among the animals,
Jesus would be born upon the Hay.

So I reckon not much has changed,
From the way it was back then;
People are still self-centered,
And there's still no room at the inn.

So lets just stand here and marvel,
At the stars that are all around;
For those stars mean more at Christmas,
Than all of the lights in town.

******

ALONE

A cowboy is used to being alone,
Just him, his horse, the sky, and wind;
And miles and miles of waving grass,
Today is just yesterday, played over again.

Sometimes he sings just to hear a sound,
Sometimes, he talks to his horse,
But there's never a voice to answer back,
No counterpoint to his discourse.

He listens to the doggies bawl,
Or the coyotes lonesome song;
Riding fence or hunting strays,
His days are hard and long.

Long before the east sky brightens,
A half days work is done;
And his workload doesn't lighten,
Until the setting of the sun.

He can spend a month out on the range,
And never see a soul,
So he sings for comfort as he works,
And remembers stories told.

Or he makes up a tale of his own,
Some wild impossible thing;
That he hopes will bring a chuckle,
At the round-up in the spring.

******

THE COWBOY BECOMES A SAILOR

I went from being a brush-popping, calf-pulling, steer-roping, cowboy, to being a sailor in Uncle Sam's Navy, and this is the way it happened.

I was nineteen that summer, and was working on the C-Bar ranch in Oklahoma. I had been cowboying since I was fourteen, and didn'tknow anything else, and didn't want to know anything else.

We had run out of tobacco at the ranch, and if you know anything about cowboys, you will know that when they are out of tobacco, things get real tense around the bunk-house. So they had sent me down to the store in Wesley Valley to get some Bull Duram, and some Red-man.

As I was riding down the dusty road that led to Wesley, I spotted the tracks of two of the biggest snakes I had ever seen. One track ran straight as a string, while the other kind of weaved around a little. Now there was an old snake-oil Doctor who lived up Gude Holler, and he would pay us cowboys twenty-five cents a piece for snakes that we brought him. Since we were only making $2.50 a day then, that was pretty big money. So we were always on the look-out for snakes.

Well, I started following those tracks, thinking that I might even get a quarter or two for two as big
as these. So I rode with my head down, following those tracks, and trying to figure out what kind of snakes they might be.

Suddenly my horse stopped and when I looked up, I saw that I was at Wesley store. The snake tracks curved on around towards the back of the store, and I figgured sure as the dickens, some other cowboy was going to get that four-bit piece for the snakes. Then I noticed that there was a stranger sitting on the porch, and he was strange looking too. He was dressed all in white with a flap hanging down from the back of the collar, and sort of a black bandanna knotted about the middle of his chest. He also wore a white hat that didn't appear to have any brim at all.

He stood up and said, " Hello there cowboy, I saw you looking at the ground as you rode up, what are you looking at?"

Well, I got down, tied my horse, then I told him about those snakes tracks I had been following. He looked at me kinda funny like for a second or two, then he motioned me over to a table he had set up on the porch and said, "I'll tell you what cowboy. I know all about those snakes, and if you will sign this piece of paper that I've got over there I'll show you where they are."

Well, I had been following those tracks for more than two miles, and I wasn't going to miss seeing those snakes, so I took that piece of paper that he gave me and signed it. He smiled, shook my hand, and said, " Congradulations, you are a proud member of the U. S. Navy. Now lets go see those snakes."
.....You know, that is the first time I ever saw a bicycle.

******

An old cowboy, and former Navy Seal, recalls the hell of
war, - and the scourge, - and blessing of death.

DEATH

I saw him first by battles glow
When hope and sanity fled;
Where strong men screamed, and cursed their God's,
As they fought and died and bled.
There were no fabled distant drums,
Nor trumpets on the wind;
Just that tattered specter, with his scythe,
And pain that will never end.

He danced upon that bloody ground,
Where reason was eclipsed;
He raised his bony hands on high,
And laughed through vanished lips.
He scrampered through that carnage site,
As young men breathed their last;
His well-worn scythe, like winter wind,
'Caught their souls, and held them fast.

As the battle waned, I saw him fade,
And leave that man-made hell;
But in the days and months to come,
I grew to know him well.
I never felt his cold embrace,
Nor touched his fleshless hand,
But I knew some day he would come for me,
As he comes for every man.

Now I walk with halting steps,
To where my journey soon will end.
I can see him waiting patiently,
And I greet him as a friend.
I do not fear his cold embrace,
Nor regret that the journey's done,
For soon I'll walk another path,
By the light of a different sun.

******

Lucky wrote this fine piece as a memmorial to our departed comrade, Wayne Naylor, who crossed over the divide, July 15, 2000.

WAYNE

I first met him at agatherin'
Down at Mountain View, Arkansas;
And he fit the image of a cowboy
Just about the best I ever saw.

His hips were lean, his shoulders wide
His hands were large and work-hardened
And the scars and rope burns on those hands
Told you he didn't get them in a garden.

His broad belt held a buckle
That said, "Champion 1999"
I never got to see him rope
But they tell me he was really fine.

When he stopped to talk to you
He looked you straight in the eye
And he had a smile as big and wide
As a cloudless, blue Texas sky.

Today I learned he had crossed the Great Divide
That my cowboy friend had gone on
God must have needed a good top-hand
For he called a real good cowboy home.

******

L. R. "Lucky" Glasscock   Poet/Reciter/Humorist
7607 C. R. 3080
Mountain View, MO   65548

Lucky spent his teen years working on ranches in Oklahoma and Texas. Lucky is retired from the United States Navy, and presently lives on his small ranch near Mountain View, Missouri. In May of 1998, Lucky was selected as Poet of The Month, by the Clanton Gang on Internet. He has appeared at "Good Times" in Atlanta, Georgia, and routinely does charity work at nursing homes, and senior citizen gatherings.

Reflections:
        "I was just a month shy of being fifteen when I achieved my life's ambition. I secured a riding job with the C-Bar Ranch in Wesley, Oklahoma. In a way I was carrying om a tradition, for my father worked on the C-Bar before I was born.
        Later I went on to work other ranches in Oklahoma and Texas, but I always ended up returning to the C-Bar, and it was there that I learned lesons that benefited me throughout my lifetime. I learned patience, how to endure hardship without complaining, to find the humor in any situation, and to judge every person as an individual.
        At age ninteen I said god-bye to the cowboy life and joined the U. S. Navy where I remained for twenty years. After retiring from the Navy, I became a store manager for a large department store chain, until my retirement in 1994. But as I grow older, my thoughts keep returning to those days when the work was long and hard and the pay was small. But when everything was compensated by a feeling of freedom and accomplishment. Looking back, for almost fifty years, I find that those days when I rode unfettered through the woods and meadows of my boyhood, were the happiest days of my life.
        These poems and stories are based on actual ebents in my life, some tall atles that I heard around camp fires that I have collected over the years. I hope that you enjoy reading them as much as I have enjoyed writing them down."

Note: Unfortunately Lucky suffered a sever stroke in the fall of 2000, and is no longer able to write the fine material that is exemplified in his very gripping emotional poem on "Death", See page 122.

LONG-AGO VERSION OF 'MARRY A MILLIONAIRE' WORKS OUT FINE

The TV show "Who Wants to Marry a Millionaire" reminds Me of the story of John and Eliza Hemry of Ray County.

John was born in Carroll County, Ohio, in 1837. He came to Ray County in about 1861 and bought a 120 acre farm south of Polo, near Sandals. He built a log house and other buildings, and was getting along very well.

In 1863, he decided he needed a wife, but where was one to be found? The county, being new, was settled mostly by young couples, so girls of marriageable age were few and far between.

By chance, he heard of a man at Edinburg, near Trenton, who had four young girls.

He waited till he had his corn planted, then rigged up a covered wagon with cooking utensils and food for the two day journey of 54 miles.

On the third day, he arrived at the man's house, called him out and introduced himself.

He told him he was hunting for a wife, and that he had heard that he had four daughters of marrying age, and he intended to collect one for his wife.

He stayed with them three days, and on the fourth day, he made his choice and called in a justice of the peace, and they were married. They started home the next day.

He could not have made a better choice. She was a good housekeeper, excellent cook and a wonderful mother of their four children.

They live a happy life until she died of malarial fever Nov. 7, 1888, at the age of 46.

Six years later, John developed stomach cancer. Because of the unbearable pain, he ended his life with a self-inflicted gunshot May 27, 1894.

******

FUNNEL CAKE

Just last August one hot day
Went to the engine show instead of pitching hay.
Saw the engines and tractors of my dreams
That I hadn't thought of since my teens.
Thought I'd brought money 'nuff
To eat some junk food and stuff.
Cost four dollars to get in the gate.
Only had 50 cents left after buying a J.C.Penney Plate.
Took in all the sights and sounds,
Even heard the whistle blow up town.
Long bout half way "tween noon and dark

Couldn't been nothing but a lark.
Just remembered while resting my feet
That I hadn't had nothing to eat.
Stopped at the Focus eat tent and studied their fare.
Looked in my wallet, not enough there.
Stopped at Lions shack to get me a steak,
They just waved when I said, "Give me a break!"
Past the Legion stand, just went on by
When I saw Mac he give me the eye.

Sat on a log feeling a flake
When I saw the big sign Funnel Cake.
I was getting hungry, bout as I've been.
Stomach growling from belt to chin.
Got over there as quick as I could
On my one short leg and the other of wood.
The hump on my back don't slow me none,
Helps to keep my face out of the sun.
My one bad eye don't affect my sight
When I hold my head up just right.

Hope that funnel cake is soft
Cause I broke my teeth when I fell in the trough.
Put the coins on the shelf and waited my turn.
If I just had some lotion for this bad sunburn.
The lady didn't even grin
When she saw where my chin shoulda been.
She didn't even glance
At the rip in my shirt or the tear in my pants.
It don't bother me when they do stare
Didn't they ever see a guy without any hair?
She handed it out with cinnamon on top.
I wolfed it down without wasting a drop.
Though I saw her wipe a tear
When I yelled, "See you next year?"
Couldn't figure it out as I crawled through the fence,
How did I get that funnel cake for only 50 Cents?

******

COUNT YOUR BLESSINGS WHERE EVER THEY ARE

The other day while going to town
Got to thinking, "Why do people frown?"
Couldn't be because they don't believe in Santa Clause.
Why it's a sight,
Must be because their hat is on too tight.
Take me, I'm happy as a lark
If I can make it home before dark
So I can see the kids before they go to bed
To dream bout sugarplums dancing in their heads.
Course I got to get out 'fore daylight and get the chores all done
So I can be to work at the rising of the sun.
Can't believe that people would rather whittle on a cob
Than sweat and work at my job.
Boss came by the other day,
Said if I kept it up he's increase my pay, maybe 10 or 15 cents a day.
Why I've worked up to the head stall,
Don't seem like any time at all.
I started at the end of the line,
Where they bring in the oldest and toughest most of the time.
Up here where I work I get to rest
Because they only bring me the best.
Why just look at my pile layin' outside,
There isn't a cut in any hide.
Why, they don't care if I sit right down on a horse and eat my dinner
And laugh and joke with all the other skinners.
Heard the Mrs. Singing and humming a tune.
Said she was due in about one more moon.
Old Doc says she's just right on time
Everything goes right it will make us nine.
She's pretty as a picture and does just fine
With the cooking & the washin' & scrubbin' the floor of pine.
Course, Grandpa helps all he could.
Carryin' water and choppin' wood.
He looks after the chickens in the coup and carries Grandma crackers
and soup
Cause she's sick and fast in bed up in the second stoop.
Old Doc says she's sure to last
If she can survive the wintry blast.
Just thinkin' how can I be so blest
To have a good family to stand the test.

Why you don't need to be a star
To count the blessings where you are.
I'm just thanking the Lord for this job and givin' Him a great big grin
Cause they just brought me one more horse to skin.

******

HOG DAY ENDS IN TRAGEDY

Several years ago about a mine east of Bonanza, Mo., a family was butchering hogs. In the process of killing one, a rifle bullet was misfired. It was ejected onto the ground.

The little boy of 4 or 5 years of age was there playing with a broken piece of an old rifle; it didn't even have a stock. Everybody was busy with the butchering and didn't notice him pick up the misfired cartridge.

He put the bullet in the old gun and walked up to his grandfather. He pointed the barrel at the old man's stomach and said, "Grandpa, I'm gonna shoot you." This time the the misfired cartridge fired. They boy's grandpa died a day or so later.

******

WOLF AND HUNTER DIE SIDE BY SIDE

Back years ago, the sighting of a wolf would usually bring several hunters, who would track or drive the wolf until he was killed.

Such as the case near Bonanza, Mo., during World War II.

A group of hunters had surrounded a wolf in a small patch of woods. When the wolf finally ran, one of hunters was too close, and was accidently shot along with the wolf.

Doctor Wilbur from Polo, Mo., was called, as he was coroner of Caldwell County. He said it was sad, for when when he arrived he found the body of the hunter and and a few feet away the dead wolf.

******

UNCLE KNEW HOW TO HAWK ANYTHING

My uncle, Albert Eddy Malotte, was born in 1880 near Craig, Mo.

He taught country school in that area many years. He came to Kingston as school superintendent in 1910.

Besides teaching school, he worked at a grocery store. One time, the owner of the store had a lot of boxed dry macaroni that wasn't selling. So he offered a bonus to any employee that could get rid of it.

Uncle Edd being wise in human nature from his years of teaching — dumped all boxes on a table and put up a sign reading, "Limit two per customer." The macaroni was all gone in a week or two.

BROWN-BAGGING IT ON CHRISTMAS OUTING

Back in the 1950s, a trip to St. Joe to Christmas shop was a real treat to us kids who were raised out in the sticks.

The Christmas time smell of the dime stores downtown is something I'll never forget.

One time, my brother and I got to go to St. Joe with our aunt and uncle to Christmas shop. They parked the car and we all went our own way.

My brother and I did our shopping at the Army surplus store and, of course, the dime stores.

We were to meet at the car at a certain time to go home. We got there a little early, so we ate our candy and read the comic books we had.

Our uncle came carrying a little brown sack shaped like a bottle. As he got in the car, he slid it under the front seat. He said he always had a few calves get sick in the winter, so he always kept a bottle of that "calf medicine" in the barn.

We were sure he kept the bottle in the barn, but both of us bet the calves didn't get any of it.

******

HAT COVER-UP AT CHURCH ON SUNDAY RECOUNTED

My neighbor, Charlie Mayes, told me several stories about Bonanza, Mo., when he was a young man. This is one of his stories.

After the town died, the people of Bonanza and the surrounding area still attended church there.

One Sunday morning, a young lady came to church on horse back. Instead of dismounting like a man (which would have been unlady like), she just slid off one side. Her dress caught on the saddle horn and was jerked up over her head. She just hung there all exposed to the elements.

The preacher, seeing her dilemma, ran over and took off his hat, then held it in front of her and yelled, "More hats! More hats!"

******

AN APPLE A DAY KEEPS THE BORDER PATROL AWAY

Back in the 1930s, my uncle and his family lived in Washington state. They're in the orchard business, so when they traveled, they always took their own apples along.

They started for a trip to California. At the California border, the police searched their car for fruit so no disease could be carried into the state by tourists.

The police were going to take the apples away from the, so Uncle Harold made his five daughters sit down right there and eat all the apples they had left.

NORTHERNER CALLED THEIR BLUFF

My great-grandfather, Thomas Clark Fort, came from Knightstown, Ind., and settled northwest of Kingston in 1865.

He was an ex Union soldier of the Civil War, a Northerner and, of course, a Lincoln Republican.

Some of the older settlers around Kingston were Democrats and sympathetic to the South. They had passed the word around that the damn Yankees had better stay out of Kingston on election day.

Great-grandpa Fort didn't own a gun, so he borrowed a "Navy" pistol, strapped it on and went to Kingston and voted without any trouble.

******

RFD

Old Ebineezer Lee, Carried mail for RFD.
He made the rounds again and again, In his black car made of tin.

He delivered most everything during his years of hire,
Whether the roads were dry or just a great big mire.

You could order anything from clothes to castor oil,
Tools to fix the neighor's fence, things to till the soil.

Old Eb always brought it out and put it in the box,
If the item was too big he'd come to the door and knock.

The only thing he didn't like, It really made him ticked,
Was every spring he had to haul those blasted baby chicks.

For every farm wife, no matter what her age,
Would order out those little chicks, it seemed to be the rage.

They started with the orders about February Trey
And ran right up to summer, hardly missing any day.

He heard the constant cheeping, it almost made him scream,
Even after going to sleep, he heard them in his dreams.

One day an idea struck him, it was a devious plan,
That hit him one day while in his motor can.

He drove on into town, to the hatchery he did go,
Got one of those little boxes, they send chickens in you know.

He waits till the thermometer says 40 odd below,
And high up on a tall Indian, is the depth of all the snow.

Out to his car with zest, he took the little box,
With a little length of cord, he ties it on the top.

It only takes a couple days of driving the route around,
To see the women looking out wearing worried frowns.

They call him cruel, heartless,, mean; bad names all around,
He just smiles from the silence of his car and says,
"Wonder why baby chicken orders are down?"

******

Dale Hartly   Poet/Reciter
3594 Windgate
Kingston, MO   64650

Dale Hartley was born in 1939 in Kingston, Missouri. After his graduation from Penny High School in Hamilton, Missouri, he spent eight years in the U. S. Marine Reserves, VMF 113Fighter Squadron. Dale and his wife Kay, have five children and have been farming since 1958. Dale is now serving his third term as Elected Presiding Commissioner of Caldwell County.

THEIR BOOTS ARE TOUGH

I've seen cowboy boots all polished
An manicured for society's praise
I've seen them fresh from the corral
Where cowpiles had over glazed.

I've seem them cracked and wrinkled
With worn soles and rundown heels
But they were tough beyond a doubt
That shaped the feet that seemed unreal.

I've seen them in display windows
Without a scar and polished bright
But never belonged to cowboy life
For they were shown for delight.

Boots render a vital service
Besides comfort and protection
They are the roadways of the mind,
The buckboards of transportation.

They are servants that will carry
Where ever we choose to go
Down the trail of self destruction
Or upward to Heavenly plateaus.

******

COWBOY JED

"Lord, I believe all things are right in Heaven
Just the way they oughta be, but down here,
Lord, I'm a feelin's things just ain't so good
Frettin' and complainin' is about all I hear.

W'y I just found myself flat out a grippin'
The other day because things weren't goin' right.
And I said, "Lord, it's time You're a doin' somethin'
Like blessin' this old parch land tonight."

The cricks and water holes are a dryin' up,
The hot, sweltering, burning winds are a scorchin'

The cattle's a bawlin' "Lord, don't you care?
Why don't You send rain like it's always been?"

Well, I slunked off to sleep in my old bedroll
Not knowin' what tomorrow would bring,
And I dreamt about lightin' and thunder
And a downpour that was a frightenin' thing,

It was a restless night, but when I awakened
The good Lord had come by with lots of rain.
The cricks were a flowin', the water holes a fillin',
And the rain had come to freshen once again.

Then I cried, "Lord forgive my belly achin',
And compainin', and how I questioned You.
Please help this ol' cowboy to know that
You're a watchin', and will always see us through."

******

THE GREAT ROUNDUP

Flinching from the darts of sleet
They rode that cold November night
While the north wind cut to the bone
Determined to fulfill their plight.

To rescue two hundred head of cattle
Stranded by a fierce snowstorm.
In Devil's Gulch time was of essence
And difficult the task to perform.

But these leather skinned cowboys
Daring as hell rode through the night
The trails obliterated and dangerous
But the bawling cows steered them right.

When daybreak came they found
The only rescue of the cattle
Was by a ravine blocked by drifts.
All day long they gave battle.

By riding the horses up and back
Until evening the snow was packed
Till the restless bovine moved out
Headed where the hay was stacked.

The cattle now home, the mission over,
We think of the Great Roundup
When Jesus the Master said
To His servants "Go! Hurry up!

Invite mavericks to my feast
To eat of My Kingdom Bread
Seek them! Call them! Bring them!
To escape the hell they dread.

Time is short and life is eternal.
Brother, will you go one more time
To tell your friend of Jesus' love
For we are living on borrowed time.

******

A KINDRED SPIRIT

I've never owned a horse
A saddle, lariat or a steer.
I've never owned grazing land
And for a cowboy that is queer.

I've never owned a cow or calf
So a cowboy I just haven't been
I've tried to be a cowboy poet,
But prizes I'll never win.

And when it comes to recitin'
I can't remember a single line.
And when I begin to read,
I'm already slippin' in decline.

From all the features listed above
It makes me feel sorta sad.
When tempted to be a cowboy
I think of the hanging chad.

So I'll never be a cowboy,
But how I love the cowboy way,
The simple life, the love of nature
Just downright honest folks are they.

I love their creative songs and poems
I love their smiles and friendliness,
Their handshakes and the hugs.
I love the meetings I confess.

I love to sit around the campfires
When the evening shadows fall
Listening to our many poets
And musicians who give their all.

Their warm spirits burst into flame
Like the fire around the wood
But the flame of kindred spirit
Burned brighter than the wood.

Cowboy friends, each a library,
An epitome of love and care
These are the fires that warm most
There is nothing to compare.

From the glow of many campfires,
The meetings in Mountain View,
The winter Watts's meetings,
And the honor of bidding adieu.

These meetings I highly treasure
For they represent the old West,
The cowboy's place in history
And the fellowship of the best.

From down on the ol' Texas trail
I yearn to ride back some day
For the music and the poems,
And hugs the good old cowboy way.

******

This poem was written by Rev. Rex Henderson, to commemorate the untimely death of Rev. Ron Ratliff's nine year old grandson, Cody. - Ed.

MEMORY OF LOVE

Lord, we've given up little Cody
And our lives feel empty now.
Lord, give us love, something to love.
In sorrow we pray somehow.

Then Heaven begins to open up
You marked his pattern true.
Not a thing would we change
His life and ways we pursue.

The way he walked down the path
His little body wiggling along
The way he said his words
My, how his voice lingers on.

His little ways of doing things
His temper and his child-like tears
And the cheer he brought to us
Brings deeper joy than appears.

So little Cody left his blessings,
And we have so much to love.
He left us invaluable riches
That guides us to his home above.

Where he's holy, healthy and happy
In the home Jesus prepared
Where the holy angels serve
And some day we will share.

******

Rex Henderson   Poet'Reciter/Sky Pilot
8613 Serenity Way
Denton, TX   76205

Rex Henderson was born in Bartlesville, Oklahoma and grew up on a farm in southeast Kansas where he was exposed to horses and cattle. At age nineteen he entered the Ministry, and later earned graduate degrees from the New Orleans Baptist Theological Seminary. After serving churches some fifty years, he began writing Western poems for two newspapers and recitation.

Rex, a "Sky Pilot", was originally a Major Member of the Missouri Cowboy Poets Association, but became an Associate Member when he moved to Denton, Texas in the fall of 2000. He is also a member of the Oklahoma Western Heritage Association. He currently lives at 8613 Serenity Way, Denton, Texas 76210.

Phone: 940-271-2701   e-mail: rexermalee@earthlink.net

SALE DAY

She spun around and snorted
and sorta squared up on all fours
One horn broken off short
and her shoulders wider than the big barn door.

My legs squeezed Ol' Doc
when I saw her paw at the dirt
but before I could pull him around
that crooked black horn hooked us right in the girt.

I keep my gear all oiled up just right
and the cinches on my saddle in good shape
who knows someday I might get
a Saturday night date.

So that girt held tight
when she hit us on the side
we were all 3 tangled up for a 3 spinner,
quadruple, Texas Long Horn kind'a ride.

She was bellorin' like a Mississippi fog horn at night
Ol' Doc's eye got bigger than silver dollars,
when she picked us both up
and swung us around like a little boy's kite.

The dust was flyin' around
and I couldn't see a thing in sight
So I just held the horn with both hands
and began to pray with all my might.

She threw us up and threw us down
I couldn't tell left from right
but I still recall that wicked snortin' sound
it must'a lasted half the night.

Hour after hour
she began to slow a bit
'bout the time the moon showed up
I could tell she would soon wear down and quit.
And finally, she tipped her head
and let us down in the dirt

the world just kept on spinnin'
and I knew me or Ol' Doc, one had to be hurt.

While we both got back to our senses,
she just sort'a ambled away for this story for me to tell
and I guess that's one ol' heifer
I just ain't quite ready to sell.

******

ALWAYS BEEN A COWBOY
(Song)

I've always been a cowboy
A'ridin' the range
With my horse and my saddle
Through the wind and the rain.

Never knew lonely
Or felt quiet pain
Till I rode into Laredo
And you called my name.

(Chorus)

Hello there cowboy! How are you?
Come here and sit yourself down.

I been lookin' for you near all my life,
And so glad it's you I have found.
We sat there and talked
For hours on end
We talked of our lost love
And forgotten friends.

We held each other
Till the mornin' light
When we rode out of town
And clear out'a sight.

(Chorus)

From the mountains I bring 'em down
Where the grass is greener down low
But now when I close my eyes in the night
I dream of a girl I did know.

(Chorus)

******

Cody Holmes   Poet/Reciter/ Singer/Musician/Song writer
7618 perkins Rd
Mountain Grove, MO   65711

Cody, Is a Major Member of the Missouri Cowboy Poets Association. He is a poet, musician, singer, song writer, and story teller. He runs a cow, calf operation in Mountain Grove, Missouri.

COW IN THE HOOP
Or I Would've Laughed if I Warn't Prayin' so Hard

Ever now an' then, one of our cows goes olympic on us, springin' like a gazelle over the pasture fence. When we catch'er, we pen her up, hopin' to break her of the habit. If not, it's off to the sale barn with'er. Well, one Saturday one of those wayward bovines was penned behind the house. After dinner, I looked out the back door and couldn't believe my eyes.

"Honey, come quick," I hollered. "Ya gotta see this!"

In the corner of the pen, hubby had stored a couple of round hay bale feeders on their sides, like two big hoops. Ol' Jumpin' Jewel had walked into one of those hops and made the mistake of turning left to exit. Her hips were too wide, so there she was, frothin' an' bawlin', draggin' that feeder around the lot. Her front out the side of the thing, but her hind end was caught in the ring. One of the rungs between the two metal rounds was rubbing her hip raw, and another, her hind leg.

We pulled on our boots and tore out there, minds racin'. How on earth would we get that thing off'n her? So, hubby herded the frightened bovine to a corner near a post, and hollered, "See that rope on the ground? Go get it and I'll tie the feeder to that post." He figgured maybe he could cut the thing off'n her if he could hold it still. I clomped over and picked up the rope, only to see that the end was buried in a foot of dried up muck. I tugged and tugged, but I couldn't budge it. Meanwhile, Jewel decided to light out, with hubby in tow. There he was hangin' on to the feeder for all he was worth, gallopin' as best he could to keep up with 'er.

"Head her off," he hollered, so I planted myself in front of her and waved my arms. Well, the wild eyed beast didn't take kindly to that, and about the time she lowered her head and pawed the ground, I knew I'd better be the one to high tail it out of there. I took off runnin' and tripped over a big ol' dirt clod, down I went, right in a cow pie. Out of the corner of my eye, I could see this cow bearin' down on me, and I wondered if I was about to meet my Maker. Hubby says her hooves missed me by 'bout four inches. I stumbled to my feet, and she was just standin' there, minus the feeder. In my stupor, I hollered, "It worked," as though we had planned the whole thing.

Heart pounding and knees quiverin', I asked hubby how it was that she had missed me, and how in tarnation that feeder had come off'n her, he told me, "When she commenced to charge my little wife, I gave the feeder one big, sideways jerk, and off it come, turning her just enough to miss ya!"

Thank You Lord, is all I have to say.

Well, when Jumpin' Jewel quit frothin, Hubby doctored the poor thing's raw hide, and we don't store round bale feeders on end in cattle pens no more. Ol' Jewel? Well, she was so glad to get away from that big ol' hoop that was chasin' her, she humbly joined up with the herd, and never did jump another fence.

******

LIFE ON THE HOWSER FARM
Topsy Turvey as Usual

Most cows are pretty good mothers. They just naturally know what to do with their offspring, especially after they've calved a few times. But, once in a while. something goes haywire, and the two don't get together. Maybe mom's teats are too clogged and sore for the calf to nurse, or, especially with first time heifers, she rejects the little one.

When one of the above happens, we try to get the two together, hand milking the cow if needed, to get things flowing as nature intended, We had one such pair in the pen, and mama cow snorted and crashed and charged each time we approached her. She didn't seem to want anything to do with the poor little fellow who had wandered off, either.

Well, we put her in the chute to milk her, and she practically tore apart the apparatus trying to get free. We bottle fed the baby, but that didn't get the two together. So, hubby thought, maybe if we put the little one in the chute, and her in the alley way, facing her offspring, the two of them would bond. Now hubby had built that alley with heavy beams and high board fencing, to hold in the wildest cattle, and he blocked her in so all she could do was to stand there, nose to nose with her baby. So he said, "Let's go in and grab a bite to eat and leave the two to get acquainted,"

About an hour later, hubby went out to see how things were coming, and minutes later he raced in hollering, "Call Chuck and tell him to get down here." Chuck is our big, strapping son who lives down the road. I conveyed the urgency in his Dad's voice to Chuck, and then ran out to see what hubby was so worked up about/ I couldn't believe my eyes. I saw four hooves sticking up in that alley way, thrashing in the air! That ol' cow had tried to climb out and gone over backward!

It was a funny sight, but if you know anything about cattle, you know that they can't live long in that position, and there was no room in there for her to right herself, which explained hubby's excitement. Well. Chuck came down and the two of them hurriedly dismantled and removed the chute, then dragged mama cow out of the alley into the open where they could help roll her over.

I don't recommend the above as a cow-taming proceedure, but I must say she was a different cow after that, and finally let her wayward calf nurse. Thank God, only three or four such crazy things have happened in the past ten years, and knock on wood, all is quiet at the Howser Farm for the moment.

******

Judy Howser   Story Teller
Rt 1   Box 158
Fort Scott, KS   66701

Judy Howser was formerly associated with the Fort Scott Community College. She is one of the major members of the steering committe that founded and continues to produce the annual "Echos of the Trail Cowboy Poetry Gathering" at Fort Scott, Kansas.

YOUR STRENGTH

Lord, here I stand with hat in hand
Looking out across the land.

Some folks think I've a lucky lot
That being a cowboy is glamorous
But we know it's not.

This life I live it's sure not for some
It's a lot of hard work
Something always needs to be done.

Up early every morning, often working late into night.
The livestock always comes first
No other way would be right.

What with the wind and the rain, the cold and the ice
My working conditions aren't always real nice.
Then, there's the heat and the sun, the flies and the dust
It's enough to make this cowboy cuss.

And financially speaking,
I'm operating on trust
And if things don't change, I'm going to go bust.

There are times, I admait, when I wanted to quit.
When I've fely plumb dicouraged
And down in the pits.

But, then something will happen that will cause me to think
And the next thing I know
I'm not on the brink.

Like this evening, Lord
With the sun setting low. The shy is all awash in colors aglow
And the reds and the purples, the violets and blues
Act as a gentle reminder, I need come talk to you.

Your grandeur before me makes my troubles seem small
And the time spent with you
Seems like no time at all.

Yup, life here on earth can be mighty rough
But with you as a partner,
Your strength is enough.

****

THE LOOK

His face is etched and weathered
His hands are callused and gnarled from wear.
His step is still spry
He's got a look in his eye
Though the years have whitened his hair.

I heard this old cowboy a'talkin'
To a young buckaroo in the fray.
Who was just starting out
To find what life was about
Living the "cowboy" way.

The old man said:
"Oh. I could have read about being a cowboy,
All about roping and riding the land.
But for me what it took
Why, I couldn't have got from a book
It took years to make this waddie a hand.

Ya see,
It's a hunger.
A need.
A want to.
When it makes no sense to some folks to even try.
And you'll know from the start
'Cause it comes from deep in your heart.
And you can tell
By the look
In the eye."

******

MID-SUMMER NIGHT'S MEMORY

When you live a rural life, there are sounds and
sights and smells that are an integral part of this lifestyle.

The Whippoorwill are calling
In the late hours of the night.

As summer breezes, waltz slowly,
With white gossamer curtains at the window in the moonlight.

The heady, sweet scent fo the honeysuckle and new mown hay
Are the evening's intoxicating perfumre.

Soft, creamy white moonbeams, lie entwined
With lacy, black tree bough shadows
On the iron bed, in this old room.

The locust and the katydid, the crickets and the frogs
Orchestrate a melodious, lovers serenade
That fills our sleepy repose with song.

******

DNA

I love this life. It is the core of my very being
It is who I am. I don't know where I stop and
outside influences begin.

So entwined in my daily existance are:

The sounds of
A hoof kick against a wood plank wall,
The soft low nicker of a mare for her foal
A blanket being placed on a horses back,
The slap of stirrup against saddle seat while cinching
The creak of leather,
The jingle of bits
The bawl of cattle
The rustle of grass as livestock pass by.
The whisper of a breeze through the pine.

The smell of
Rain on the wind
My favorite horse
Cattle pens
The damp sourness of horse sweat in saddle blankets
New mown hay
A well kept barn
Leather.

The sight of
Intricate Cobwebs woven in fence lines
Bejeweled with sparkling crystal dewdrops
Slow rising bedded cattle, which stretch and hump their backs
before moving on
Daybreah streaking across the shy and sunsets lingering in the dusk.

The feel of
The sun on my back
Cold biting wind on my cheeks sliding down my neck, cutting through
to the bone
Sweat trickling between my shoulder blases
The weight of good bridlereins in my hand
My saddle between my legs.

******

RANCHER'S WIFE

I'll never be a rancher's wife; it's a life I'll never know.
But, it has been a dream of mine, since oh, so long ago.
I always figured I'd meet someone along the way,
While I was learning to make a hand, ridin' horses for my pay.

I wasn't expecting no firewoprks, no knight in shiny armor to sweep me
off my feet
Just someone honest, polite and kind, was the type I wanted to meet.
Oh, I figured he'd be a little ornery, with a twinkle in his eye.
But if we ever said, "I do." We'd "Do' till the day we died.

Now I was working on all the attributes I thought a rancher's wife should posses.
Starting colts, building fence and looking good in high heels and a dress.

Stretching pennies into dollars, getting up early to do the chores
and when there was an extra mouth to feed, making room at the table for just
one more.

Playing midwife to mares and heifers, doctoring colts and calves
and thanking God at the end of the day, for all the things I have.
Like; the majestic beauty of sunrises in the morning, and the clean, crisp smell
and feel of fall
the wonder of life in a newborn calf and miles of wide-open prairie spaces
and some of my favorite things of all.

But then I turned 40 and decided no one was coming down the ranch's mile long
drive a'looking for a wife.
So I moved to town, got a job - now I breathe the smog and put up with
constant strife
Of houses set too close together, and apartment living is even worse.
With too thin walls between you so that you hear your neighbor's curse.

Now my days are filled with driving in rush hour traffic, fighting crowds and
honking horns.
Working in small confining spaces, sometimes gazing out the window looking
wistful and forlorn.

'Cause, I still think about how my life used to be, and what it has now become,
remembering what I left behind and the dreams I dreamt when I was young.
Dreams of cattle grazing on the hillside on a place we would call home
and all the puppies, ponies and pickups that we would surly own.

I guess everything in life is a trade-off, 'cause I'm finally able to put money in
the bank,
But since I stopped working ranches I've gained 30 pounds and there is a
noticeable swelling
in my flanks.

I still use my black iron skillets and cook enough to feed a branding crew,
But, I sometime get to wondering, would I have made the change if I'd only
knew?

How much of my heart I'd leave in pieces scattered out upon the Texas plains,
in the yelp of the coyote, or that it would cause me so much pain
to watch the sun come up between tall buildings
instead of from some horse's back

and as the years now stretch before me it becomes more and more a fact -
that I'll never be a ranchers wife
it's a life I'll never know.

******

In 1870 two brothers named Benjamin, came from Russia and settled on the Missouri prairie, a half a day's horseback ride from Kansas City. That land is still in the Benjamine family today, and is better known as Benjamime Ranch. In 1957, Howard Benjamine and stock contractoerFloyd Rumford put on the 1st Annual Kansas City 4th of July Rodeo. There was no written contractbetween the two, just two men's word sealed with a handshake.

In '57 Howard and Floyd were young men and their sons were small children. In 1996, for the 39th Annual Rodeo, their grandchildren were working as pick-up men and vendors at the rodeo. I worked for Benjamine Ranch and I also had my boot shine stand at the 39th rodeo. People would stop and tell me how they had been coming to the 4th of July rodeo for years. How their parents use to bring them when they were little, and as adults they were now bringing their own children. It was a family tradition.

Which got me to thinking, about all the rodeos that had been put on in the pastand all the people who have been a part of those rodeos. I thought about the partnership and friendship that had developed over the years between Floyd and Howard and what it must have taken to make this agreement still work on hust a handshake. An I though about all the changes that have occurred in our society and the rodeo world since '57, and how the rodeo has still continued on.

On the last night of that rodeo, during opening ceremonies, as I watched Howard and Floyd do their long-standing handshake, from horseback, in the center of the arena, I wrote this poem:

39 YEARS OF TRADITION

39 years of tradition sealed in a handshake and a smile,
Betwixt two good friends, who for each other, go an extra mile.

39 years of tradition, with nary a conflict unresolved.
What started with Floyd and Howard, now has 3 generations involved.

39 years of tradition, in the heat and the dust and the mud.
Bringing to Kansas City, cowboy rodeo fun.

With wild chuck wagon races, palomonos pulling stages and rodeo queens
by the score.
Crazy bullfighters, determined bronc riders, and barrel races galore.

Down through the ages, through 4 decades of changes, Jerry Taylor's voice
has made the call.
The grand entry's aprade, specialty acts on display and the contestant's names
one and all.
39 years of tradition all wrapped up in a handshake among friends
39 years of memories, may the tradition and friendship never end.

The following year, in the spring of 1997, Floyd Rumford suffered a stroke and Howard Benjamine was fighting Leukemia. For that year's 40th annual rodeo, they did their traditional handshake from the seat of a horse drawn buggy, instead of horseback. Floyd Rumford died March of 1998, and Howard Benjamine was buried 10 days after the 1998 rodeo was over.

******

MISSING YOU

There is a lover's moon a shinning
Its full and silvery white
The stars up in the heavens
Are a dancing, twinkling sight
The campfire, it's a crackling
Burning, warm and bright.

And I'm sitting here remembering
Missing you tonight.

Soft, as a lover's caress
The evening breeze in flight.
As it dances, then it lingers
Upon my cheek clenched tight.
That gentle breeze, among the trees
Whispers sighs, into the night.

And I'm sitting here remembering
Missing you tonight.
Somewhere in the darkness
A Lobo laments its plight.

And I'm sitting here remembering
Missing you, tonight.

******

SHOEING SWEETIE

It was a Kodak moment
A once in a lifetime - first time
Three generations standing there
Grandfather, father, and son.

The boy was only ten years old and all his life he'd seen
Grandpa and dad shoeing horses.

And Sweetie, she was a three-year-old, gentle, but not broke, in
Grandpa's trading string.
She came with a good mond and a want-to-get-along kind of attitude.
Thje boy had taken a liking to her, because she was just his size.
Not too big, but not a pony either. And the boy and the mare fit,
Like they were made for each other.

So he worked with her every day. Grandpa helped him with her in the
round pen
And then they ventured out into the arena and then the open fields.
The first horse the boy had really trained;and they went everywhere that
summer.
Gathering livestock, crossing rivers, playing tag on horseback, racing
through pastures.

So it seemed only a natural progression og things when the boy asked
"Grandpa, can you teach me to shoe? Can I shoe Sweetie?"
And a smile and a look passed between the two fathers.

The shoeing apron came up to his armpitts and hung clear down to his
toes.
And the rasp was as long as his shinbone from ankle to knee.

Grandpa supplied the ballast, as he stood behind the boy, steady as a
rock
While Dad knelt and helped hold Sweetie's foot up
And the boy supplied the sweat and muscle, as he nipped, and rasped
and tapped.
Listening to words of wisdom about how and where and why.
Small hands gripping with doubled-up choke holds an hamdles of
equipment
Intended for a grown man's large, stout hands.

It was hard work; it wasn't easy as it looked. Not anything like playing
on the anvil
Hammering on thrown away shoes and straightening bent nails.

What Sweetie didn't know was she was part of an eternal equation of
turnmig
little boys into men. A passing on of knowledge, a torch bearer to a new

generation of horsemen to a boy following footsteps left behind by a
Great grandfather, Grandfather, and Father.

And the boy, if he continues in the footsteps put before him, may one
day have a grandchild of his own who says ..."Grandpa, teach me to
shoe." And hopefully, there will be a "Sweetie" tp learn on.

******

REALITY

Sometime the nights get mighty lonely and I wonder why I try
Working way out on these ranches where I watch the eagle fly.
And the brightest lights a shining are those that twinkle up above
And my miond gets to thinking about leaving this life I love.

'Cause reality is sinking in; I don't bounce like I did when I was young
Any more I'm not eat up with being brave and things seem to hurt more when
they get sprung,
Or bruised or broken and I seem to bleed a little more profuse.
My back and joints are aching from all the physical abuse.

I guess I've finally ,atured, 'cause health insurance seems more important than
my saddle or my hat
Why, always before I could pick up on a moments notice, all I needed was
transportation and my tack.

Use to be I loved to travel, seeing sights and having fun.
Strangers were just friends I hadn't met, and I never knew which ione
Would turn into my best buddy, or a mentor who helped my horse skills to
progress.
And my life is all the richer for the ones who've ahowed me that success
Is not so much in the winning but in the process of the try.
And if I'd truly done my best, when there wasn't any reason why
I shouldn't hold my head up proudly, smile and give God a heart felt "Thanks"
For the opportunity and ability and for all the times that truly rank
As some of my best memories, moments forever etched upon my heart
Of true friends, good dogs and great horses, from this life I never would depart.

But 40's just around the corner; it's knocking ay my door,
Even though I'm still plenty able, I've started to think that there's more
To life than riding horses, and doctoring cattle for my pay
Or coming home bone tired at the end of a long hard day.

Honestly, I never thought I'd see this day a'coming, why, I was going to cowboy
my whole life
Figgured I'd keep on thraing horses for different ranches until I became some
cowboy's wife.

As a single woman I've no retirement, nor one of them 401K's
With the way Social Security is, I need to start putting away
Some kind of savings, something I can look forward too, ... but heck,
On cowboy wages thers's always more month left, than money in the check.

Here lately, I want my own curtains at the windows and pictures on the walls,
And color coordinated throw rugs lying scattered down the hall.
Someplace I can come home to and know it's mine to keep
But to buy a piece of land, for me, the price is just too steep.

So, I've been thinking about moving to the city and learning how to type
On one of them computers that you're always hearing so much hype.
About, how it's the wave of the future, but all this while I've been living
in the past
And I'm afraid if I get much older... well my life will have just gone by too fast.

It truly is a struggle, about the hardest thing I have ever done
Deciding if I stay with what I'm doing, or go back to something I know is not
much fun.

See, years ago I left the city and office work behind
Decided I'd pack up and follow my heart's desire, working horses was more my
kind.
So I've traveled round the country lerning my trade from some of the best
Working long hours, hard work with low pay to see if I'd meet the test.

I've got to do what others only dream of, and I've never had one regret
But now I lay at night thinking and I struggle and I fret
And the decision I'm about to make cuts me like a knife
'Cause npothing ever stays the same - that's the reality of life.

******

    In 1988 my sister and her family came from Kansas City to Dallas, for Christmas. I got
3 days off from the U-$ Ranch in Sealty, Texas to join them. We went to Fort Worth, stopped at
Leddy's Saddle shop, the Cadillac of saddle makers. A wonderful place, full of fine handcrafted
equipment and intoxicating new leather smell. My nephew was an inquistive 4 year old: open, and
straightforward you never know what he would say/ A cowboy entered the shop and from the quiet
assuredness about him, his faded jeans, the stack of the pant leg, the fit and shape of his hat, and the

weathered creases on his face, he had the look of a hand. Kress walked up, stopped square in fronyt of him; eyed him up and down, then looked him straight in the eye and said, "Are you a REAL cowboy?" The room became still, the man looked Kress straight in the eye, a moment passed, then a slow smile came across his face and he quietly replied, "Yes son, you could call me a "Real" cowboy."

******

AM I A COWBOY YET?

I've dug postholes, built fence and started colts
Did chores at 5 a. m. after being up all night with a sick heifer
Manned every position there is in working cattle,
operating the catch gate, wormed, tagged and inoculated,
as well as pushed up the stragglers in the chute.

Pulled calves that weighed less than I did
Been soaking wet from the top of my head to the tip of my toes
from sudden showers while riding fence.

Drove old cars and pickups. Worked for room, beef and $500 a month
Taped my boots with gray duct tape 'cause payday was still two weeks a way.
Choose the company of my dog, and horses over some male aquaintances I've known.

Been bit, kicked, bucked off, fell off and got off
Mowed hay and bucked bales.

Danced the night away: after a rodeo under the stars, or in some smokey bar, or musty old local community center or crowded street dance and then rode colts all day long the next.

Checked pastures, riding fence, counting cattle, making sure floats in water tanks still worked
And repaired broken water lines on Christmas Day
Did the job because it needed doing and I was the only one to do it.
Prayed to God Almighty to get me through
Because it was just Him and me and guts and determination, and the me part was questionable in the -10 degree weather.

I've seen a bald eagle swoop through the trees and catch a fish in the creek and fly overgead to roost in an old snag just ahead while out gathering pastures,

Rode just as dawn streaked red across the horizon to the rythmic creek of leathewr, clip clop of hooves, and jingle of bits.

While white misty fog lightly blanketed low lying brush and cattle.
Spoke quite, one word commands to black and white border collies, noislessly
streking through mist and dark and waking cows who were slow raising
apparitions up through the fog with deliberate hog-back humps in backs and
limbering one leg stretches.

Or had mini-vacations and I never left the place as I walked in a warm summer
shower, picking plump, juicy dewberries as big as my thumb that stood stirrup
high and dried off in the warm sunshine.

Wormed, inoculated and ear tagged 100n head of new cattle when the wind chill
was so cold it would ice up the gun.

Or been so hot that I sweat trickle down my back and dust laid like fine face
powder stching black lines in the creases of my face and neck as we worked in
the heat and the sun.

******

Dear Lola,

*I started this poem the day I heard Floyd passed away. I was so sad and as I thought
about all that you and your family had lost, the first few stanza just wrote themselves, The poem
doesn't do Floyd justice, but it captures the essence of the Floyd Rumford I came to know.*

A GOOD MAN PASSED THIS WAY
In memory of Floyd Rumford
Cowboy, PRCA Stock Contractor, and Horseman Delux.

They say your life is never the same, when someone good passes your way.
And favors you with a handshakeand smiles and calls you "friend"
For a little while.

Well.....
A good man passed away today.
The lives he touched won't be the same.

Empty arms and gaping holes in hearts
Were left behind with Floyd's depart.

He was more than lover, father, grandfather, friend.
He was a true confident, upon whom you could depend.

An honorable man with a Godly heart
You knew where he stood, right from the start.

A dapper cowboy in his hat and jeans
The life he loved made him spry and lean.

A fun-loving prankster with a disarming grin,
He was always quick to help you up
Or take you in.

A mentor to all who came along,
He taught each one right from wrong.
On caring for livestock, or
Riding and driving horses and mules.
From a wealth of knowledge
He'd not found in schools.

There are many that mourn his passing away and
I know they join mewhen I say:
"Knowing Floyd was one of life's true pleasures
And his gift of friendship can never be measured.

Fot the legacy of love he left behind
Is something rare and hard to find.

******

Judith Johnston   Poet/Reciter
2000 E. 125th Street
Kansas City, MO   64146-1446

RODEO CLOWN

It was a small town rodeo
Sponsored by the local Jaycees
And the clown they'd hired
Was a splendid example of rule by committee.

Some two bit circus
Must have bit the dust
And the clown they'd had
Was taking all jobs as a hungry man must.

But it was obvious to those
Who were in the know
That the man in the mask
Was taking part in his very first rodeo.

He wore a big red nose
And a painted on smile
And those long shoes that he wore
Seemed to stretch out a mile.

All in all
He was a right funny fellow
And in one hand
He carried a tiny, red, silk umbrella.

He done all right
During the broncs and the roping
Kept a lot of folks laughing
With his clowning and joking.

Then came the bulls
And things were changed around
He didn't roll out a barrel
In fact he couldn't be found.

Then a Jaycee spotted him
Sitting high in the crowd
And the argument that followed
Got heated and loud.

He'd seen those bulls
When in the pens they were loaded
They wanted him down there
When those chute gates exploded.

Well, he must have been broke
Or just lacked common sense
Cause he came down from the crowd
And climbed over the fence.

The crowd got quiet
When they saw what he was doin'
It was spooky and sad
Like when a storm, or a wedding was brewin'.

He stood lonely and lost
Out in front of that crowd
Then the chute gates popped open
And things really got loud.

It was the luck of the draw
The first bull he would face
Pure hated the cowboys
And the whole human race.

He bucked off his rider
And the crowd gave a groan
As the bull spun toward the clown
And then froze still as stone.

Now, I've never considered
If a bull could have dreams
I think dogs can
And maybe some mules that I've seen.

But that bull must have thought
That it hit paradise
Or maybe entered the lottery
And won the first prize.

He lowered his head
And went charging to get 'em

The clown tried to run
But those long shoes wouldn't let 'em.

He knocked the clown down
Then gave a loud painful bellow
As he got stuck in the eye
With a tiny, red, silk umbrella.

The clown used that umbrella
Like he was fightin' a duel
But the beating he took
Was both painful and cruel.

The cowboys leaped in
Through the dust and confusion
And pulled that clown out
With only minor contusions.

Everyone was amazed
That no bones were broken
Because that bull had been busy
With his kicking and poking.

His big red nose was gone
Of course his real one was still there
Then that bull started hacking
And shot his nose through the air.

One of his long shoes
Now hung from a horn
And from the other horn dangled
The red wig he had worn.

He'd lost his tiny, red silk umbrella
It seemed no one knew where
But for weeks that bull bellowed
When he hiked his tail in the air.

He was battered and beaten
And when his voice could be found
He announced his retirement
As a rodeo clown.

******

ROWDY

I guess at the time
Rowdy was eighteen or so
He was riding the bulls
At the small rodeos.

He had a bull out on Sunday
But on Saturday night
He was shoeing a horse
When it decided to fight.

When the dust had all settled
That horse had new shoes
But right-handed Rowdy
Had his riding hand bruised.

He also had ribs
That had been pawed all around
And a bruise in his Wranglers
Where the W was found.

With his riding hand wasted
And bruised neck to thigh
Rowdy was too hurt to ride
Too proud not to try.

He'd never rode southpaw
But they say need inspired
And in the rodeo sport
Riding hurt is required.

So on Sunday he was back
Of the rodeo chutes
Putting rosin on his rope
And spurs on his boots.

The bull he had drawn
Was an ornery old cuss
Who left most of his riders
Down biting the dust.

He wrapped his left hand
Then asked for the gate
Although he felt awkward
He was riding for eight.

The bull bucked out left
Then spun to the right
Old Rowdy was hooking
And hanging on tight.

Then he slid to the side
Dropped down in the well
He was hung on a ton
Of pure bucking Hell.

The clowns knew their jobs
And broke loose his hold
But not before Rowdy
Was plumb knocked out cold.

The ambulance was there
When he first came around
They said he was headed
For the clinic downtown.

But Rowdy stood up
Though he was dizzy and pained
Told the medic he was fine
His whole body was just sprained.

Now looking back
Some twenty years or more
I can see the next problem
Was the belt buckle he wore.

It was silver and heavy
The first buckle he'd won
And it seemed to remind him
Of things he had done.

Now, unknown to Rowdy
While unconcious he lay there
They'd loosened his britches
To give him some air.

When he pushed through the crowd
That had gathered around
That heavy old buckle
Pulled his britches right down.

His belt got all tangled
With the spurs that he wore
And with one working hand
He couldn't pull up his drawers.

A thousand spectators
Roared with delight
And cameras were flashing
As they recorded the sight.

One of his friends
Finally rushed to his side
Helped him pull up his pants
Find a good place to hide.

Rowdy's injuries soon healed
But his pride was sure hurt
When the paper ran his picture
With his pants in the dirt.

He later told his friends
That his Mom had good sense
When she said wear clean underwear
In case of any accidents.

******

RIDING FOR THE BRAND
(Song)

The trip retraced the trail that he had traveled
As a young man with a new bride by his side
Now the old man rode his horse in lonely silence
Six months ago his lovely wife had died.

The trail he rode was dim and rarely traveled
But he knew each twist and turn it took by heart
And well he knew the place the trail would lead him
He'd be there long before the day got dark.

For high up in the mountains was a valley
By a gurgling creek there was a ledge of sand

Where 50 years ago sat two young lovers
Together tracing out their ranching brand.

He viewed the trail through eyes grown dim with memories
A mind that saw things clearly from the past
Her young face seemed to float along beside him
As he rode the trail he knew would be his last.

Behind him was the ranch they'd built together
With cows and horses grazing on the land
On each flank was clearly burned the symbol
Their sons and daughters proudly called their brand.

And high up in the mountains was a valley
Where eagles dived and danced upon the wind
A love was formed that lasted past forever
A place he had to see just once again.

The pain deep in his chest was getting stronger
The past and present seemed somehow to blend
At last his eyes cleared up to search the heavens
And saw the eagles dancing on the wind.

He hung his bridle carefully on the saddle
Slapped his horse and watched it race away
Then lay down on the sand ledge in the valley
To watch the final darkness take the day.

And high up in the mountains was a valley
By a gurgling creek there was a ledge of sand
Where 50 years ago sat two young lovers
Together tracing out their ranching brand.

Together they rode only for the brand.

******

THE MOUTHPIECE

The old man perched on the bucking chute
Watching the young guys ride
He cocked a weathered brow at me
As I sat down by his side.

His clothes were old and faded
And his thinning hair was white
But when he turned to talk to me
His eyes were full of life.

He said, "Now look at these young peacocks
With padded vests and fancy chaps
Hell, back when I was young and riding
There warn't one dared look like that.

Our gear was stained and dirty
With here and there a tear
And our smiles would usually show some gaps
Because no mouthpiece did we wear.

Now, after biting my tongue a time or two
And getting yanked down on some horns
I figured that by age twenty-some
I'd be smooth-mouth as a baby born.

So I bought a big tobacco plug
And I crammed up both cheeks full
Thinking that plug would cushion my teeth
As I crawled down on that bull.

Now. I know what you are thinking
But it weren't that way at all
You're thinking that after a jump or two
I swallowed that big old chaw.

Nosiree, that tobacco worked
Kept my teeth and tongue intact
As that bull warmed up to bucking
I just chewed and hugged his back.

Since I'd never been a chewing man
Real quick I had to expectorate
I was smart enough to spit downwind
But I lost the wind back at the gate.

Now, I know what you are thinking
But it weren't that way at all
You're thinking I swallowed all that juice
I'd worked up from that big chaw.

Nosiree, I just puckered up
Thought, where it goes, it goes
Looking back it was pure bad luck
That I spit on that bull's nose.

Now, you'd think a cud-chewing critter
Would be more tolerant than a horse or mule
But that big bull just went plumb wild
When he inhaled that juice I'd chewed.

The next jump I went flying high
Kinda sailplaned through the air
I was looking for soft ground to land
But where I lit, it wasn't there.

Now, I know what you are thinking
But it weren't that way at all
You're thinking I swallowed that big old quid
But I had it locked tight in my jaw.

Yessiree, my plan had worked
I'd protected my tongue and teeth
I couldn't wait to tell my friends
About my new, and safe, mouthpiece.

It stayed with me through each spin and jump
Even lasted through the fall
Then they announced my ride scored ninty-one
And I swallowed that big old chaw."

******

THE HORSE WHISPERER

While surfing channels one rainy day
I found a program on PBS
Where a man trained horses by whispering
Sounded like something I needed to test.

This grabbed my attention right away
For my training was more like a battle
It involved whips and spurs and four letter words
Along with ear biting, blindfolds, and old saddles.

This guy claimed he could take a wild horse
And ride him on the same day he met him
It sounded much better than the method I used
Which was climb on, buck off, and go get him.

He said the whole secret was observing
Every move that the green horse made
To watch his ears, and his mouth, and his movement
To have the horse bond, instead of being afraid.

So I went out to the wild horse auction
Where I purchased a six year old stud
I wanted a good test for my skill as a whisperer
And in the pen he seemed of calm blood.

When I hauled him he tore up my trailer
When I stalled him he tore up my barn
So I turned him loose in my stud pen
Figuring there he couldn't do harm.

I spent three days patching my stud pen
Had to order more lumber and nails
When he switched from kicking to jumping
I had to go up a couple more rails.

After three weeks of life in the stud pen
Three weeks of hauling him water and grain
He quit trying to bust down the fences
So I decided he was ready to tame.

According to the book I had purchased
I was to get him to trot or to lope
In a circle around the enclosure
Gently urging him with a soft length of rope.

Rope in hand I entered the fence gate
Sure enough he started to run
You don't need a whole herd for a stampede
With the right critter you can do it with one.

For two hours we ran the arena
I chased him a few rounds, then him me
My career as a horse whisperer trainer
So far just relied on my speed.

The book said he would start chewing
And then he would start to slow down
When he wanted to stop I should let him
Then walk away and he'd follow me around.

Sure enough he started chewing and halted
I turned my back and strolled slowly away
When he nudged me. I was sure we had bonded
Then he bit me, just where I won't say.

When I spun around to correct him
All I saw was sharp teeth and big feet
I banged his nose with the book on horse whispering
To gain time for my speedy retreat.

I sure regretted those two extra railings
That I'd added to get the fence way up high
But with that stud snapping teeth at my backside
I easily cleared it on my very first try.

That stallion was squalling and raging
Made it plain he'd never be tamed
So I borrowed my bankers new trailer
And turned him loose way out on the range.

Now I'm back to my old training methods
And I ignore all these trendy new schemes
I know now why they call it "horse whispering"
That's what happens when you run out of screams.

******

GUNS

His face was angry, worn and weathered
But he kept his temper tightly tethered
As he eyed the school board that called him here
His boots and Levis were clean and worn
His stetson pulled down for a storm
When he rose to speak his voice was strong and clear.

He faced a dentist, preacher, lawyer
Banker's wife, and rich old sawyer

All elected by the People to the Board
But being elected don't mean flawless
And though the rancher was not lawless
The rights he had, he would always closely hoard.

He said, "My son was expelled a week ago
Though he'll graduate in a month or so
And the reason you gave me was he had a gun
I won't argue this cause it's a fact
But a cab locked rifle's no criminal act
Especially if you are a working rancher's son.

My son had chores that he must do
Miles from home and miles from school
My foreman dropped his horse out there that day
A neighbor saw some steers of mine
That had drifted past my northern line
So after school my son was chasing strays.

Now this ain't no school of city breds
We're mostly farm and ranching spreads
Every family member helps to do the chores
I've known most these kids 'bout all their life
Their folks I've neighbored storm and strife
No finer kids have crossed a school house floor.

To a ranch raised kid a gun's a tool
But our sons and daughters are no fools
They know a 30-30 is not a toy
But it durn sure ain't no big AK
Or Uzie with it's deadly spray
And it's never pointed at another girl or boy.

You'll never find these kids at school
Breaking God's most sacred rule
By shooting classmates down with random aim
That small brief time of national story
For these children holds no glory
They know life is not a movie or a game.

This canyon where my son was heading
Has rattle snakes with deadly venom
I killed a cattle-eating couger there last year.
There's some grizzlies up that high
If your horse is hurt, you might get by
By shooting an elk or maybe a deer.

I guess the point that I'm a'making
Is you can't stop a kid from graduating
Just because he has a gun locked in his truck
He has fencing tools and fly dope there
A saddle, bridle, feed for his mare
Shovels to dig out cattle that are stuck.

We've set his college money by
But without high school he can't even try
To take our ranch through this millenium
Right now the boy's confused and mad
His work shop is his pick-up cab
Where he keeps his working gear, including guns."

The school board said, "We understand
But schools have rules and firearms are banned."
"Then change the rules.", the cattle rancher thundered.
The school board members flinched and ducked
But the audience present all spoke up
Until the elected ones could see that they had blundered.

Then and there they took a vote
Decided rules wrote wrong could be rewrote
And changed the way the regulations read
But fearful of the Eastern press
They still banned guns like all the rest
Just scratched out firearms - wrote BB guns instead.

******

KATIES KISS

He'd been long upon the circuit
Ranked top twenty fourteen times
But the stock was getting tougher
And the road a long hard grind.

He needed one more year of effort
To meet the goals that he had set
To raise the big down payment
For the ranch they planned to get.

But his wife was getting mulish
Said he needed to retire
They had enough to buy the ranch
Just make the loan a little higher.

She said that little Katie
Needed him to be at home
A little girl needs more from father
Than a voice on a telephone.

But his pick-up was all loaded
It was time for him to leave
He gently kissed away their tears
And asked them not to grieve.

Katie grabbed her mother's purse
Smeared lipstick on her lips
He smiled down at the little girl he loved
And turned his cheek for the red lipped kiss.

But Katie jumped in the pick-up cab
Gave the rear view mirror a kiss
Said, "Now when you look behind you
You'll think of the ones you miss."

He gave them both a final hug
And started down the road
He had a show to make tomorrow
And a lot of miles to go.

But Katie's words stayed with him
And he knew his wife was right
That little girl needed more from him
Than long distance every night.

In the corner of the mirror
Was the center of his soul
He cranked that pick-up truck around
He'd just retired from rodeo.

******

    In 1855 Congress gave Jefferson Davis, the head of the War
Department, a $30,00 appropiation, and Major Henry Wayne was assigned the
task of traveling overseas to the Middle East, where he bought 33 camels to be
used by the U. S. Cavalry in the desert Southwest. Lt. Edward Beale was
assigned the task of getting them in service. The start of the Civil War stopped
the "Great Experiment." Most of the animals escaped into the desert. For many
years the animals were seen wandering the desert around the Gila and the
Colorado rivers. Some say they are still there.

THE COWBOY AND THE CAMEL

The young cub reporter
Was out searching for tales
Met an old Southwest cowboy
Who was fresh out of jail.

Who agreed for a meal
And a drink he'd supply
A tail of suvival
The cub's boss would surely buy .

His story was ancient
Back before the big fight
When the Blue claimed the wrong
And the Grey claimed the right.

Arizona was the place
Of the story he'd relate
And the whole thing happened
In eighteen fifty eight.

His horse had died
Some three hours ago
When the cowboy staggered in
To the small water hole.

The Arizona deserts
A bad place to be lost
And many a traveler
Had paid the high cost.

He still carried his saddle
His bridle, canteen, and rope
But it was far to next water
And he had little hope.

But he filled up his canteen
From the small, shrinking pool
And decided to leave
In the night desert cool.

When he saw walking toward him
From out of the sun
Such a strange looking beast
His hand went to his gun.

But a quick second look
Showed four legs and a hide
And to a true western cowboy
That meant something to ride.

So grabbing his rope
He dug down in the sand
If his luck would hold out
He'd ride out of this land.

As the beast moved in closer
He furrowed his brow
For some parts looked horsey
Some mulish, and some cow.

It was ewe necked and spavined
With a real ugly face
And the gait that it favored
Was a big rolling pace.

It had hooves like an oxen
And a wimpy old tail
And he wasn't right certain
If it was female or male.

But most striking of all
Was the shape of its back
It had a hump like a grizzly
Only bigger, and further back.

As it moved even closer
He could tell it knew man
It had a brass ring in it's nose
And a U. S. for a brand.

His first toss was true
On a front leg it closed

He worked up the rope
And grabbed the ring in its nose.

Then he was faced with the chore
Of trying to saddle
A creature that was built like
Neither horses or cattle.

The girth was too short
If his saddle centered the hump
But if he moved it on back
It slipped off its rump.

His reins wouldn't reach
On the bridle he had
And he figured that bit
Would just make it plumb mad.

So he decided on bareback
Though his tack would be lost
He was bent on survival
Whatever the cost.

He cut up his rope
Tho it was new just this year
He'd use that nose ring for steering
And maybe also for gears.

He pulled down on that ring
And the beast slowly knelt
For the first time in hours
A faint hope he then felt.

He crawled up on its back
Kinda straddled the hump
Gripped the rope to its nose ring
And gave its ribs a good thump.

Then rocking and swaying
On the beast from the sands
He rode out of the desert
To more favorable lands.

The young cub reporter
Gave the old man a stare
Then tore up his notes
Let'em fall through the air.

He called the old man a liar
Then spun on his heels
The old cowboy smiled sadly
And turned back to his meal.

But not before pulling
Out a pouch by its string
And pouring out in his palm
A big old brass ring.

******

ME AND GOD

Me and God went walking
Through a shady Ozark glen
No other man moved out with us
Just me out walking with Him.

We traced a clear spring's gurgling path
To where a river flowed
Just quietly, slowly, moved along
Enjoying what He'd bestowed.

Me and God sat on a log
And looked us all around
At chipmunks, squirrels, a browsing deer
And heard the woodland sounds.

Me and God looked high above
The rolling, wooded hills
At soaring birds and floating clouds
And heights I don't know still.

We talked of woes of mortal man
The sickness, grief, and death
The greed and hate and jealousy
That birth gives man's first breath.

We talked about the deep, deep love
Man shared with God and family
And how that love can conquer all
If man would stop and see.

The sunset framed the river
The fires being lit beyond
Where my brother waited with grey-clad men
For the battle lines of dawn.

He knew nothing of my presence
I knew of his by chance
The choice was mine alone to make
Alone, to take a stance.

My horse was tethered, waiting
And a U. S. brand he wore
I slowly stepped to leather
Looked again at yonder shore.

Dawn would find me missing
The Blue could stand one less
I pulled my horse's head around
And headed him due west.

I tore off my own blue tunic
Thought I felt Him give a nod
Some choices lie for us to make
And we made it, - Me and God.

******

THE HOMESTEADERS

He fled the Appalachians
Left the tired and bitter soil
For a homestead out in Kansas
Where he might profit from his toil.

He believed the tales told by land agents
Of a deep and fertile loam
How crops would spring up overnight
Where the buffalo once roamed.

He hitched two mules to wagon
Loaded three kids and a wife
Said farewell to friends and kin
And set out for his new life.

The trip was long and brutal
Many rivers must they cross
One small grave they left behind
Each frontier has its cost.

At last they entered Kansas
Staked out 160 as their own
Used their plow to break the sod
Into squares to build a home.

They took their mules and wagon
To a tree grove miles away
Where they cut some logs for roofing
Over which more sod would lay.

They scraped deer hide thin for windows
Used leather straps to hang the doors
Hauled fireplace stones from a nearby creek
Packed the dirt they called a floor.

They draped cloth below the ceiling
To catch dirt that dribbled down
Used buffalo chips for all their fires
Since no firewood was close around.

The prairie soil was virgin
And yielded slowly to the plow
The three-day trip to town was made
Bought a bull and two good cows.

Each year they made some progress
Each spring more land was cropped
The children came in stair steps
More hands for chores that never stopped.

Two tiny graves well tended
Were on a grassy wind-swept hill
Where the wild flowers added beauty
And gave life where life was stilled.

The woman's beauty faded
Drained by toil and Kansas sun
The man grew lean but rawhide tough
From work that was never done.

Twice they fought off Indians
Many times they fought a drought
A twister picked up their outhouse
Set it down some three miles out.

But they proved up on their homestead
And even bought the farm next door
No one could call them wealthy
But at last they were not poor.

Nine kids suvived the hardships
And each one left in time
But they all came back to visit
The proud parents left behind.

The old sod house finally vanished
Replaced by lumber brought by rail
And the outside world moved closer
As the Fed's improved the mail.

Their youngest son stayed with them
Because he too was born to till
And when the couple died two days apart
He dug their graves upon the hill.

The land they loved has passed to me
A descendant of their line
Their weathered graves are tended still
And a fence protects their shrine.

Sometimes when shadows lengthen
And memories flood the land
I walk the ground they worked and loved
And take pride in who I am.

******

John D. "Jay" Jones   Poet/Reciter/Story Teller/Song Writer
1715 Aspen Circle
Columbia, MO   65202

Jay Jones is a Major Member of The Missouri Cowboy Poets Association, and is the present editor of the MCPA News Letter. Jay is a native Missourian, and a former rodeo performer. His specialty in rodeo was that as a Bull Rider. Jay's poetry, and stories, is a reflection of his true life experiences. The stories and poems of his youthful rodeo days are apticulerly colorful. Jay has recently picked up his old guitar and written some very fine Western songs.

DEAR ALLISON

I went to the barn quite early to do the morning chores
Like forkin' down hay and feedin' grain, and swingin' wide the doors.
I caught up that bay colt, to do a favorite thing
Ridin' in the pasture, checkin' calves, in early spring.

Now that colt, like you, is just a kid; his schoolin's just begun.
And he's got to learn to pay attention; other times for fun.
He'll take the bit, and stand quiet, when the saddle's swung in place,
And though he might want to, he won't bolt, it's me who'll set the pace.

Just like you learn your ABC's, he's got to learn his too,
And that takes practice, and hard work, so he'll know what to do.
When you're grown, you'll make good use of everything you've learned.
And if he tries, why, so will he; into a cow horse he's turned.

So I opened up the gate and walked us both outside
He eased his back and let a sigh, when I settled down astride.
We went along the meadow then, the dew just sparklin' in the light
Of early mornin' sun rays, and the meadow larks singing bright.

Until we came to the pasture gate, and I stepped down to do
The opening, then the shutting, of it when he passed through.
The cows looked up from grazing when we ventured near,
The little calves watched with eyes of curiosity, not fear.

Now there's a heifer, whos time is close, I've watched the last few days,
But now don't see her with the herd, Guess she's hidin'up aways.
Along the creek. Ho! There she goes. The colt watches her run east
Then stop, and look back west, to the buckbrush beneath the trees.

She's calved alright, that's where we'll look, to see what we can find.
She watches us go down the draw, then she follows aways behind.
It's hard to see down in the brush, but we hunt back and forth
Until I see the tracks she made, and they lead back north.

To a thicket, and lookin' hard, I just can see a tiny ear
Flicker once, then lie still. but that's enough, because I'm near.
And I push through and find him there, nose stretched out on the ground
And still as hope, just frightened eyes, lashes flutterin' at my sound.

And then I see your balloon in shreds, and the note that you set free;
"Dear Finder, When you find this, won't you send it back to me?
And tell me where it came to rest, how far it's journey's run
Away from Kansas City. Love Allison.

******

SCHOOL WORK

My boy's just like a lot of 'em, I suppose.
He'd rather be in boots and jeans than got up in town clothes.
And he'll vow to do most anything, even fixin' fence,
If he thinks it keeps him home from school, and off the teacher's bench.

Now, fetchin' pliers and bailin' wire ain't no kind of fun,
But he swears it beats a day in school, and, well... he is my son.
But we make him go a bunch, and hope that he does well,
And will use his time effectively in that God-forsaken cell.

Sometimes, he'll forget himself, and even have some fun,
And bring us home a tale about some stunt some kid has done.
Or, in his haste to get outside some cookies and some milk,
Papers spill out of his books that reveal the student' ilk.

And so it came to pass one night, when I'd come in from chores,
And picked a piece of paper up off of the kitchen floor.
His assignment was to write in prose, correct and neat,
Three things he'd have if he should snare a leprechaun's hind feet.

The first that he wrote down was money. Now that makes good sense to me,
Or to anyone who's doctored calves through a cold spring's damp and freeze.
But he'd not keep it for himself. Why, he'd divvy it all out.
Piles for Ma and Pa, and teachers too. Nope, he'd wouldn't leave her out!

Oh, he'd keep a little for himself, just enough for gettin' by,
To keep stocked up in candy canes, and have one good horse to ride.
The second thing was World Peace, to abolish crime and vice,
And to have everybody get along, to just "Be nice."

But the third one he wrote down made me give his mom a wink,
And reckon, "Maybe everything we've said has not gone down the sink."
For what he wants makes good advice for people, low or high.
It's for everyone to be trustworthy and never tell a lie.

Johnny Kindrick   Poet/Reciter/Musician/Singer/Song Writer
RR Box 25
Richards, Mo. 64778

Johnny is a true professional performer. He plays and sings old time favorites as well as some of his own songs, and recites mostly his own poems. Johnny and his family run a few cows on their home-place at the edge of the Great Plains where Kansas meets Missouri. He has been a journalist, Musician, and educator. An authority on the cowboy mythology, his presentastion is a historical overview through stories, and song of the evolution of the cowboy image.

A VISIT FROM THE VET

With an old cow down,
A flat tire on the truck,
The ponds all froze over,
And the tractor still stuck.

I said to myself,
What the heck can I do?
There's been days like this
In fact quite a few.

As for the old downer cow,
I'll just call the vet.
He might get her a goin',
But it's not a sure bet.

Cause my neighbor once called him
When down on his luck,
And the next vehicle along
Was a dead animal truck.

But he came anyway
With a gleam in his eye,
He gave her a shot,
And bid a hasty good-bye.

As he left spinning gravel
I wondered somehow
Was the farewell for me?
Or was it good-bye to the cow?

Must have been for the cow,
For with the shot and good-bye,
He left her a laying,
Her feet propped on the sky.

Then I looked up the road,
And to my dismay,
A dead animal wagon
Was heading my way.

I'm much smarter now
As Doc heads back to town
For I know why the dead wagons
All follow him around.

And I thought to myself
As I oft had before,
Well, I should have known better,
I don't need Dr. Moore!

As for my truck and the tractor,
There's still some remorse,
For I got rid of them both,
And have bought a dumb horse.

******

WHEN OLD AGE STRIKES

When old age strikes,
You just can't win.
You lose your memory
And grow more skin.

When you can't find your tools,
You look and you look,
But can't find a thing
That nobody took.

You'll go to the bathroom
Almost every night,
And dribble the floor
Before you can turn on the light.

You'll stub your toe on a chair,
Though it hurts like sin,
You'll turn right around
And do it again.

You lose your glasses,
Can't find your cane.
When it's time for action,
It's all in vain.

And speaking of romance,
Believe it or not;
There's no use to strike
Cause the iron's not hot.

With the hearing aid lost,
And a hump in your back,
It's not worth the effort
To crawl out of the sack.

But you shimmey out of bed,
With a touch of the gout,
And put on your clothes,
But they're wrong side out.

Then you slap in your teeth,
But you look like a clown,
Cause just like yesterday,
You got them upside down.

You look in the mirror,
Oh what a sight,
You've been through a battle
But you've lost the fight.

You don't dare see a doctor,
It will just make him grin,
When he gets his hooks in your wallet
And says - "Come back again."

Old age can be cruel,
It's one thing that's true.
It's no respector of persons,
It might catch up with you.

And the only way
That you'll ever shuck it
Is just turn up your toes,
And kick the bucket!

******

NO SUNSET

Old cowboys never die,
At least that's what they say,
But I never had the proof of it
'Till long about last May.

Old cowboy George was riding range
With thunder in the sky,
When lightening struck and killed his horse,
We thought old George would die.

With eyes rolled back, his hair all singed,
And the buzzards circling round,
All though the time had surely come
To plant him in the ground.

When all at once he gave a kick,
And then let out a yell,
Get me a horse I'm here to work
I've had my taste of hell.

You know old cowboys never die.
We are a hardy bunch.
Get of of my way I'm here to stay,
And it's brown beans for my lunch.

They'll ride the range, they'll mend the fence.
They'll even put up hay,
But true old cowboys never die
They just smell that way.

******

Shelby Lane   Poet/Reciter/Singer Musician
Rt 1 Box 113
Elkland, MO   65644

Shelby Lane is a small cattle rancher. He sings, and plays guitar and other instuments. He performs at church and class reunions, jam sessions, and other civic events.

EDITH

Slowly he opened his eyes from surgery'
And patted his wife's hand.
His leg was broken and cast to the hip,
ICU was still in demand.

"Edith, you were there with me, my sweet little wife,
When the cow hooked me last fall.
And you were there when the tractor turned over,
In fact you saw it all.

It was you who bandaged my arm up,
When the chain saw made it's assault.
And there when the hay baler ate my other arm,
Due to a mechanical default.

You were there when the dun horse bucked me off,
Blacked my eye and cut my head
And there when I dallied my finger up
Left it cut, swollen and red.

You were there when the handy-man jack fell,
And my chest was crushed by the truck.
Now I've come to one final conclusion,
Edith, you're just bad luck.

******

BETWEEN FATHER AND SON

They sat and reminisced the tales,
This father and his boy.
Laughed with open laughter now,
Of things they did enjoy.

Mother hearing now the tales,
Of things to her unknown.
She'd never heard the stories,
Until her child was grown.

"Remember Dad, that cow we penned,
The one that fought so bad?

We shipped her then that very day,
For all the hell we'd had."

"Yep, that's the same old cow son.
When we hauled her into town,
When you went to unload her,
She turned and knocked you down."

"What about that big dun cow?
The one that hooked your mare.
Knocked her down with you astride,
Sure gave me quite a scare."

The mother's thoughts turned backward,
Her mind did calculate.
She said, "When did this happen?"
Her son said, "I was eight."

Dad whata 'bout the time your bull
Hooked me right in the butt.
Wallowed me around the pen,
We sure did leave a rut."

"That day Danny bucked you off,
He threw you pretty high.
Got you up and dusted you off,
Said you were learnin' to fly."

Once again mother's thoughts went back.
As laughter filled the den.
All these things had happend back,
When her child was only ten.

She'd never known of their wrecks.
Protective of her son,
For if she had ever found out,
She'd raise hell with everyone.

Their secrets, kept to themselves,
In silence they did abide.
Until this day, twenty years past,
They set there side by side.

******

THE RIGHT TO VOTE

The sheriff after serving many years,
Now was up for re-election,
Because he was old, he knew that the young
Would vote in his opponent's direction.

He knew he simply needed more votes,
To win back his own terrain.
Somehow He'd get the much needed votes,
The lead he just had to regain.

Taking his wife of fifty years,
He played the old election game,
Collecting names from the local grave-yard,
To boost up votes in his name.

They started at the right hand corner,
Worked their way to the grave-yard center.
The sheriff stopped, but his wife went on
As more names in her book she would enter.

"Woman, what are you doing?, he asked,
"Our talley does now surpass
The amount of votes I'm needing
To out vote my opponent with class."

"I know dear," came his wife's reply,
"But it's just not dignified,
The ones over here have the same right to vote
As the ones on the other side."

******

SWEET THING

Looking through the Caller Times,
Ole Jim Bob by chance read.
The advice page by "Dear Abby,"
Absorbed every word she said.

She spoke of the perfect match,
Between man and his mate.
Common interest she did stress,
For the perfect syndicate.

Now Jim Bob had one interest,
His love was roping steers,
Had to find a gal who roped,
For marriage to persevere.

It wasn't long before he met
His perfect little chick.
She threw a real good heel loop,
Yes, roping was her nic.

In time they marched down the aisle,
Became they man and wife.
He didn't know the role she'd play,
This implant on his life.

But soon the honeymoon shut down,
And Jim Bob had the urge.
To pen his trusty steers and rope,
When Sweet Thing did emerge.

"I think I'm going to rope with you,
So don't call Rick to heel.
The way he's been missing
He would only cost us bills.

And anyway he always brings,
His case of Miller Lite.
That stuff will rot your liver,
I'll ice you down some Sprite.

Put your snuff can on the post,
You sure don't need a dip.
I don't like the spray I get,
While riding at your hip.

I don't load steers in the chute,
I sure don't rope no horns.
Daddy did all this for me,
From time that I was born."

The first steer she heeled him,
She cold trailed half the night,
Jim Bob kept yelling, "Now rope."
She'd yell back, "Things ain't just right."

She wouldn't rope ole number five,
He did not pull real straight.
Came out ahead of number six,
Turned him back at the gate.

"You didn't handle that steer right."
Was often her complaint.
"If you think I'm Camarillo,
Then think again I ain't."

Jim Bob went through years of life,
Of husband, wife team work.
Never lost his cool one time,
He never went beserk.

But often wished for times that were,
When Rick would heel his steers.
To dip his snuff when er he pleased,
To drink just one cold beer.

He quietly got a plan in mind,
That would cause no remorse.
He went to a barrel futurity,
Bought a winning barrel horse.

Now Sweet Thing runs her barrel race,
And Jim Bob ropes his steers.
Their life a perfect marriage;
Has endured twenty years.

******

COWBOY GATHERING

I went to a cowboy gatherin'
'Twas back a month or two.
Thought I'd write a cowboy poem
Like the paid performers do.

Fixed myself with pen and paper
And wuz workin' overtime
But about three verses later
I noticed the words don't rhyme.

Now rhymin' sure makes a poem
Sound a whole lot better,

An' writin' poems ain't as easy
As writin' down a letter.

Them big performers come on stage
I heard'em do their thing
I listen to their songs and poems
Until my poor ears ring.

Now they make it look so easy
It's hard for me to bear,
Then I noticed one thing common,
Them folks all have facial hair.

It really must have took some time
To grow that hair s'long.
Does it help 'em with a poem
Or to write a cowboy song?

Some of them are down-right wooley
With hair up on their cheeks.
They're always twistin' on the ends
Which curl up in pointed peaks.

I'll bet that hair's like Cypress knees,
It helps 'em get more air.
It may supply some vitamins
That improves their wordy fair.

But you can't argue with success,
And I'll not even try,
That hair a'growin' on their face
May be just the reason why.

They can write them fancy poems
And never break a sweat,
But when I try to do the same
I just end up in a fret.

I guess there's something in my genes
That has to do with hair.
I've even fertilized my face
But it just stays slick and bare.

Folks, I've sure 'nough thought it over,
Which turned my mind to hash.
The reason I can't write a poem;
I can't grow a big mustache!

THIS OLE BOOK

He pulled his hat down on his head,
His jacket pulled up tight
Around his neck to fight the wind
And rode out through the night.

Some miles away from camp he stopped,
Reached for his little book,
Then looked skyward toward the stars
With a thankful cowboy look.

"Now Lord I know it's Christmas Eve
And I'm not much on praying,
But hope you'll lend an ear to me
And hear the words I'm saying.

I ner been in your church's door.
Can't stand the frustration
That comes when large crowds gather
At your local congrgation.

But I got your book here by my side
Carried it pert near fifty years.
It got me through in laughter,
In sorrow and in tears.

It's pages Lord are tattered
And torn with years of use.
Rode miles in this ole saddle bag,
And suffered through abuse.

It's been with me down cattle trails
Roped many a steer that's tough.
Has flooded streams and rivers
With waters high and rough.

Has doctored calves, fixed tractor tires
It's lived the cowboy life.
It's raised up three good children
And gave me one fine wife.

But on this special night each year,
Just have to have my say,
And thank you Lord for this ole book
You gave me on your birthday."

Jimmi Naylor   Poet
HC 67 Box 536
Ash Flat, AR   71523

Jimmi Naylor is a Memorial Life Associate Member of the MCPA. She was born in the country of South Texas, and grew up on the hard knocks of cowboy life. She now calls Agnos, Arkansas home. She teaches 8th grade much of the time, but she still enjoys running barrels. and a good horse. Although Jimmi writes beautiful poetry, she will not appear before an audience, therefore before his untimely death her devoted cowboy husband, Wayne, recited Jinni's poems at every opportunity. Wayne, an MCPA member, died from a heart attack in July 2000. "Edith" was Wayne's favorite of Jimmi's poems.

THE COWBOY IN HEAVEN

I was awakened one night from a deep sleep
    By a blinding, bright light, my maker to meet.
What is the meaning of this? I asked with alarm,
    A deep but gentle voice replied,
"This is your heavenly Father. I'll do you no harm."
    There must be a mistake - I'm not dead!
"I have a job for you," the Voice from within said.

    "You see, the devil has been stealing souls away from me.
And disguises them as cattle for eternity.
    I need a good cowboy that is tough and keen,
Who doesn't mind riding hard and living on sourdough and bean.
    For it will be hot and dusty, dry as a gourd,
Rocks and rattlers to keep you from being bored.
    Scrub brush, ticks and chiggers to make you complain.
Only the importance of the job is to keep you from going insane.
    The cows have long horns pointed like pins,
But remember, they have all paid for their earthly sins.
    I want you to bring them back however you can.
To green pasture and cool water, away from the desert sand."

    What is my second choice? I ask. *This job is too rough for me.*
The soft voice growled, "How about Hell for eternity?"
    Sir, begging your pardon, the difference I don't see,
Maybe you could kindly explain it to me.
    "The difference is quite simple, I'm sure you'll agree.
You'll spend eternity herding cows with the best horses to ride.
    But most important, you'll be on MY SIDE."

******

WHAT YOU SEE

You say I look like an old hippie
But I'm much older than that
You can tell by the callous on my seat
From the saddles I have sat
    I was born in the year of '41
    I was born to ride a horse
    Born to be a cowboy, I'm what you see, I'm what you see.

Go ahead and look down your nose at me
Pretend that I'm not here
Because I won't change the length of my hair
For any woman my dear
> I was born to be a cowboy
> Born to live free
> Born to breath the fresh night air, I'm what you see, I'm what you see.

I won't try to change you my dear
I'll except you as you are
With your frilly clothes and lacy hose
Our love will carry us far
> I was born to be a cowboy
> I wasn't born to be alone
> And you're the one that I chose, to be my woman, to be my woman.

I can't be something that I'm not
Or live by another man's code
So I'll just walk in my own boots
And carry my own heavy load
> I was born to be a cowboy
> That's all I'll ever be
> So look down your nose at my dusty clothes
> > But please don't try to change me
> > Please don't try to change me
> > For I'm what you see.

******

CHRISTMAS CHEER

I was camped down on the Piney,
  It was that time of year
Out of a job, very little money,
  Didn't have much Christmas cheer.
The wind was blowing cold
  With a hint of snow in the air.
I was feeling sorry for myself,
  Life sure is unfair.
The fire was being obstinate
  Not wanting to go.
So I ate a can of cold beans
  Then crawled down in my bedroll.

Maybe things would be better
   Come the break of morn.
Now I just want to sleep
   And to get warm.
Sleep came quickly
   Too soon it was bright as day.
I slept fast, I thought to myself,
   As I pushed the blankets away.
But morning hadn't come
   Much to my surprise.
Just a brilliant light surrounded me
   That nearly blinded my eyes.
A calm silence came over
   Me like a fresh snow.
Like Adam I wanted to hide
   But there was no place to go.
The light and silence were penetrating
   They quickly engulfed my being and soul.
Giving the feeling of the
   Warmest peace I'll ever know.
Then both were gone
   Again it was windy and cold.
Was I dreaming that night?
   Well I really can not say
But it changed this cowboy's life
   On that Christmas day.
That peace has been with
   Me now thru out the years
And here's wishing you that same
   Happiness, Peace and CHRISTMAS CHEER.

******

BORROWED TIME

I'm just here on borrow time
       don't have long to stay.
Not much time to correct mistakes I make,
       before my Lord comes to take me away.

Borrowed time is all there is,
       be it a minute or a hundred years.
So I'll spend my time with care
       and try to bring more happiness than tears.

There is an example I must set
    for the stranger I haven't yet met.
May he see some glory in my eyes
    to carry with him until he dies.

I don't want to be a hero or a king
    just a plain and simple cowboy, let me be.
Let me shine with a light for all to see
    the love of God all over me.

When this borrowed time is gone
    and it is time for me to move along
Let a memory of me remain
    to praise the glory of THY NAME.

Borrowed time is going fast,
    just don't know how long it will last
This may be my last chance to pray
    before my Lord comes to take me away.

Yes, this may be my last chance to pray
    before my Lord takes me away.

******

TIME TO GO

Get up, you riders, it's time to go.
  Get the lead out, don't be so slow!
The moon's gone down, the sun's on the rise.
  Have a cup of coffee, wipe the sleep from your eyes.

There's mountains to climb, valleys to see;
  Cliffs so high they make you dizzy
Roaring rivers to ford, so clean and deep,
  Will burn memories in your mind to forever keep.

How can one not want to ride by the hour?
  To smell the fresh forest and the wild prairie flowers.
God made this for all mankind to enjoy,
  So help keep it pretty and clean, don't help to destroy.

A good horse to ride and no phones to ring,
  Hum a soft ballad or listen to the birds sing.
Spend time with the spirit that's deep within,
  To know yourself is to be your own best friend.

BUCKAROO JIM

Out in Missouri in the days of old.

Lived a young cowboy so brave and bold.

I would like to say that he is tall and slim

BUT HE'S NOT!

Buckaroo Jim, Buckaroo Jim

Pride of the west and we all love him.

Down on the Piney they went for a ride.

Jiggs stopped in the crick, Buckaroo kicked him in the side.

With a jump and a kick

Jiggs threw Buckaroo in the crick.

Buckaroo Jim, Buckaroo Jim

If you're going to play in the crick you need to learn to swim.

A yearling heifer got a bee under her skin.

Chased Buckaroo around the catch pen.

Sing to her Jim that will common her down.

"My mind is willing," he replied,

But my feet won't stay on the ground.

Buckaroo Jim, Buckaroo Jim

I think I'll work the cows from the outside of the pen.

******

COWBOY

Hey Cowboy where you been? I asked of my old friend.
Well I've been up in County General, a young colt tried to do me in.
I would like to talk to you if you don't mind.
Something happened there that I just can't define.
Set me down and tell me what it's about
Together I'm sure we can figure it out.
There was this bright place where my troubles ceased
With a feeling of complete security and peace
And I was drawn up a path to a gate
But it was locked, I arrived too late
And I couldn't get thru but an Angel standing guard
Said Cowboy take that trail around to the front yard.
I started on down the trail but it was rocky and rough
Couldn't walk it without boots, my barefeet weren't tough.
I went back and told the Angel without my boots I couldn't get to the front gate
And the Angel told me to go get my boots, that heaven would wait.
When I awoke, called for a nurse, need my boots quick
I need to go home, but she said I was too sick.
So here I am and I don't know what to believe
Except the Dr. said he thought he had lost me.
But one thing I for sure know
I want to have my boots on when it's time to go.
Well time passed and I drifted to a far away range
Hadn't seen Cowboy in many a year, when a telegram came
Informing me that Cowboy was down, not expected to survive
He asked for me to come before he died.
I left a note for my boss telling him of my flight
Saddled my best horse and rode off into the night.
Arrived in Marshall, Texas, a two day ride.
I went straight to County General to be by my friend's side
The family said Cowboy was in a coma, was running out of time
I walked in, stepped up and took his hand in mine
Much to my shock and surprise
He squeezed my hand and opened his eyes
Raised up and said I've been waiting for you old friend.
I want you to fill my last request when I cash in.
I want my boots on before they lay me in the ground
Before I hit that narrow, rough trail I want my feet sound
It will be done, I promise to see to your last request.
Cowboy layed back, closed his eyes and said I need to rest.
I went back into the hallway, set down to wait
For I knew Cowboy was ready for his second trip to Heavens gate.

I dose off to sleep. It had been a long ride
Worth every minute to be at my friend's side.
Something startled me awake, I knew Cowboy was gone
I looked to Heaven said "goodbye Cowboy
I'll make sure you have your boots on."

******

Ronald D. Pappan, DVM   Poet/Reciter/Singer/Musician
P. O. Box 250
Richwoods, MO 63071-0250

Ronald Pappan, was born a cowboy in Oklahoma in 1941 to share cropper parents. Part Indian, French, Irish, and English. He grew up living the cowboy life with cattle, horses, hay, and wheat. He graduated from Kansas State University with degrees in Animal Husbandry and Veterinary Medicine. He has lived in the St. Louis area since 1971. He practices veterinary medicine, raise quarter horses, trail ride, show, judge, and sing cowboy and traditional country songs around the campfire.

TH' COWBOY WAY

They glared at one other. Toe to toe it'd been one hell of a fight;
Friends for years, they'd duked it out, each thinkin' he was right.

Joe a black eye, Tom a fat lip. It looked as though neither had won;
Now they stood cuffed, th' two old cowboys, feelin' real sheepish an' dumb.

Th' bookin' desk officer looked at th' cowpokes, turned aside an' grinned;
"You fellers have a disagreement? I thought you two was friends."

"Got to hold you 'till tomorrow. It's probably just as well."
He called th' jailer in an' said, "Take'em down to a holdin' cell."

Once there, th' hours passed slowly, so they each had time t' think;
To dwell upon their folly. Joe's eye so swole he couldn't blink.

Tom, he finally spoke up - "What we did sure was a bust!"
Joe looked at 'im with his good eye. "You're right, ya crusty ol' cuss!"

They began to yell an' beller, to get Sarge's attention;
Sarge ignored them 'em for a spell - that was his intention -

T' let'em dwell on what they'd done. On that he did intend;
Wanted th' cowpokes to remember they really was best friends.

An' when about four hours had passed, he walked up to their cell;
Th' two ol' codgers on th' bunk looked like they'd been through hell.

"Have you had time t' think it over, what you two have done?
'Cause, from th' looks on yer faces, neither of ya won."

Ol' Tom, he looked at Joe. Joe looked back at'im and grinned;
"We just had a little tussel - but we're still th' best of friends."

"Ya, see, Sarge, we're from th' old school. That's about all we can say.
Ya duke it out, then ya shake hands. That's th' cowboy way!

Sarge, got a key, stepped up to th' door. "Ya both get outa here."
It just saves me paperwork", he told'em with a sneer.

They walked out on th' street together. Neither had much t' say;
But they stopped on th' corner an' they shook hands

IT WAS JEST TH' COWBOY WAY.

TH' STORY OF TH' SADDLE BAGS

Th' cowboy leaned against his horse, tied to a hitchin' rail;
Th' cowpoke looked as if he'd rode in right off th' dusty trail.
I walked up to th' cowpoke, an' he flashed a wolfish grin
He asked if I'd care t' hear 'bout th' predicament he was in.
Now, me bein' a real friendly sort, I told 'im that I would;
An' offered my assistance, in any way I could.
Now, he held a pair of saddle bags, stained an' grayish brown;
Said they'd fallen off a mule he'd passed on his way into th' town.
Th' woman ridin' on that mule ignored his strident shouts;
As he tried to catch her eye as he waved th' bags about.
"I follered her aways," he said. "She plumb ignored my cries
An' m' voice fell on deaf ears, an' her unseeing eyes.
I asked about 'er from th' owner of the' gen'ral store.
He said she was a strange one, but he didn't know much more.
Now, ya see I didn't want no one t' think I stole these bags;
'Specially from a woman -- even if she be a hag!
An' just when I though th' bags was mine, th' ol' woman, she appeared,
As if by magic, on that mule. She looked at me an' sneered.
Accused me then of stealin' 'em, but that I did deny.
Then she drawed a pistol on me -- I feared I'd surely die.
Then, I drawed m' gun an' shot her dead, an' she fell off that mule;
No cowpoke, puncher or no hag should take me for a fool!"
My eyes were wide, my mouth agape as I listened to his tale;
How could he act so nonchalant, a' leanin' on that rail?
If he'd just killed a woman fer a pair o' saddle bags!
What made th' bags so valuable, t' make him shoot the hag?
My curiousity got me, an' I warmed up t' the' task
"What's in them bags there, Mister" I jest had t' ask.
Th' cowpoke looked at me, grinned an' then replied:
"It took ya long enough, boy, t' ask me what's inside!
Ya see, I been a' punchin' cows. Ain't been here fer a spell
An' funnin's hard t' come by, I can tell ya, sure as hell!
But, I'll tell ya what's inside these bags, since you fell fer my' yarn
It's the same b.s. that you'll find, son, in any rancher's barn!!!"

******

I AIN'T RIDIN' SIDESADDLE!

Some folks jest don't relish life
Like they ought to do
Don't rowdy it and randy it,
Paint th' town a bright red hue.

They live their life "conservative,"
Never riskin' a great deal;
How do they know they've experienced
What it's possible to feel?
I want t'ride my horse full out
Feel th' cool wind in my hair;
Feel th' power underneath me,
That's his an' mine to share.
No, I ain't ridin' sidesaddle;
I want to sit with pride
My body meldin' with th' horse,
An' match him stride for stride!
An', I'll dare to go full out
For th' things in life I love;
So, I ain't ridin' sidesaddle!
I swear to God above!
Let me relish each new day
Drink it in an' gulp it down;
You may not think my manners great
Upon me you might frown
But I ain't ridin' sidesaddle!
Let me tell you that, my friend,
Just let me meet MY life headon
Until I go 'round th' bend!
So, till th' Bassman calls me in
I AIN'T RIDIN' SIDESADDLE!!!

******

THE HORSE AUCTION

Th' horse was old, past his prime when they led him in th' ring;
Had a cut on his knee, but his eye was kind. I wondered what he would
    bring.

Was huntin' a mount for my grandson. Wanted somethin' I could trust;
Th' horse didn't limp. Didn't look bad, if you ignored th' dull coat an' th' dust.

Th' auctioneer started makin' his spiel, said th' horse was 16 years old;
An' that geldin' handled like a champ -- th' kind that's worth pure gold.

I put up my hand when he started at Three, t'see how th' biddin' would go;
But someone else had th' same idea, an' his price began t' grow.

After awhile th' bids started t' lag. I was hopin' against hope,
That I would prevail an' buy this ol' horse, but so did some other folk.

My grandson's birthday was in just two days. He wanted a horse real bad;
I wanted to make him into a horseman like I had made of his dad.

Th' bid was at Eight Hundred an' Five. They headed th' horse toward th' door;
My bid was low, not quite up to snuff, so I bid Twenty Five more.

Th' woman sittin' across th' way must o' wanted th' horse just as bad;
She raised m' bid by Ten an' looked real smug. Was startin' to make me mad!

Th' price was now at Eight Hundred an' Forty. I was beginnin' to feel real low;
How would I feel if I went home without him? Was runnin' low on dough.

I decided then to bid one more time. After that I'd have to go home;
An' to my delight, the woman quit, too, an' that surprised me some.

Later I loaded th' horse in my trailer an' I noticed across th' way,
That same woman loadin' a pony, an' I heard her girlfriend say:

"You got a good price for ol' Buck over there. But don't ya feel some remorse?
Takin' some dumb cowboy for a ride by biddin' on your own horse?"

******

RIDIN' NIGHT WATCH

I drew short straw, ridin' watch tonight, circlin' th' herd t'
keep'm tight;
Th' moon is full an' shinin' bright
An' all's right with th' world.

My hoss is watchful, stridin' loose, ears up an' a'listenin;
To th' sounds of th' bedded herd, horns pointed skyward,
hides a'glishenin'
An' all's right with th' world!

No night storm is a brewin', no heat lightnin' t' be seen;
Ridin' night hawk on a night like this is every cowboy's dream.
When all's right with th' world!

Cows a talkin' to their calves; steers a callin' low;
Music to a cowpokes ears. Some cowboy's singin' down
below.
An' all's right with th' world!!

Th' smell of sage an' dew an' cow - t' me, they're just th' best!
An' if I had t' die right now, I'd make just one request
That all cowpokes a ridin' night watch be given such a night;
When th' herd's content an' bedded down, an' th' prairie's lit
up bright --

AN' ALL'S RIGHT WITH TH' WORLD!

******

IF THEY DON'T GET PERTIER AS TH' NIGHT WEARS ON

She sat on a stool at th' end of th' bar, where she'd sat many times before;
Never mind there was some kinda overhand, an' her makeup had been a chore.
When she sauntered in th' door that night, she'd passed a cowboy comin' in;
Looked like he'd been on th' range a spell - three day whiskers on his chin.

For th' best part of th' evenin' now he'd drank beer, chased it with gin;
An' looked over at her a couple o' times - gave her a cowboy grin.
Now she began to turn on th' charm, showed her dimples deep an' large;
Gave him her best 'come on' glance - a look that was supercharged.

Th' cowpoke got up - he'd took th' bait. Walked up an' tipped his hat;
"Mind if I sit down here with ya, ma'am?" She thought it was simple as that.

But, it was a shock when he sat down. up close, she warnt no beauty!
He hoped that as th' night wore on, she'd turn into a cutie.
But, that never happened, to his chagrin, though she wanted him to stay;
He mumbled to her as he got up. "Tomorrow's another work day."

There's a point this story gets to, arrived at in roundabout course -
If the ugly ones don't get pertier as the night wears on -

IT'S TIME TO GO HOME TO YER HORSE!!!

******

TH' REAL BULL

Th' bull pawed th' ground an' spouted out steam
From nostrils red, eyes gleamin' mean.
He'd been the King of the Pasture 'till now
Had had his pick of jest any ol' cow.
But here was somethin' he'd not seen before,
What looked like a bovine in the corral next door.

But somethin' was not right - different somehow;
  Th' thing had a motor, but horns like a cow.
Th' bossman rode in on his cuttin' horse colt,
Took after th' thing, an' it turned with a jolt.
Then it made a sound like it was changin' gears;
  A sound that was new to the ol' bull's ears.

Now th' thing was a challenge - a nuisance to him;
  Peered at it with eyes that anger made dim.
An' th' bull took a run and cleared th' fence full.
To th' rider's surprise, he now faced th' bull,
Instead of the mechanical cuttin' horse steer.
  Turned the calf fast - said, "We're outa here!"

But to his utter surprise, he was not Toro's aim -
  It was th' steer - th' mechanical thing!
Th' ol' bull charged it, tossed it up high;
  It came down on his horns for another try.
Trampled it under foot, ripped th' horns from it's head.
  He was certain now th' bovine thing was dead!

To make this here story short an' sweet,
  Th' bull fought th' thing 'till he fell on his seat.
An' he felt so silly as th' cows gathered 'round
To look at this thing makin' whirrin' sounds,
As it reared up feebly, he let out a snort - an'
  Th' cuttin' steer finally pulled up short.

An' th' bull wasn't quite sure jest what he had done;
  It wasn't a battle that he'd really won.
An' th' cows thought him silly fer losing his cool,
It had not made him look like a very smart bull.
So, th' moral of this story is perty darn clear
  Jest make sure ya know a bull from a steer!!!

******

TIN LIZZIE

Th' cowboy'd been on the range for a spell -- decided he'd head into town.
Saddled his hoss an' away he did ride - then he was Wichita bound.
On th' outskirts of th' city, he came on a curious sight;
'Twas a four wheeled, smoke spoutin' monster, an' it put his hoss t' flight.
The cayouse forgot he knew th' word 'whoa' - an' snortin', away he did run;
Th' driver of th' Tin Lizzie though it was wonderful fun!

He laughed with such gusto, an' slapped his thigh - as he watched that ole
cayouse buck;
Th' cowboy was doin' some ridin' as ol' Roanie dodged and ducked.
Then, after th' geldin' had come t' a halt, th' cowboy spun him around.
T' face th' shakin', shudderin' monster -- but this time they held their ground.
He was mad an' in awe, both at th' same time as he faced that Lizzie machine;
But, th' driver a'laughin' inside her made th' cowboy plumb mean!
Now, th' cowpoke didn't take kindly to th' driver a'makin' fun;
So, he pulled his trusty six shooter - an' now th' driver was under th' gun!
"Jest what th' hell's so funny?" asked th' cowpoke of th' driver man;
Shore as shootin', he wiped off his smirk -- was sweatin' t' beat th' band.
"I truly am sorry, mister. Didn't mean t' spook yore horse."
He thought he'd get off lightly, that it was a matter of course.
Th' cowboy took a spell t' answer, but this is what he said:
"You go around treatin' people this way, you just might end up dead!
But, I ain't never seen nothin' like this here contraption;
I been a long time on th' range,"
Th' cowpoke gazed at th' driver, who still looked a little strange.
"An', I don't cotton t' you makin' fun of someone ya don't even know;
An' if ya got any sense at all, son, ya better fire it up an' go.
Th' driver had lost his cavalier mood, an' he got out t' turn th' crank;
Th' cowpoke saw all th' work that it took, put his heel in his horse's flank --
So, turnin' his horse, away he did ride -- took hisself to th' nearest bar,
An' later that night, while more than jest tipsy, told of meetin' with th' car.
An' now at th' end of this story, a conclusion must be seen;
Neither th' cowpoke nor none of his listeners could know what th' Lizzies would
mean --
They were th' beginnin' of th' gasoline age, th' ignition of th' torch,
That would burn themselves into history as th' end of th' cowboy an' horse.

**

That it marked th' beginnin' or th' end for th' workin' cowboy, who had made
his livin' on a horse.
Which brings to mind a sayin' of Will Rogers -- " America will be the first
nation in history to go to the poorhouse in an automobile!"

******

Donna Penley   Poet/Reciter
6548 S. Osage
Wichita, KS   67217

Donna Penley is a cowgirl poet now living in Kansas, but who was born in Missouri. She has been writing poetry for over twenty years. She has focused on cowboy poetry for the last six years. Donna writes about all phases of cowboy life, and includes a lot of cowboy humor in her writing. Her poem, "Carrie Nation," hangs in the Carrie Nation Museum in Medicine Lodge, Kansas. Great Empire Broadcasting Company has honored Donna by producing a cassette tape of her poetry, which was distributed to all the public libraries in the state of Kansas for the benefit of the blind and sight impaired.

Donna has three other books. They are: "NO PRESERVATIVES ADDED", "LETTERS FORM A COWBOY", and "TALL TALES & LESSONS LEARNED".

Look at Donna's exciting web page on the net at: donnapenley.com.

FAVORITE SEASON

The air was cool and crisp, the a sun was shining bright
   the kind of day I live for
If God would grant me my greatest wish
   I couldn't ask for more.

I walked to the barn and saddled a horse
   then set out to make my rounds
It wasn't all that necessary, but,
   a good excuse to get out where nature abounds.

The saddle squeaked and my spurs were jingling
   as we set out at a jog
I rode like that for an hour or so
   then rested on a fresh fallen log.

I threw a leg up on the log
   as my horse was catchung his air
Then my mind started drifting
   off, out there somewhere.

The sun was warm there out of the wind
   so I pushed back into the shade
As I started thinking about the things I had
   and the way that I was made.

It wasn't arrogant or prideful
   cause I'd learned a long time ago
God has made us with different likes
   that's His business, He'd ought to know.

while some of us need fresh air
   and green grass beneath our feet
Some are content to live in town
   and walk on concrete.

So I just thanked Him for these old cows,
   this good horse and this kind of life.
But, mostly I thanked Him for my sons
   and especially for my wife.

And I thanked Him for this time of year
   and the way the seasons change so fast
This truly is my favorite time of year, jacket and chaps weather
   flys are gone and hayin's done at last.

Then I started thinking
   how a man's life changes much the same
And, if you think about it
   you can just about name,

The day and the year
   when seasons begin to over lap
And I thought about the Springtime of my life,
   cuddling with my Momma and setting on daddy's lap.

As we drove the old truck to town
   And how Summer came and my world started spinning round
As I met this girl who became the center of my life
   and I remember the day she and I became husband and wife.

The long Summer of hard work and play
   as the boys came along,
I thought those days would last forever,
   but, it's another day.

Now, I'm not saying I've entered the fall of my life
   but Indian Summer has begun
And I guess the greatest thrill to this point
   is seeing my sons have sons.

Well maybe it's not as simple as I thought
   maybe I am getting old
One things for sure, I'm getting to where
   I really don't mind the cold.

Then that old log sort of interrupted my thoughts
   so I pulled the cinch and gave the stirrup a test
Then I paused and bowed my head one more time and said
"I just thank you Lord, for each Season seems to be the Best."

******

BULLSNAKE SURPRISE

"The Encyclopedia of Rawhide and Leather Braiding",
   a book I'd received as a gift
Soon became an obsession with me
   and danged near caused our marriage a rift.

It wasn't long until my wife was referring to it
   as my "Braiding Bible"
And as I got into that thing, I thought
   "Why I might just libel....

To get as good as them vaqueros
   or who knows?
I might become as proficient
   as them Peruvian Gouchos."

The first thing I did was build me some tools
   amandrel, a splitter and a fid
Then I began to procure me some hides
   colt and calf and kid.

My first project was a three strand mystery braid
   followed be 4 round then 6 and eight
I braided over rawhide cores, ropes and metal rings
   man, I was doing great!

It wasn't long till my projects were filing my room
   the best I'd ever seen.
There were braided reins and headstalls, romals, quirts, and hobbles
   why I was a regular braiding machine!

I turned out Spanish Ring Knots by the dozen
   Pineapples by the score
Chinese Buttons, Gaucho Buttons,
   Lone Star Buttons and more.

But all of this was just practice for a project I'd set my eye on
   since the day that I'd been bit..
A custom made, weighted handled
   Bullsnake Whip.

I cut my strings long and tapered
  beveled and straight and true
A 12 strand braid, ten feet long
  and the popper added two.

That thing became an extension of my right arm
  I practiced day and night
I could pop it to the front, pop it to the back
  pop it to the left and to the right.

Now, my horses were getting skittish
  and my cows were downright shy
And I noticed my dog kept watching me
  from the corner of his eye.

Then came the day I made my fatal mistake
A judgement error that proved the demise of my trusty Bullsnake

We were walking from the truck to the house
  and the wife was just slightly ahead
When I noticed, hanging from the seat of her pants,
  a long, white fuzzy thread.

Temptation ruled, I sorta held back,
  let her get out there just about right
Then, KAWOP!, Oh, I could tell by the sound
  that snake had took a bite!

She turned on her heel and clawed at the string
Then she just glared at me and pointed at that "thing".

Then, without a spoken word she went into the house
  I slithered into my chair
While she was cooking supper
  I was saying my prayers.

I could tell by the pounding and clattering she made
  that she was still hurting and mad
As I sat there and reflected
  on the good marriage we'd had.

Then she came to the door and hollered,
  "It's ready, are you?"
I entered the kitchen...
  and stared at the stew.

She dipped me a bowl and passed it to me
  then she caught my eyes
"Eat hardy honey. it's your favorite,
  Bullsnake Surprise!"

She'd chopped it up and boiled it
  the rawhide was floating like tripe
I had no recourse but to eat it,
  I knew better than gripe.

So ends the tale (tail?) of the Bullsnake whip,
  a story that's true but sad
And as I reflect upon that stew, you know,
  It was better thab most I've had!

******

     This is the first poem I ever wrote. A lot of folks don't realize that a preacher writes about a book a year just in sermons, not counting all of the Bible studies and other things we do. Usually, these sermons are used only once, and usually as quickly forgotten by the listeners. Once in a while you really preach a good one and if you're not careful you can get big-headed. But, the Lord seems to delight in keeping His servents humble. This poem is not a Cowboy poem, and it didn't really happen, but it is the greatest fear of any man speaking in public.

HUMBLED

I preached a hot one Sunday
  man you could feel the heat
The youth, they paid attention
  not one deacon went to sleep.
My exegesis was perfect,
  my illustrations were the best
I allowed how God would save the righteous
  but He'd bedamn the rest.

I pounded and stomped and shouted
   till my voice was hoarse
That sermon I delivered
   with Supernatural Force.
Every time I'd rounded that pulpit
   that crowd would catch its breath
Man, I was getting nervous,
   afraid I'd scare someone to death!
Their eyes were wide, expressions transfixed,
   I had them in my hand
I led them through the Wilderness
   right into Beulah Land.
"Oh, you are quite the preacher", I proudly thought
   "You are one crowd gripper."
It was only later that I humbly learned
   I'd forgot to zip my zipper!

******

KNOT IN YOUR ROPE

Folks who don't believe in miraculous cures
   ain't never fooled with the bovine
You can have an old cow who can just barely go
   till you take a rope or needle - then suddenly they're just fine!

Now, this little story I'm about to relate
   will prove what I'm sayin' is true
And if you listen real close to the words that I say
   you might extract a moral or two.

I was checking my cows, it was calving time
   late May or early June
I don't recall the precise date
   but it was during the Missouri Monsoon.

Those cows of mine are kind of a religious bunch
   a Catholic/Baptist version
They like to baptise their babies at birth
   but they do it by immersion!

On this particular day the babies were fine
   but one old cow could just barely go
Probably foot rot, the weathers so wet
   or maybe a thorn betwixt her toes.

I rode up beside her she paid me no mind
   her foot was all swollen and sore
Now, me thinks, "I'll just rope her and tie her to a tree
   I've done it a hundred times before."

As I took down my rope she began to move off
   I built my loop she moved to a trot
By the time I was cranking and looking to throw
   she was splitting the wind and blowing snot!

And she was headed down hill right for the brush
   not my favorite place to be
But, I whipped up behind her and made a desperate throw
   as she ducked 'neath the branch of a tree.

Now, I wasn't tied on, didn't go for a daly
   I never even jerked the slack from my twine.
Hey. I thought I had missed, besides
   I had something more pressing in mind.

I was ducking my head and pulling up hard
   trying to avoid a crash
When suddenly the rope jerked out of my hand
   and disappeared like a snake in the grass.

Just my luck, I'd snagged her,
   like a new shirt in a barbed wire fence
This was going to be fun, I'd have to run her down a'foot
   the brush was so dad blamed dence.

A turn of events, now
   It's my horse that's tied to a tree
about a hundred yards into the brush,
   I saw her, glaring back at me.

I managed somehow to get hold of the rope
   and was looking for a tree to daly around
But, that's hard to do when everything's a blur
   that old rip was covering the ground.

But, I was keeping up - like a flag in a gale
  when she broke out into the clear
I was taking about 40 feet a jump
  then she shifted into high gear!

The next thing I knew, my buckle was plowing a furry
  and my nose was breaking the way
But my hands had burned down to the "rosebud"
  so I knew I was there to stay.

We was slipping and sliding through that grass
  so tall and wet I thought I'd surely drown.
When suddenly, that old cow just up and collapsed
  I guess I wore her down.

So ends the tale of the miraculous cure
  but the moral's all about hope
When you're down on your luck and you can barely hold on
  you'd best have a knot in your rope.

(The knot in my rope is Jesus Christ - I John 5:4,5)

******

WHEN COWBOYS REPENT

We arrive at the arena in mid-afternoon
  and observe the usual sights
Cowboys and would-bes are starting to arrive
  getting ready for showtime later tonight.

Already I'm starting to get nervous
  butterflies are flittering inside
And I can't help but thimk, "It's been a long drive,
  and it's still a long wait - just for an 8 second ride.

Seems there's never a breeze in these places,
  it's either raining or hot
But I cowboy up, go pay my dues
  then wander down to see what I got.

My bronc is called "X3,(something or the other Skoal)"
   he's Roman nosed with a long tangly mane
As I look him over, I'm thinking Mama was right
   "You cowboys are all insane!"

This horse is pure outlaw
   one glass eye, and four huge feet
And he ain't no mixer: surly and suspicious,
   something tells me I'm dead meat.

But, his most undesirable trait ain't his disposition
   the thing that's causing me to hedge
Is the way his backbone sticks up out of his withers
   like a 2x4 on edge!

Not knowing anything about this horse
   I start to ask around
"He'll take a run, then suck back."
   "Be easy in the chute, but don't fool around."
     "That old wider maker will do anything to peel you,
     then kick you when you're down."

"Better screw your hat down boy,
   I had him last Friday night
Marked him out real good and rode him 3 hard jumps
   then somebody turned out the lights!"

All this good advice done got my butterflies in a lather
   my belly's one big knot.
The cowboy who says he ain't scared or nervous
   is lying or crazy, both of which I'm not.

Ain't it funny how time
   can simultaneously crawl and fly
The first thing I know they're finally loading the chutes
   and the colors are riding by.

And old "X3 something or other Skoal"
   makes his way to chute number one
He acts like he cain't hardl wait
   that ornery son-of-a-gun.

I'm all chapped up and spurred
   so I hustle up and set riggin' in style
That old bronc takes it like a pro, don't flinch a muscle,
   but, I swear I seen him smile.

I sweat out the Grand Entry, try to loosen up
   get myself in a positive mode
In those few moments of pagentry
   I'd hate to guess how many broncs I've rode.

Then, they play the National Anthem
   and without a spoken word
Every cowboy takes off his hat, bows his head,
   and starts to bargain with the Lord.

"Oh, say can you see?"
   brings to mind every wicked thing I ever said or did
"By the rockets red glare"
   brings to mind all those fears I thought I had hid.

"Lord, if you'll get me through this thing
   I swear as long as I live
I'll never say another cuss word, and if you bless me to win
   why, the tithes I'll surely give."

"Lord, please don't let my hand get hung again
   and forgive us of our sin
And about me being a preacher, well,
   after this ride, we'll talk again?"

Now, folks I ain't trying to be irreverent
   that's not at all my intent
But, when they play the National Anthem
   that's when cowboys repent!

******

NOW THERE'S A COWBOY

Many attempts have been made to define the attributes
   of a Real American Cowboy and Buckaroo
Definitions vary from the job that he does and clothes that he wears
   to what he drinks or smokes or chews.

I ain't here to set no records straight
   nor bust anybodies balloon
But, I'd sure like to tell you 'bout one sure 'nough Cowboy
   I met one Sunday afternoon.

It was at Lamoni, Iowa, at a jackpot ropin'
  back in eighty three or four
Indoor arena in the winter months
  calves weighing 300#'s and more.

They were big, black baldies, that had fought
  many a good hand to the 2 minutes allowed
12's and 16's would get you a check
  and polite applause from the crowd.

In the novice section this fellow rode in
  I judged to be about twenty
Ridin' a big dun gelding, aged but well built
  with cow-sence a plenty.

He rode into the arena and built his loop
  just inside the gate
That's when we noticed his left arm was pinned to his shirt
  and just hung there like some dead weight.

His hand just drooped like frost bit Lilies
  the arm was withered beneath
He backed his horse into the box
  then put the reins in his teeth.

His rope was short, just long enough
  to run from the horn and neck rope and back
He nodded for his calf and about 50 feet out
  that cowboy was pitchin' his slack.

For the next 2 minutes and 54 seconds
  we watched a battle of will
That calf bucked and kicked and bawled and butted
  but, that cowboy kept comin' on still.

Every man, woman, child and horse in that barn
  was glued to the scene
It was stone silent, not a word was said, but tears were shed
  by some of the toughest guys I've seen.

His hat was kicked off, shirt jerked out
  then torn from bottom to top
Then that left arm came loose from the pin
  and like a flag in a gale just flipped and flopped.

Two minutes came and two minutes went
   without any sounding of the bell
But the time keeper was caught up in the fight
   between this angel of light, and that demon straight from hell!

Then with every last ounc of his strength, energy and will
   he legged that calf to the ground
Held its front leg in the crook of his arm
   took 2 laps and a huey and tied that calf down.

That barn erupted in shouts and cheers and applause
   and not one dry eye
'Cause we'd just watched 150 pounds of Cowboy
   packed with a trainload of Try.

******

HATS

Cowboy hats are the darndest invention
   I've spent enough on 'em to have a pretty good pension
But, in all my days, I never wore
   a hat I just brought home from the store.

I just can't wait to get home
   and put on some steam
So I can reshape
   the hat of my dreams.

It don't matter the crease,
   Quarter Horse, RCA, or Gus
I'm never content till I bend it and roll it
   and I fuss and fuss.

I dip the brim
   and square up the front
Then work on the crown
   for the shape that I want.

I'll boil a tea pot 'bout bone dry
   for hours I try and try
Till finally, I give up, soak it, shape it
   then leave it to dry.

So, if you see me with a hat
  that looks sorely departed
All I can say is,
  "You should have seen it before I started.

******

ALL FOR NAUGHT

He was makin' his points with great compassion
  this preacher was getting down to brass tacks
He delivered his sermon in a most powerful fasion
  and was taking us all to task.
To drunkards and harlots and backslidein' Christians
  (not to mention elders and bishops and deacons)
Cowboys and farmers, bankers and musicians
  no one escaped his piercing rendition.
"Repent and confess or to hell you are doomed!"
  it was quiet as death as he came to a close
But, his false teeth dislodged as his voice finally boomed
  and in slow motion, it seemed, were launched 3 rows!

******

ODE TO SCOTTY DEE

You're getting gray old friend
  and your back is starting to sway
But, you always gave your best
  whether at work or at play
You're the best old hoss
  a man could ever hope to own
But, it won't be long:
  till you be movin' on.
I surely believe that the Lord takes horses to heaven
  and I know you're gonna be
The pick of the bunch,
  just watin' there for me.
And when the Lord comes chargin',
  on that Stallion of White
We'll be with Him for that final gather
  to make all wrong things right.

When we get old Satan cornered
   I'll throw a loop that will never miss
And you can drive him by the heels
   right up to the Great Abyss
Some cowboy will brand him "DOOMED"
   and roll him off the edge
Then we'll shut the door on hell's great gate
   and chunk it with a wedge.
Then, you and me, old Scotty Dee
   will ride in with the Lord
All in my way of thinking
   that will be my great reward.

******

Ron Ratliff   Poet/Reciter/Braider/Carver/Sky Pilot
403 South Main
Pattonsburg, Mo. 64670

Ron Ratliff is a Charter Major Member of the Missouri Cowboy Poets Association, and one of the MCPA "Sky Pilots". He was born in Northwest Missouri in 1950. He is a Southern Baptist minister, leather craftsman, welder and cowboy. His experience in the Rodeo arena, raising "valuable" beef, and his heart for the "Cowboy Way" lend themselves to some humorous stories in rhyme. Ron recites his original poetry in melodic and energetic form that captures the attention of the listener.

SURVIVAL

She trimed the wick at twilight
And pulled the curtains closed;
The stew was simmering happily
And the cat was in repose.

The chicks had flown up hours ago
As darkness crossed the land —
She'd milked Old Bess and fed the stock
And now sat with book in hand.

The days were long and breaks were few as
She washed and ironed the clothes,
Prepared the meals and cleaned the house
And kept the garden hosed.

That book was her unwinding from
The rigors of this life —
It took her far in time and place
And she'd forget the strife.

It told of fairy princesses,
Of castles and of kings;
It told of days from long ago
And many other things.

So when she was downhearted
Or just had time alone,
She got a book and opened it
And read till the cows came home!

******

THE QUILT

The quilt was made a block at a time
Of dresses and aprons and shirts;
Each piece held a memory
Full of laughter and tears and hurts.

The scraps were kept in a bag by the chair
Cut from clothing her family had worn —
Homespun cotton, calico, native wool,
Often mended from being torn.

That blue calico was the first shirt she made
For a new husband to wear to the dance;
It matched the blue in his twinkling eyes
That had captured her in one glance.

The lace covered piece was from her wedding day,
Soft flannel from the baby's gown,
Checked gingham covered the window
That had been sent in from town.

The pink with tiny flowers was from
Her daughter's first day of class;
She'd made it with love, just bursting with pride,
But wept as she grew up too fast.

The brown homespun was from a shirt
Her son had worn off to war.
He was too young to go and fight,
Too young to come home no more.

She smoothed the quilt with trembling hands
As it warmed her fragile bones;
Her mind went back through the journey of life
As she lay on the bed all alone.

Each piece of her life was in that quilt;
Each piece brought a memory to mind.
Put together, the parts made a whole —
As each block her life had defined.

******

Times change with each generation,
and we all have selective memories.
Go back for a while to a slower, quieter pace,
when you didn't lock the door at night . . .
When you slept outside in the summertime . . .
when you bought a sack of flour based on
the color and print of the fabric.
When movies cost a dime.

******

GOLD METAL FLOUR AND PRINCE ALBERT IN A CAN

O on Saturdays we'd get right up
    An' feed an' milk real fast —
All week we worked from sun to sun
But weekend's here at last.

We'd knock off early in the day—
The chores all done up right;
Clean overalls an' faces scrubbed—
Here was Saturday night!

We's pile into the old black Ford
An' start off down the road,
Anticipation on every face—
Forgot the corn we'd hoed.

To buy the sugar, coffee, flour,
We traded eggs an' milk—
Ma picked each flour sack careful, like
That new dress would be silk.

Papa gathered up the egg crates
An' took them in to sell;
I watched old Troy candle them—
None else did it so well.

As two by two the eggs he'd lift
An' hold up to the light—
No spot too small for him to find—
He sorted them out right.

We visited neighbors, kids, an' friends—
We'd seen them just last week—
Men talked cattle, crops, an' drouth, as
They stood there on the street.

Women clustered with little ones
While we took off alone;
Bought nickel cokes an' looked at girls
An' wished that we were grown.

With dime in hand we met our friends
Outside the picture show;
We watched the feature, cartoons, news,
Together in a row.

We watched it twice, then went outside
An' played it out again---
Took turns bringing Justice, to make
The West the way it'd been.

Too soon the daylight faded out
An' twilight cast its spell---
Time to find the family an'
Decide which tales to tell.

As evening fell on Ma an' me
We went off to the stores;
We walked the blocks an' window shopped
Till we could look no more.

"Go get your Pa; it's time to go."
The one command she gave,
An' I'd go in the pool hall there
An' squint through smoky haze.

A mysterious rite occurred
In that murky atmosphere---
It might have had a sign out front:
"No women 'lowed in here."

The clacking balls an' cigarettes
Bespoke a world of men;
Bare light bulbs hung on fraying cords
An' flickered now an' then.

The lighted cigarettes glowed red---
Both Wings an' Lucky Strike---
You could walk a mile for a Camel
Or--whatever brand you'd like.

The strong scent of burnt tobacco
Hung heavy in the air,
For many rolled their own those days
An' filter tips were rare.

So boys grew up with smoke filled lungs
An' took it as their due---
No one gave thought back then just
What that tar would do.

One final stop as we went home
Down roads of dusty red:
An ice cream cone from the drug store
Before we went to bed.

I laid my head in Mama's lap
To make that long drive home---
She talked to Papa 'bout the day
An hummed a Sunday song.

The work was hard when I was young
But I grew up all right,
An' I'd never trade a single one
Of those magic Saturday nights.

******

AMERICA'S HEROES

Our heros have always been "cowboys"
But what does that really mean?
Is it Vince, or George, or John Wayne,
In a big hat and faded jeans?

Is it Saturday morning serials,
Where Tim and Hoppy rode?
Is it Tom and B-Grade Westerns
Where the hero was never throwed?

Could it be the Lone Ranger lunchbox,
Or paper dolls of Roy and Dale,
Or the rodeo at the fairgrounds,
Or shaking hands with Gene at the rail?

Could it be lessons from Daddy?
"Carry your load and beyond."
"Share a meal with a traveler."
"Let your word be your bond."

Could it be that it's all of the above?
With other things thrown in, too---
Like Granpas and daddys standing tall,
Showing us what to do?

The movies and toys and music
Remind us of days long ago
When men were honest, truthful, and just,
So kids knew which way to grow.

Those cowboys *are* America's heroes
And lived the Cowboy Code---
Loved God and Mama and horses,
Proud of the trail they rode.

But the greatest hero of all
At least that I've ever knowed
Was the man who was my daddy---
He lived the Cowboy Code.

He never talked to be talking,
Just when he'd something to say.
He never took without asking,
Always wanted to pay.

His handshake was good as a contract---
His word he wouldn't break;
He knew a man's name's important
When his reputation's at stake.

He always worked harder than most---
Earned his day wages fair;
Knew how to get along with the boss
And treat his partners square.

Never let a man go away
Hungry outside the door---
He'd feed him first, then let him work,
Then pay him something more.

He asked no questions of the strays---
Expected honest work.
He knew each one could have been him
Had God not been at work.

Married his sweetheart and loved her
Through years of good and bad;
Corn and cattle won't make you rich---
They did with what they had.

He raised his fam'ly trusting God
For food and health and rain---
When he saw strength was running out,
He'd pray and not complain.

Throughout the years as pain increased,
He smiled and loved us more;
Remembered not the times I'd failed---
He'd not been keeping score.

So this man's always my hero;
Gave wisdom to the end---
He'd led in the right directions
And always been my friend.

Yes, I grew up with a cowboy
And learned the Code of the West;
I gauge my heroes next to him---
Make sure they pass the test.

******

FIXIN' TO GET EXCITIN'

T h' brandin' irons were ready
On that cloudless summer day,
While Lester an' th' other boys
Looked on with some dismay.

Ol' Reb had built hisself a loop
An' picked him out a stray---
He swore that little critter
Would wear his brand today.

Th' hoolihan had settled sweet
Aroun' that snowy head,
But Baby wouldn't have it--for
He'd seen them irons was red!

So a bellerin' an' a bawlin'
He cut roun' an' in between
Th' hind legs of Reb's horse--an'
Took off towards Abilene.

"It's fixin' to get excitin'"
Said Lester, "I'll be bound"
Then Will got tangled in his spurs
An' tumbled to th' ground.

"Look out." says Andy, cautious-like,
As Buster took a jump,
Cause mama cow was a-aimin'
Those horns at Buster's rump.

Th' prickly pears was waitin' there
As Buster made his leap,
An' Reb found new disaster
With pears an' cowpies---deep.

Then Lester dropped his cigarette
He'd took so long in makin'---
Still had th' pouch-string in his mouth
When he saw the turn they'd taken.

Now Buster still is runnin' with
That cow attached behind,
An' Reb's still holdin' on th' rope,
Somewhat all entwined.

Reb's chaps were cut to ribbons
An' his shirt was all askew,
An' where he fin'lly lost his hat
Nobody ever knew.

But when all th' dust got settled,
Reb shook his head once more---
He found he'd branded Lester---
An' Les was mighty sore.

Th' baby butted 'gainst his ma
An' give the boys a glare---
His little tail still held its arch;
His little hide, its hair.

******

LICKING THE ICING BOWL

My mind goes back to long ago
　　when I was just a kid,
When skies were blue and days were long
　and future things were hid.

I'd mount that broomstick every day
　and down the trails I'd ride
To catch the robbers, gold in hand,
　the collie at my side.

The afternoons would never end
　till tuckered out once more,
I'd find the way back to the house
　and tie the stickhorse to the door.

My mother cooked and canned and baked
　from garden stuff we'd pick;
She made three-layer birthday cakes
　with icing deep and thick.

She mixed the cocoa, sugar, milk,
　and beat it all by hand;
Anticipating chocolate dreams
　was more than I could stand.

The icing made, she poured it on
　and added peaks and swirls,
Then left some extra in the bowl
　for a delighted little girl.

It was so good and rich and smooth---
　lay sweetly on the tonque---
I'd scrape the bowl and lick the spoon
　where bits of icing hung.

I spent my days at work and play
　with memories made of gold,
But my favorite thing in all the world
　was licking the icing bowl.

******

BABY CHICKS

B aby chicks are bits of fluff
  Demanding hours of care;
They have to be fed, and watered, and warm,
And they're awful easy to scare.

My folks used to raise those chicks
And worked from dawn to dark---
They kept the brooder house just the right temp
And doctored each little mark.

See, some were not quite so fuzzy
As others of their kind,
Cause some would get an obsession
With peckin' each other's behind.

So Mom would sit there amongst 'em
And spot 'em running past---
She'd grab those cheepers one at a time
And apply that medicine fast.

Some started growing feathers;
Some just gave up the ghost---
Lost a few to coyotes and such,
But we fried, baked and stewed the most!

******

A COWBOY CHRISTMAS

S ure is cold out here on this hill
  That fire just ain't big enough;
Spendin' Christmas Eve out here alone
Sure seems mighty rough.

But somebody had to see after th' stock
An' Bud---he's got him a wife,
An' Sonny went to check on his Ma---
She won't be long in this life.

An' Charley now has got all them kids---
Couldn't miss bringin' 'em toys.
He'd whittled out whistles an' tops an' dolls
Every minute he'd spent with us boys.

So I was the one who got to ride herd—
Didn't have no fam'ly near,
An' it's mighty cold in this line camp,
But, say, ain't th' sky awful clear?

There's stars hangin' low, almost to touch,
An' snow sparkles here on th' ground
Peaceful as can be on this Miracle Night—
A lonely coyote's th' only sound.

I remember th' stories Ma used to read
From th' Bible, big an' black,
'Bout how God sent His Son to be born on this night
To point men to th' right track.

She told me 'bout Mary an' Joseph
An' Wise Men an' shepherds that came—
Like me—'cept I'm keepin' cattle, not woolies,
But I reckon it's sorta th' same.

An' on that long-ago night, men saw th' star
An' followed it to where He lay,
Just like men still look for God
Each an' ev'ry day.

So sure, it's cold out here tonight
An' lonely by th' fire,
But I'll just remember that other time
An' listen for th' angel choir.

An' maybe *I'm* th' lucky one,
Spendin' tonight out here,
'Cause stars hang low in a prairie sky
An' th' Child seems mighty near.

So thank you, Father, for your Gift
An' for lovin' us so much—
I'll look an' wonder just which Star was
Th' sign of your heavenly touch.

******

ROLL ON

Tumbleweed rollin' 'cross th' plain
Pullin' my soul along,
Loneliness achin' deep within---
Sometimes I don't belong.

Tumbleweed rushin' before th' wind,
You take my hopes an' fears---
Could be th' next time you pass by,
You'll also take my tears.

Tumbleweed snaggin' agin th' sage,
Looks like you're waitin' for me---
Take my hurt an' roll it away---
Leave my heart empty but free.

Tumbleweed desolate in th' field,
Hearts all tied up with string,
Full of desires an' promises broke---
What will th' tumbleweed bring?

Tumbleweed blowin' wild in th' wind,
What other lives will you touch?
Take my dreams an' deliver them
Tied with ribbons an' such.

Tumbleweed tumbling once again
Across th' empty sky---
My love is like th' tumbleweed,
Sayin' a sad goodbye.

******

IT'S SADDLIN" UP TIME

Billy's mole is growing; Grandma's found a lump---
All these problems put your ropin' in a slump.
Don't know the answers, though you used to be wise---
Lots of questions are starting to rise......

Every person has a story to tell
Of someone they'd known for quite a spell---
Someone who's lucky and had it made,
But now something's happened, and they're afraid.

The key word is Fear - Universal Fear;
It strikes our hearts - Its message is clear;
You're never too young, too old, or too smart
For those icy fingers to grip your heart.

Cancer's a killer that we can defeat,
A challenge that cowboys are ready to meet.
Don't ever think it won't happen to you---
It hits one in three, so what can you do?

You can lock your doors and protect your place,
But cancer sneaks in right in front of your face,
It lurks in the corners and laughs with glee---
It rides behind as you try to flee.

It's sneaky and silent---attacks your soul,
Invades your life, and you pay the toll.
It travels with Death, with Pain, and with Grief---
It steals your health like a common thief.

It hurts your marriage, your home, and your kids---
There's not just one victim - the whole family is.
It doesn't care if you're a king or a star;
Cancer can get you whoever you are.

You leave your family, and neighbors, and friends---
A quality life may come to an end;
You lose self-respect, dignity, pride---
At a certain point, there's no re-ride.

I lost my father, my teacher, my friend---
He never quit till right at the end.
He conquered drouth, and floods, and wild cattle,
But the Big C came and won the battle.

Potential was there, unrealized---
Things taken for granted now highly prized.
The saddest result of life diminished
Is having to leave with things unfinished.

So until researchers find a cure,
Notice all changes, however obscure---
Be alert to growth in lumps or spots;
Say, "Was it like yesterday---or not?"

Now my Mom's a surviver and still around
'Cause she called a doctor when the lump was found---
She had radiation to kill those cells
And now--five years later--she's totally well!

It's saddlin' up time for the Cowboy Way---
The Code of the West will make cancer pay;
We want all the cowpokes to stay alive---
It's time for the last great cowboy drive.

Though Big C is wicked without a doubt,
Research and awareness can stamp it out---
Cowpokes of all ages can help with this raid
And join West Quest in the Cowboy Cancer Crusade!

******

Francine Robison   Poet/Author
15 Hardesty Dr
Shawnee, OK   74804

Francine Robison traded in teaching high school classroom to go on the road with Cowboy Poetry. However, retirement didn't last long, and she is now an adjunct teacher at Oklahoma Baptist University. She has also taught summer sessions in Mexico and China.

Francine's background includes a farmer dad and a Schoolmarm. She writes from personal experience or from family stories passed down from her parents, with most of the settings in southern Oklahoma and the Arbuckle Mountains.

Farm life included a horse, a collie dog, and numerous cats. She didn't walk five miles in the snow to school, but did walk down the cattle guard to catch the school bus, carrying her homework and Roy Rogers lunch box.

She believes that the West is an important part of our history and that people should be reminded of the hopes and dreams, as well as the sacrifices and courage, of our ancestors as they settled new lands and raised families.

She has appeared in numerous poetry gatherings as well as a couple of pig roasts.

Francine has been named **Cowboy Poet Laureate of Oklahoma** and is endorsed by **West Quest.**

GRANT ROPE AND WYETH SADDLE

Back in the summer of '88 I took a job up near Paradise, Missouri. One day my mare, Rose, and me was checkin' out a pasture that had a lot of old fence around it. As we was lookin' it over, we found a good-sized dead limb layin' on the fence. There was a ditch about 25 or 30 yards from where the dead limb was, so we was gonna drag the limb off the fence and into the near-by ditch.

Well, I ain't much of a roper, but I always carry a 33-foot Dub Grant on my Wyeth saddle with me to do needed tasks. So, I put a loop on the big end of the limb and tied the tail of the rope to the saddle-horn. The mare walks the slack out, and leans into the strain, and we drag the dead limb to the ditch. Well, I re-coils the rope an' casually lays it over the saddle horn, not botherin' to un-tie the tail, an' we go on checkin' the fence. A short time later, we came to a pen. may 5-6 acres in size, all growed-up with weeds about as tall as a horse's back. As we start through this patch, up jumped a little White-tail buck. An' Rose, bein' in a ropin' mode, does her job, puttin' me as close as she could to the deer's flank, an' the young buck takes right down the fence-line. Now, it occurs to me, there's three of us in this deal, an' I"m the only one not playin' my part. So, I builds me a short loop an' makes my throw. Must have been the tall weeds that deflected my loop,(or could it have been my lack of ropin' skill?), but that loop settled perfect on one of those six inch hedge fence posts. Now Rose is still doin' her job, she's keepin' right on that deer's hind-quarter, but that Grant Rope, my Wyeth saddle an' ME quit the chase right there, EXACTLY thirty-three feet from that hedge Fence-Post!

******

THE RANCHER AND THE COWBOY

*An example of how independent cowboys are, and how
they value the dignity of labor over the fruits of labor.*

The rancher said to the cowboy;
"I know what I've asked of you ain't very much fun,
But if you're gonna work for me,
You gotta do what needs to be done.

You can go back to twistin' broncs and punchin' cows,
When you're through puttin' up this hay.
But right now, take holt of that pitchfork
And start to earn you're pay."

The cowboy said to the rancher; "I done my part,
Pitchin' hay, and diggin' holes. 'fore I left home.
I painted barns and strung fence. Ya' see Mr. Cattle-man,
That's why I left our ranch, to roam.

  So when you need a hand
  To round up and work the herd,
  I'll work from sunup 'til after dark
  With never a cross word.

But while you're puttin' up the hay
To winter feed your cattle,
I'll be in town havin' some fun
And soapin'-up my Saddle."

     ******

THE COWBOY COUNTRY SALUTE

  I'm sure you've noticed
  When you travel farm and ranch roads
  The salutation you receive,
  It's the cowboy country code.

    When you meet a feller
    Comin' the other way.
    An' he waves a salute,
    To wish you a "Good- day".

An' when you send a letter,
You post agreeting at the top,
Why not do the same when,
You're off the black-top?

    It seems like to me,
    It's a natural thing to wave,
    Show's folks you Respect 'em
    An that you're well behaved.

RESPECT... ummh, there's a word,
We need to practice more.
If we'd show more of IT,
Folks might not act so sore.

Respect in farm country is,
A nod, a wave, a tip of the hat.
City folks, and town people,
Don't seem to understand that.

They see other folks as obstacles,
Just objects in their way.
By recognizin' an' respectin' folks,
They'd learn the cowboy country way.

Be it far from me to say,
The city folks are wrong,
But out on the ranch roads,
Where folks wave to show their respect,
IS WHERE I'M PROUD TO CALL HOME!

******

THE MASTER'S HAND IN THE SPRING

I believe it's the time of year,
When the Master makes his majesty plain.
'Cause I shore can see his majesty all around me,
In the re-birth that takes place in the spring.

Some folks don't believe in God.
That's God with a capital "G".
They say that we evolved from some amoeba,
That crawled up outta the sea.

Oh! they worship, as they rush through life,
In their materialistic glee.
Their possessions are their god,
That's god with a very small "g".

This is mighty sad, and dangerous,
An' a awful puny way to explain.
If they'd open their eyes, to this springtime paradise,
They's see the Master's hand in the spring.

Just look at the pattern of those spots, on the mare,
The bright dandelion flowers, with leaves so green,
Those cotton-candy clouds, in that azure sky.
Yes, I see the Master's hand in everything.

> In the bright colored calves and colts
> Born to life in early spring,
> In the new foals on their wobbly legs,
> Who don't yet know fear of any-thing.

I'm told God's *Grace* is, un-merited favor
An' *Faith* is the substance of things unseen.
Then it seems plain to me, I'll bet you'll agree,
We are blessed in everything.

> God's gift is free for the askin',
> Just admit that you were born into sin.
> He'll be your companion and pardner,
> If you'll just ride life's trails with Him.

******

DAD'S BOOTS

> A little more than a year ago
> I watched as Dad slipped away so slow.

> > He had lived a full life with Mom,
> > Now he was goin' to a better home.
> > To watch him suffer like he did,
> > Hurt me more'n some.

> I wanted to take the pain away
> I sat and held his hand.
> I'd never known, or even seen,
> Such an enduring man.

> > Remembering when I was small,
> > The times he'd hold me and
> > Tell me not to bawl.

The comfort that I felt
When I would touch the whiskers on his face.
The calmness that came over me
After his embrace.

As we were cleaning up his house
Gettin' ready for the sale,
I came across a pair of boots,
My daddy used to fill.

I stood there just a holdin' 'em.
Looked at 'em for awhile.
As I reflected on the lessons learned
It brought back a smile.

'Bout then it really hit me,
As the tears began to spill.
Now the job was my responsibility,
Those boots won't be easy to fill.

It' been more'n a year now,
And I haven't put those boots on.
Today I decided it was time,
As I was stayin' home.

I pulled 'em on my feet
With gentle love and care.
They fit the size and shape of my foot,
As I walked around the house there.

I wore them for an hour or more
Workin' with the horses,
And doin' my other chores.

The boots were mighty comfortable on my feet
And it shore felt good.
To know I was standin'
Where such a mighty man had stood.

I looked down at those boots with admiration.
Before I pulled 'em off the end of my leg.
To set them back up in the closet.
Those boots shore seemed mighty BIG!
******

WOMEN FOLK

The old cowboy that told this story to me said, "I spent most
of my money on beer and women, the rest of it, I just wasted."

Womenfolk are such lovely,
Unpredictable things,
But they're way too much trouble
For the pleasure they bring.

> One year durin' brandin',
> I met a gal named Sue.
> She could rope an' brand an' castrate,
> But she'd always burn the stew.

Then I met up with Arlene,
In a sheep camp late one fall,
She got homesick before spring,
She'd just sit in the wagon an' bawl.

> Then I got to courtin' Judy,
> Linda, Brenda, Anne, and Sandy,
> Each one started gettin' cranky,
> 'Cause I wasn't always handy.

At a dance one moon-lit night,
Believe it was back in seventy-two,
I fell in love again.
Her name was Betty Lou.

> Soon, the dance was over.
> My, how the time had flew.
> 'But my money ran-out.
> 'Bout that time, so did Betty Lou.

Then at Billy Bob's in Ft. Worth,
I fell in love with Norma.
Well, it didn't last long either,
She couldn't leave her Momma.

> So I swore off womenfolk
> For purt-near three days, MCPA
> But movin' west love struck again,
> At a party near Ft. Hays.

It was there I met Peggy,
An' man she was a looker.
We was talkin' marriage,
When I learned she was a hooker.

Well, that was the end of that.
I hit the road again.
I wondered about life,
An' how this all would end.

I was workin' cattle in Arkansas,
An' wearin' a fancy boot,
When I met a widder-woman
By th name of Bonnie Cute.

Well, we started courtin' an' snortin',
In the spring of seventy-nine.
And by the Fourth of July,
We were gettin' on just fine.

Then there was a little squabble,
'Bout who'd pay the bills.
I headed west again,
An' left her there in the hills.

This time I swore off for good,
Prob'ly a month or so.
I had this itchin' in my boots
That constantly said, "Go."

In Kansas I met an Alaskan gal,
She was puttin' up hay.
She wudden hard to look at.
I thought, "She's tough enough to stay."

An stay she did too,
For neigh on half a year,
Before her mukluks took her
Back to the Alaskan Frontier.

Now they tell me,
An' I reckon it's true,
"A rollin' stone
Gathers no moss."

One thing I know,
When a man is young
An' havin' lots'a fun,
He never considers the cost.

The women folk have moved on,
An' my money's all gone.
SHOOT! I should'a just
KISSED MY HOSS!!!

******

CALICO ROCK RODEO

I was in Calico Rock, Arkansas in the spring of seventy-seven
If you've never seen the rodeo there
Then man you've not been livin'.

This extravaganza is really somethin'
You should take the time to go see.
There is just nothin' like it from the mountains of Wyoming
To the hills of Tennessee.

They bring in the roughest stock,
I mean, this stuff is snaky and rank.
Nobody even tries to ride these animals
Til' they've had plenty to drink.

These animals are tough, their hide's really thick.
No matter how hard you hooked 'em,
Your spurs just wouldn't stick.
This stuff's been runnin' loose in the hills all winter.

Just one look makes the toughest cowboy shiver,
But not the folks in Calico.
They'd saddle 'em up and climb right on
And set up there, like they's usin' the telephone.

When the Grand Entry came in the gate,
Let me tell you friend, it was worth the wait.

Now if you were thinkin' that I was talkin'
About the contestant's stock,
You've got a wrong assumption.
I'm talkin' 'bout the animals
In the Grand Entry, at Calico Rock.

> A contestant in this rodeo, you don't have to be.
> All you need is somethin' with hair
> And you can ride in the Grand Entry.

As soon as the flags came through the entrance gate.
I saw the wildest scene. anyone could appreciate.
There was people layin' here, and people layin' there.

One rather heavy woman. 'bout the first one bucked down,
Was layin' in the midst of this chaos, sprawled out on the ground.

The paramedics was tryin' to get to her, through all this confusion,
To drag her to safety, with the equipment they had,
Through all this confusion,
And relieve her contusions.

> The ambulance they had, looked about World War One.
> They's tryin' to get her rolled onto a stretcher,
> While dartin', dodgin' and duckin',
>   it shore looked like fun.

Finally they got her loaded up, to take her to the cripple cart.
Now that World War One ambulance died, and refused to start.
While I was watchin' I heard an explosion sound
Then I saw underneath it. Fire was shootin' down the ground.

> Well, with all this ruckus, here comes the fire brigade.
> Two guys with firefightin' equipment, a 5 gallon cooler of gatorade.

Soon the fire was under control, and the arena mostly clear,
If they could just get that ambulance out, we could have a rodeo here.

A couple of calf ropers looped onto the front end
And drug the ambulance out beside the buckin' chutes, into the loadin' pen.

All this time that woman in the back, had been recuperatin'
And she was startin' to scream and shout! It sounded excruciatin'!
After a thorough examination, the old lady was just fine.
Now we can get on with the rodeo, it was way past time.

You may think that rodeos are crazy, wild and hostile,
But after you've seen the Grand Entry at Calico Rock
All the rest of 'em look plumb halcyon, tame and docile.

******

COWBOY CAVIAR

Cowboys come in every shape
Cowboys come in every size
Some have brown or blue
Quite often they have black eyes.

Cowboys are sometimes lean
And sometimes cowboys are fat
But one thing's for shore
They've all got a big Resistol hat.

Some cowboys hardly ever eat
There's others who have holler legs and feet.
Their appetite varies, dependin' on where they are.
But. I've never met a cowboy who didn't like caviar.

They'll eat it in the hayfield
They'll eat it from a can
They'll eat it workin' cattle
They eat it at rodeos across the land.

They eat it with their fingers
They eat it with their knife
They eat it from their saddle bags
The even spred it on a bread slice.

I once saw a cowboy down a can
In eight seconds flat
As he wiped his mustache on his shirt sleeve
He said, " what kind'a score did I get for that?"

Cowboys love little morsels
They're so colorful and round

If no spoon is handy, they tilt their head back
And turn the can upside down.

Some punchers hide a can
Rolled up in their bedroll tight
If he wants a little snack
He can devour it about mid-nite.

Caviar's kept many a
Cowboy from completely starvin'
It can roll around in the floorboard of your pick-up
'Til Saturday, then you can share it with your darlin'.

The other day I found two cans of caviar in the bed of my pick-up
It was Saturday, and I was lonesome, so I called my darlin' up
Well I took her up on the mountain -- up high where the trees don't grow
We sat there on a rock eatin' caviar as it started to snow.

How cowboys can afford such expensive fare
You might not understand.
Shoot! The stuff's not high at all
Costs less than a dollar a can!

This relationship the cowboy has with caviar
Beats all I've ever seen.
Just in case you don't know what cowboy caviar is
Well! It's Ranch Style Pork and Beans!

******

THE SIGN ON THE DOOR

It was a cold winter mornin'
In Kaycee, Wyoming.
The snow-drifts were deep,
An' the wind was a'moaning.

I stopped in the hardware store;
The Rusty Spur.
Just about the time,
Folks were startin' to stir.

Bud was there,
Not quite woke-up.
He said. "Come   -in.
Coffee's done, hav'a cup."

     Then thru the door, strolls
     A rough-lookin' cowboy.
     I glanced at Bud's face,
     It registered -- ANNOY.

The cowboy walks in
Stompin' mud on the floor.
He don't worry,
'Bout shuttin the door.

     Bud saya, "Feller,
     You born in a barn."
     The cowboy says, "Sir, (sniff)
     I'd like to get warm."

"Shut the door." says Bud.
"I'm damn near froze."
The cowboy replied;
"Says OPEN -- (sniff)
It DON'T say CLOSE!"

******

RODEO MAN

I heard a voice,
And turned to see,
That there was no-one
Speakin' to me.

     I heard the chute-boss
     Say, "Get screwd down.
     You're next out
     In this go-round."

I heard the clang
Of the iron chute,
And felt the power
Of the brute.

I saw around me,
A blurry world,
As the huge beast,
Bucked and whirled.

I heard the shouts
Of the crowd.
I was floating
On a cloud.

I heard the throaty
Buzzer sound,
And felt the jar
Of hitting the ground.

I heard the applause
Of the cheering fans.
This is the life
Of a RODEO MAN.

******

Cliff Sexton
1849 95th Street
Union Town, KS   66779

Cliff was born and raised in the beautiful White River country of Northern Arkansas, farm and ranch country. His family has been in the farm-ranch business for generations. He is a promoter of Wrangler cowboy apparel, and has performed as a cowboy poet, musician and singer, at numerous Kansas City institutions. He is enshrined in the Kansas Trap Shooters Hall of Fame in Wichita, Kansas. He is a member of the P. R. C. A., and is a private pilot.

Cliff has written two books of cowboy poems.

James and Molly Smith
Cherokee Indian Performers

MCPA ANTHOLOGY   JAMES & MOLLY SMITH

---

* * * * * * * * * * * ᎠᏓᏙᎵᏍᏙᎢ ᎢᎨᎰᏅᎢ * * * * * * * * * *

ᎣᎩᏙᏓ ᏣᎳᏱ Ᏼ.Ꭳ, ᏣᎳᏉᏗᏳ ᎨᏎᏍᏗ ᏕᏣᏙᎥᎢ.
ᏣᎬᎩᏆᎦ ᎥᎦ ᎡᏏᎣᎭᎠᎢ. ᎠᏂ ᎡᎶᎧᎦ ᎤᎯᏍᏆᎤᎸ
ᏘᎶᏘᎤᎨᎢ, ᎾᏍᎩᏬ ᏣᎳᏱ ᎻᎯᏍᏆᎤᎦ.
ᎻᎥᎸᎢᎡ ᎣᏍᏆᎤᏄᏆᎥ ᎤᏱᏂ Ꭺ.Ꭳ ᎢᎦ. ᏗᎨᎤᏱ-
ᎢᏴᎥᏃ ᏎᏆᏲᏎᎢ, ᎾᏍᎩᏬ ᎻᏗᏍᏈᎡᎥᎬ ᎠᏍᏴ.
ᎠᎴ ᎳᏆᎠ ᎤᏔᎪᏴᏗ ᎥᎦ ᎤᏆᏱᏆᎤᏆᏬᏣᏴ,
ᏆᏱᏳᎳᏄᏆᎦᏆᎥᏆᎱ ᎤᏓ ᎥᎡᎢ. ᏣᎥᎦᏎᏎ
ᏣᎬᎩᏆ ᎥᎡᎢ, ᎠᎦ ᏣᎦᎮᏱᎠᏴ ᎥᎡᎢ, ᎠᎦ
ᎡᏣᎳᏉᏗᏳ ᎥᎡ ᎻᎠᏄᎠᎢ. ᎡᎹᎾᎤᎣ

---

* * * * * * * * * * * * a-da-do-li-sdo-i i-ge-ho-nv-i * * * * * * * * * * *
o-gi-do-da ga-lv-la-di he-hi, ga-lv-quo-di-yu ge-se-sdi de-tsa-do-v-i.
tsa-gv-wi-yu-hi ge-sv wi-ga-na-nu-go-i. a-ni e-lo-hi wi-ni-ga-li-sda
ha-da-nv-te-sqv-i, na-sgi-ya ga-lv-la-di tsi-ni-ga-li-sdi-ha.
ni-da-do-da-qui-sv o-ga-li-sda-yv-di sgi-v-si go-hi i-ga. di-ge-sgi-
v-si-quo-no de-sgi-du-gv-i, na-sgi-ya tsi-di-ga-yo-tsi-ne-ho tso-tsi-du-gi.
a-le tle-sdi u-da-go-le-ye-di-yi ge-sv wi-di-sgi-ya-ti-nv-sta-nv-gi,
sgi-yu-da-le-sge-sdi-quo-sgi-ni u-yo ge-sv-i. tsa-tse-li-ga-ye-no
tsa-gv-wi-yu-hi ge-sv-i, a-le tsa-li-ni-gi-di-yi ge-sv-i, a-le
e-tsa-lv-quo-di-yu ge-sv ni-go-hi-lv-i.
                                        e-me-nv

---

* * * * * * * * * * * * *   THE LORD'S PRAYER   * * * * * * * * * * * * * *
                        (PRAYER HE HAS TAUGHT US)
Our Father Heaven Dweller, hallowed be thy name. Thy Kingdom let it make
its appearance. Here upon Earth take place thy will, the same as in Heaven
is done. Daily our food give to us this day. Forgive us our debts the same
as we forgive our debtors. And do not temptation being lead us into. Deliver
us from evil existing. For thine the Kingdom is, and the power is, and the
glory is, forever.
            AMEN

The Lord's Prayer in Cherokee
Indian Translation in English

James and Molly Smith   Poet/Indian Performers
4611 Seagraves Dr
Joplin, MO   64804

Jim and Molly Smith are both Major Members of the Missouri Cowboy Poets Association, and are both Cherokee Indians. Molly is co-founder and past leader of the White River Band of the Northern Cherokee Tribe, and Jim is a registered member of the Cherokee Nation of Oklahoma. They present a beautiful performance of the Lord's prayer, while a musical version of the Lords Prayer is being played in the background. Jim recites the Lord's prayer in the Cherokee dialect, as Molly signs the prayer in Indian sign language all in synchronization with the background music. During the performance both Jim and Molly are dressed in authentic Indian regalia. The beautiful, hand made, doe skin dress that Molly wears, was made and decorated by Molly herself.

Presenting the Lord's Prayer in Cherokee Dialect and Indian sign language is their mission. They feel blessed that the Lord has enabled them to do the Lord's Prayer, and that He commissioned them to present it whenever possible. They have presented the prayer in churches, powwows, rodeos, cowboy poetry gatherings, cowboy churches, chautauquas, and "Goat Ropin's". They are active in preserving the Cherokee culture, especially for their six grandchildren.

Jim is a cowboy poet/story teller, coming from a varied background of rodeo, ranching , and teaching animal husbandry at Oklahoma State University. While at OSU, he served as horse herdsman, and was secretary of the Oklahoma quarter horse association. Named by a Cherokee Elder, he is **Nunne-Hi-Soguila, "Spirit of the Horse"**.

ECHOES IN THE WIND - A REPRISE

The old wooden windmill beckons, remnant of a day gone by.
There it stands a silent sentinel still reaching for the sky!
No ranch life mills around it; no more it's blades do spin,
But it serves as a reminder, like the echoes in the wind!

Time's pages flip so quickly; the seconds turn to years!
Technology and science are this nation's new frontiers,
But the richness of our heritage is one we cannot spend,
The cowboy's voices call to us, like the echoes in the wind!

Their spirits roam the grasslands; They're fixed in each corral.
Their whispers can be heard amongst the sage and chaparral.
The howling of each coyote seems to greet them as a friend
We can hear what they are saying in the echoes of the wind!

Tell their stories round the campfires. Sing their song with their guitars.
Keep the skill of campfire cooking. Sleep beneath the friendly stars.
Round the cattle up in springtime. Don't unsaddle till day's end.
Cowboy spirits ride beside you like the echoes in the wind!

The echoes tell of cowboys who were willing to exchange
A life of ease and comfort for the freedom of the range.
Echos tell of cowboy values that Time will not rescind,
They bring back what was best in us - those echoes in the wind!

******

A GOOD LICKIN'

I"ll tell you something about mama cows. They're protective as can be,
And they show deep attentive care to their progeny.
And one thing of which human parents might stand in awe:
Young calves are taught to pay attention. Mama's word is law!
From the time they draw their first breath,
and their eyes take their first blink,
She provides both security and discipline, as well as milk and drink.
Calves will stagger to their shaky feet and with Mama go along,
Never venturing from her safe side until they're feeling strong.
And she'll bed them down in shelter if she has to go away,
And they'll stay right there and wait for her, even if she's gone all day.

Because all of those white-faced cows to you and me may look alike,
You would think that findin' Mama might confuse the little tyke,
But to find his mama, all he has to do is just inhale,
And his nose will lead him right to his mama without fail.
For like women wearing perfume, I guess you could allow
That each mama's smell is different,
though they all wear "eau de cow!"
And if that baby calf could talk, like a small boy, he would shout,
"Really, now you've licked enough! Come on. Maw, cut it out!
I can hardly keep my balance! You're gonna knock me off my feet!
What is it with you mothers? What's so great 'bout clean and neat?"
But he'll endure his mama's fussing, and in a year he'll be all grown,
And Mama will have a new calf, so he'll be on his own.
Life's cycle pushes onward. We take each change in stride.
But there's something special about those days with mama at our side!

******

GRANDMA

I remember my old grandma in visions sharp and clear.
I can hear her, I can see her face as if she were still here.
She was a feisty lady, a working cowboy's wife,
And you could tell by looking that she'd had no easy life.

Though her wrinkles showed the years she's lived, a girl's twinkle in her smile,
And she'd waltz me 'round her kitchen in an energetic style.
She had married my grandad when she was just sixteen,
And stayed right by his side when times were good, and times were lean.

Through the children, sons and daughters, to which she joyfully gave birth,
Through the heartbreak that they faced returning one child to the earth.
Side by side they stood together; Through the years they both did toil.
They were aged oak trees sheltering us, roots firmly in the soil.

And Grandma's was the heart and hand that kept us all together.
She gumptioned up the meek of us; the wild ones, she'd tether.
And when she dished out treats, she saw that each one got his part,
But she always saved the biggest piece for Grandpa, her sweetheart.

As she patted Grandpa's head and bent to kiss him on the cheek,
More love passed between those two than words could ever speak.
I can see her figure standing by her old wood-burning stove,
Or stepping spryly up into the pickup truck she drove.

My Grandma gave me honest talk and wisdom of her years.
My Grandma gave me cookies as she wiped away my tears.
My Grandma gave me spunk an' grit to make it through each test,
But it's that love that Grandma gave that I remember best!

******

Ann Sochat   Poet/Reciter
120-A La Nell Street
Canutillo, TX   79835

Ann Sochat is an Associate Member of the Missouri Cowboy Poets Association. She is also the current presidentof the Texas Cowboy Poets Association. Ann is a poet and performer who has been featured at numerous cowboy gatherings throughout the Southwest. Ann's poetry has been published in several books and magazines. Her book "Cowhide and Calico" received the 1997 award for cowboy poetry book of the year. Her poetry entusiastically conveys the humor, action, traditions, and challenges of cowboy life, both past and present.

THIRSTY

One time when I was younger, I made a foolish mistake.
You should never tie a horse up, with something he can break.
You see, when I tied my horse, I'd forgotten where I was.
I was kneeling down, checking a track, when a rattlesnake buzzed.
That horse jerked back and scrambled, I heard the reins go pop!
Then I took yelling like a fool, at a horse that wasn't gonna stop!
I watched that horse run out of sight, high-tailing it back to the ranch.
Then a thought occurred to me, as I stood in that dry branch.
It's funny how your mind works when you know you've been a dink.
Watching my canteen disappear, I thought about needing a drink.
It was open, sagebrush desert. I looked to the left and the right.
Other'n' that snag where I tied my horse, there wasn't a tree in sight.
I stumbled along, looking for green that meant water underground,
My mouth got so dry that licking my lips made a raspy kind of sound.
The sun bore down and heat waves rose that made the cactus wiggle.
I thought of cold glasses of lemonade; the vision made me giggle.
I was staggering down a dry wash, when the tracks of a cow I found.
Some day long past, a rainstorn had passed, enough to soak the ground.
That wet sand and limestone mud had hardened up like plaster.
And there, in one of those cattle tracks, was the answer to my disaster.
I have sipped champagne in a fancy hotel; dark ale in an English pub;
I've enjoyed fresh-squeezed orange juice, and moonshine from a jug.
I've tasted some of the finest wines to be found in the vinter's rack,
But none could compare, to that green water there, in that dirty old cow track!

******

OLD FOUR-EYES

In Eighteen eighty-three, at age twenty-five, he went West.
Fresh out of Harvard Law School, with money to invest.
He was looking for a cow ranch, of which he could be boss,
And near Medora, North Dakota, he found the Maltese Cross.
He knew nothing 'bout running a cow outfit, but he was game.
Though a greenhorn, he'd give it his best shot all the same.
He was kinda sickly lookin', and on his nose those steel frames.
So, because he wore eye-glasses, "Four-Eyes" became his name.
It seemed he had a built-in grin, that trouble couldn't erase,
No matter how tough things got, that smile stayed on his face.

The chances he took made it seem he didn't have good sense,
With his large teeth, his smile looked like a white picket fence.
The West was pretty wild back then, still far from bein' tame,
And "Four-eyes'" favorite thing was goin' huntin' for wild game.
He learned to ride the "rough string", and an especially bad one,
Bucked so hard that he lost his hat, his glasses and his gun!
One night a rowdy cowboy thought this Dude could be beat,
He told everyone in the saloon, - "Boys, Four-eyes is gonna treat!"
Well, Four-eyes took it for a while, he didn't even lose his smile,
Finally saying, "If I must, I must," he flattened him, cowboy-style!
He was paid the ultimate compliment, making him "one-of-the-guys."
His name was changed to the more affectionate, "Old Four-eyes."
Some horse thieves thought this Eastern Dude to be an easy mark,
Three of them rustled some horses, one night when it was dark.
Old Four-eyes set out on their trail with his big Winchester rifle,
And those thieves found out he wasn't one with whom you'd trifle!
He ran the Maltese Cross and Elkhorn Ranches for the next 16 year,
Then he went on to bigger things, that brought his Country's cheers.
He called Western men who'd rode with him to form the Rough Riders.
And they followed him still, up San Juan Hill, 'cause he was a fighter!
He became Secretary of the Navy, and he served with strong intent,
And before he was done, he had become - our Twenty-sixth President!
Teddy Roosevelt proved anyone can be a hero, if they're cowboy tough,
To smile through adversity and danger, and never say, "Enough."
We should take a moral from this story, and take a vow not to relent,
Until we find another strong and true Cowboy - to be our President!

*****

LEARNING THE LINGO

Now cowboy poetry can be a lot of fun to listen to,
But to really understand it, you must know a thing or two,
About how cowboys talk, and the special lingo that they use.
When you hear how it came about, you won't be so confused.
Now, let's take that word, *Lingo*, there's a story behind that.
It comes from *Lingua Franca*, which is a technical kind of chat.
You see, the cowboy sort of "borrowed" some terms from Mexico,
From men already handling cows, the Mexican *"Vacquero."*
Now the B and V in Spanish tend to sound somewhat the same,
So, if the cowboy couldn't say it right, - it got a brand new name.

The Mexican who herded cows was called a *"Vacquero."*
But we couldn't quite pronounce it, and it came out "Buckaroo."
Now, when it came to talking tack, the changes came galore,
"Fiador", Mexican for throat-latch, soon became the "Theodore."
Since *"Jacquima"* was hard to say, it wound up "Hackamore."
"Mecate" was made "McCarty" and there were many more.
"Lazo" became "Lasso" and *"Caballo"*, the word for horse,
Was changed to "Cavvieyah," and butchered even worse.
"Bronco" means rough or wild. "Bronc" was more the cowboy style.
And the Vacquero's *"Chaparejos"* became "Chaps" after a while.
"Dar La Vuelta", to give a turn, became the "Dally" around the horn.
"Mesteno" became "Mustang," and a new cowboy word was born.
"Estampida" the Spanish word that means loud noise,
Was changed to mean a runaway herd, a "Stampede" to the cowboys.
Now when a cowboy celebrated, his tongue got somewhat loose.
"Calabozo" the Spanish word for dungeon, became the "Calaboose."
The *"Juzgado"*, the lockup, was slurred and stirred somehow,
To become the cowboy's word for jail, he called it the "Hoosegow."
Now that's just the beginning' no telling how far it will reach,
'Cause cowboys are still in business, making up new kinds of speech.
When he climbs on the hurricane deck of a sun-fishing crowbait,
You may hear language that I haven't even begun to investigate!
Now this kind of thing is catching, and some things that you may say
Have seeped into our language, and are said the "cowboy" way.
Terms like "ear-marked," "maverick," "hung up," and "bawling out."
All come from cowboy lingo. So, listen close, you'll figure us out!

******

MY SIDEKICK

Let me tell you 'bout my Sidekick, my Compadre, My Friend.
He sticks with me though thick 'n thin, He'll be with me to the end.
No one else can be relied on to be such a special Friend.
What a lucky guy I am to have a Sidekick!

Now, you know what a Sidekick is - he's closer than a brother!
He's the one who'll back you up - when you can't find any other!
Everybody needs a Sidekick when the goin's getting rougher!
Things can go a whole lot better with a Sidekick!

Roy Rogers had his Gabby Hayes - always there to back his play.
Gene Autry had Smiley Burnette, or Pat Buttram in his day.

The Lone Ranger had his Tonto - "Kemo Sabey" he would say.
Why, all those cowboy heroes had a Sidekick!

The Cisco Kid had Pancho - with his broad 'n happy grin.
Red Ryder had Little Beaver riding alongside of him.
Hopalong had Russell Hayden - my what trouble he got in!
Seems like everybody had a Sidekick!

Well, my Sidekick's always with me, and He whispers in my ear,
Helping me steer clear of trouble when Temptation's drawing near.
I'm careful where I take Him - 'cause bad language hurts His ears.
What a lucky guy I am to have a Sidekick.

If you'd like to have a Sidekick - to go everywhere with you...
To bring out all the very best - in all you're going through,
Then give your life to Jesus - and you know what he will do?
He'll send the Holy Spirit for your Sidekick!

How lucky you will be to have that Sidekick!

******

THE COWBOY CODE

We've heard about the Cowboy Code, also called, the Code of the West,
The reason the Code came about, was to help men live at their best.
Men were pitting themselves against the land, in a harsh environment,
And each needed to trust the other to do the right thing in any event.
There were storms, stampedes, dry deserts. wild rivers to be crossed,
Without food and water, shelter and guns, good men could be lost.
Lives depended on a man's word, complete trust was the key element.
With no law, a man's word had to be as binding as a legal document.
The hard-fisted, strict, moral code of the time was born of dire need.
It required you to hold up your end of a deal, both in word and deed.
Unless a man lived up to his word, and held true to that sacred trust,
He would be considered less than a man, for the Code was for the just.
Whole herds of cattle were bought and sold on a simple handshake,
Though it cost him all that he owned, his promise he would not break.
The Code of the West was built upon the foundation of fair play.

You treated others right, and expected them to treat you the same way.
Western hospitality required that you provide the traveler a meal,
Someday you might be the sojourner on the other end of the deal.

You didn't step down from your horse, until you have been asked.
You might earn your meal by chopping wood or some other task.
You would never ride another man's horse without his permission,
And you did not whip or mistreat his horse under any condition.
A man on foot did not put his hand on another man's bridle rein,
That indicated disrespect of his ability to keep his horse restrained.
A cowboy removed his hat for the ladies as a way of showing respect,
And he watched his language and manners, being very circumspect.
He was a knight errant on horseback, and each day was a golden quest.
The cowboy was a gentleman, for that was the Code of the West.

******

THE OLD BRONC TWISTER

He still gets up before daylight, because that's always been his way.
He says, "Anyone sleeping past sunrise has wasted most of the day!"
The cowboy coffee that he brews is strong enough to wake the dead,
But he insists that HE must make it, "cause no one else is out of bed!"

He still squints out the window, to see what the weather's gonna be,
Tho he can't ride or do chores any more, because of his bad knee.
Constant aches and pains are the price he pays for his years of rodeo.
A man can take just so much punishment - before it begins to show.

The eyes that could spot cattle on a mountain several miles away,
Now give him trouble when he tries to read the paper every day.
He always checks the obituaries to see which of his old pals died.
The day he saw Eddie Collin' name, he hung his head and cried.

Him and Eddie was partners; they followed the rodeo circuit together.
With Eddie standing at his back, there was no storm they couldn't weather.
Eddie was born at Old Agency, South Dakota, but that didn't matter to him.
'Cept he was ready to fight with anyone that called Eddie a "redskin.!"

Him and Eddie Collins were "Turtles" long before there was a P.R.C.A.
They rode in them all, from the Calgary Stampede to Cheyenne Frontier Days.
The pallbearers had led a riderless horse, with Eddie's boots in each stirrup.
They didn't notify the old man. They figured he couldn't make the trip.

He was pretty sore he missed the funeral, but South Dakota's a long ride,
And he gets uncomfortable in a car, 'cause he's busted up some inside.
He's reconciled himself to wait for death, but he mutters to himself,
"If I'd knowed I's gonna live so long, I'd ataken better care of myself!"

He's just an old busted-up cowboy, who feels he been around too long.
He plays old records on the phonograph so he can hear some cowboy songs.
Sometimes when he's asleep on the sofa, he hollers and sets up a din,
And I know that he's dreaming...that somewhere...him and Eddie ride again.

Note: Percy Kirk, a Native American, competed in rodeo under the name Eddie Collins.

******

OUT WEST

I was talking with some new friends, and the question was asked,
"Would you please tell us why you're so crazy about the West."
"Well, it's kinda hard to explain, if you haven't been out there.
But it seems there's something special about the very air.
It's clear and clean, scented with the fragrance of wild flowers
In the high mountain meadows. I could stay up there for hours!
You can almost see forever, even objects far away with amazing clarity.
Vast vistas that make man seem small. Well, that's how it affects me.
Sweeping valleys, snow-capped peaks that have a way of turning pink,
When you're out there in the evening and the sun starts to sink.
You can watch a distant rainstorm that's many, many miles away
And know you'll not need your slicker, 'cause you'll be dry today.
There are high mountain lakes that reflect the sky in deeper blue,
The green meadow grass and bright flowers add a brighter hue.
It's a big, bold, wild country, not content with half-way measures,
And it can be the enemy of those who come to take its treasures.
Cold winds can steal your body's warmth and take away your reason,
And in the high mountains, the snow can fall in almost any season.
The high altitude sun can quickly cause unprotected skin to burn,
Or the freezing cold can stop the bold, so they nevermore return.
There are howling winds that can peel the bark right off a tree,
Or soft, refreshing zephyrs that bring relief from summer heat.

Water can be a musical little rivulet, dancing over rocks and moss,
Or, a roaring, raging, whitewater river that's impossible to cross.
It's a wild place, where there's danger, where the coward dare not go.
A snapped twig can be a chipmunk, or a Grizzly bear with cubs in tow.
White antler tips above the brush might mean a trophy elk to hunt,
Or, perhaps a dangerous bull moose gone plumb crazy with the rut.
The pleasure of a good horse, strong and willing to climb the height.
Where you can look down in wonder, at a Bald Eagle in its flight.

Pine-scented forests on northern slopes where the melting snow lingers
Lifting branches Heavenward, and the wind turns them into singers
Of a ghostly choir, chanting words that you can't quite understand,
Their giant boles like Cathedral columns in a vast, enchanted land.
What do I like about the West? Well, I just can't find the words to say,
Except,...if things had worked out different, I'd still be there today."

******

KNIGHTS OF THE ROUND TABLE

I drove into town the other day, and stopped at the Tumbleweed cafe.
At the table sat Grey Wolf and Bo, drinking coffee and watching it snow.
Marge brought me coffee hot and black, n'left the pot so there'd be no lack.
I lifted the cup and took a sip. The ice in my mustache melted down my lip.
We looked at each other a minute or two, and I asked, "Well, what's new?"
Grey Wolf, with the sagacity of his race, sipped his coffee, and made a face.

Bo said, "I'll tell you what's new! Several things have got me in a stew!
Like releasing wolves in Yellowstone! Why can't they just leave things alone?
Wolves can't read boundary signs! So, they feast on sheep like yours and mine!
Did you hear they plan to poison the trout, to get the non-native species out?
The hunter the Grizz mauled the other day? They're trying to put him away!"
She about tore him to pieces! He's accused of shooting an endangered species!"
Grey Wolf sat silently there in his place, sipped his coffee and made a face.

"Somethin' else that gets my goat; the way they ram things down yer throat!
They break the land into small pieces, and then take away our grazing leases!
When the Park was created from our land, they said we could graze the B.L.M.!
Now "Tree-huggers" are in our hair, saying we can't take our herds up there!
Another thing that gripes my soul, - we can't clear land of prairie dog holes!
They want those little critters protected, and if they multiply like I've projected,
Soon there won't be an acre of ground that's not occupied by a prairie dog town!
Grey Wolf lifted his mug from its place, took another sip, and made a face.

"They'd have us stop shooting those pests, and not destroy the packrat's nests!
Now, they're pulling the silliest stunt, - tryin' to stop our local rattlesnake hunt!"
Finally, I got a word in edge-wise, "Let me tell you guys about a big surprise!
While riding out past Cooper's Draw, I found the dangest thing that I ever saw!
Shoshoni Springs is dry as a bone! Been water there since times unknown!"
Bo then put his two cents in, "Dang Corps of Engineers is building dams agin!"
Grey Wolf pushed his cup away, n'cleared his throat. He had something to say.
"Huh! Worst coffee I've ever tasted! I just drank it so it wouldn't be wasted."

"Now you know how it feels, to get caught with your pants around your heels.
To have some "Johnny-lately say, "You can't keep doing things this way!"

Fence off your access and say, "That's tough."   As if that were not insult enough,
They take your water and land, in the interest of something considered more grand.
Now you see how we Indians felt, when white men came with guns on their gelt,
Drove us from our ancestral home, the mountains and valleys we used to roam.
They gave us marginal land, outa the way, n'fought us 'til we promised to stay.
Old Chief Washakie was nobody's fool, he pretended to be the White Man's tool.
He asked for land near the Wind Rivers, a place that gave white men the shivers.

The Wind Rivers shoulder the storms aside, and leave the tall grass waving high.
Even Old Washakie never suspected - that land would be where oil was detected.
Back when the Indian ruled the palins, there was no trouble with lack of rains.
The Indian simply packs up and moves. The land was plowed by buffalo hooves.
The great herds kept the grasses at bay, yet not so short that the dirt blew away.
There was a balance of predator and prey. The herd bulls kept the wolves away.
The weak and old were the ones taken, but now that balance has been forsaken.
Some folks believe the earth's an Eden, where the weaker ones are never eaten.

If you will look carefully at things, like why there's no water at Shoshoni Springs,
You'll see the Great Spirit's plan was made to work without the help of man.
We should reason together n'look for ways - this land can be used in future days.
With reason, science and common sense, we can maybe put a gate in the fence.
With enviornmentalist and rancher working together, over time this storm we'll weather.
We have enough problems to face, getting along with the rest of the human race."
Having solved the ills of the world at large, he said, "Please, no more of that coffee, Marge!"

******

THE PRAIRIE AUTOCRAT

If ever there was an uncrowned king, it was the old chuck wagon cook.
If you wanted to find someone crankier, I don't know where you'd look.
His kingdom stretched from the campfire to the tongue of the chuck wagon.
He had the bearing of an emperor, and the disposition of a dragon.

That he was a force to reckon with, he left not the slightest doubt.
If you dared tp criticize old Cookie's grub - you just might do without!o
Just one disparaging word about his food was sometimes all it took.
Only a fool argues with a mule, a skunk or an old chuck wagon cook!

Cookie was a man of many talents, which, of course, he had to be.
His wagon was like a sailing ship, on a wind-blown, grassy sea.
Without his many different skills, the cattle drive would meet defeat.
To stay in the saddle sixteen hours a day - those cowboys had to eat!

Not only was he a teamster, with a heavy-loaded chuck wagon to drive,
His expertise as a chuck wagon cook kept the trail drive or round-up alive.
His special position in the camp gave him a host of other things to do;
He was sometimes a doctor, a dentist, a barber, and a veterinarian too.

He might hold the stakes if some sort of betting contest occurred.
He would maybe arbitrate a cowboy quarrel with a well-chosen word.
Since he kept a shovel for trenching, so his campfire didn't spread;
He might also be an undertaker, if a mishap left some cowboy dead.

His day started in the middle of the night. By 3 a.m. his fire was bright
Even on the worst rainy days, when wood was wet and hard to light.
By the time the Wrangler had driven all the horses into the rope corral,
Cookie was banging pot lids, and hollering, "Get up, it's time for Chow!"

He'd have Dutch oven baked hot biscuits, meat, dried fruit, hash browns,
And a two-gallon pot of hot coffee, made with a heaping handful of grounds.
While the cowboys roped their horses, he'd be kneading sourdough bread
Before 5 a.m., he lined his chuck wagon out...to drive fifteen miles on ahead.

Before that day ended, he'd have two more hearty meals whipped up;
Like boiled potatoes, short ribs with onions, hot bread and "spotted pup",
(That's rice and raisins cooked together), ginger bread, or Dutch oven pie.
Then, he started preparing the next days grub, which he did by lantern light.

Tho he was looked on as a despot, and a cranky, grumpy old grouch...
Old Cookie always had hot coffee, and his welcome lantern hung out.
If we had to do all of Cookies jobs, cook and bring the wagon through
While keeping old Cookies long hours, well, I reckon we'd be grumpy, too!

******

WESTERN WEAR

The tourist looked at the cowboy, her eyes filled with curiosity.
She had never seen such a get-up, and she wondered how it came to be.
"Mr, Cowboy, can you tell me why your choice of clothing is so strange?
Is there some reason why you dress that way to work out on the range?"
The cowboy sighed and rolled his eyes, he'd been through all this before.
Yet, he answered her politely, and he went through it all once more.

"Ma'm, this big sombrero that I'm wearing is a pure necessity.
It shades me from the sun, and keeps the rain and snow off me.
It will fan a campfire into flame, or carry water to douse one out.
These bonnet strings anchor it in a storm, or when I'm riding "flat out".
The silk kerchief around my neck is also a very necessary thing,
It's a face wipe, dust mask, sling, tourniquet or even a pigging string!"

"A coat would just encumber my arms, but this snug vest fills the bill,
It won't catch on the saddle horn, and it wards off the morning chill.
These jeans are made with the seam outside, so the saddle won't rub me raw,
And when I really need protection, I've got the best chaps you ever saw.
Not the kind you see in rodeos, or like they wear in the big parades,
But I can ride through brush and cactus, and never have to be afraid.

"Now, these tall boots are lifesavers, They protect my lower leg, you see,
'Cause my horse might brush against a fence, or whack my leg against a tree.
And the high heels won't let my feet go through the stirrups when they're slick,
I'm not wearing spurs, but when I do, I have a much better hoss.
I seldom use 'em, but their jingle-jangle reminds him who's the boss."

"Now, Miss Tourist, I hope you don't think it's impertinent of me,
If I turn this quiz around to you, and have you explain just what I see.
You're wearing big sunglasses, the briefest shorts, the tiniest swimsuit top,
With white stuff painted on your nose, I guess, to make your sunburn stop.
Your feet are shod with funny clogs, made from someone's old used tires.
And you're asking me why I look strange. I think somebody crossed your
wires!"

******

Neal Torrey
665 N. Lemmon Av
Bolivar, MO   65613

Neal both recites and reads his own unique poetry from his true experiences that truly tell it like it was by one who has lived the life. He was born in Putnam County, Missouri in 1935. He has worked a wide variety of jobs to pay his way through college. He has used his writing skills to enjoy a career in broadcast advertising, and as a Radio-TV director. Neal has been involved in law enforcement, and as Captain of the Sheriff's Search and Rescue unit in Teton County, Wyoming. He was writing cowboy poetry before it became popular, and has published, and illustrated, a book of his original poems. Neal and his wife, Rurh, have raised Quarter Horses and Appaloosas for over 30 years.

Stability
Photograph by Rachael

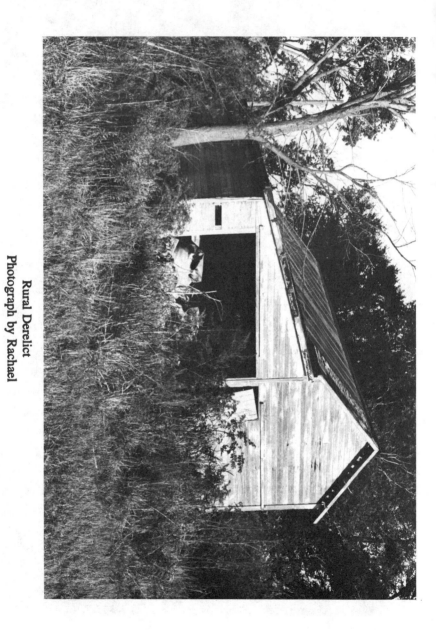

Rural Derelict
Photograph by Rachael

Abandoned
Photograph by Rachael

Portal To The Past
Photograph by Rachael

Rachael Tucker
P. O. box 107
Covington, GA   30015

Rachael Couch is a textile design artist who received her training at the University of Kansas. Relying onher training in architexture and in textile desig, she devotes time to photography, especially rural scenes. Rachael has completed a childrens book in which she used photography and other art media to illustrate a Western rural poem. She and her husband, Steve, presently preside in Covington, Georgia.

COWBOY HEAVEN

When the sun goes down on the prairie
The sky is all tinged with crimson
Sage fills the air with it's flavor
And I know, this is real cowboy heaven.

This is the time that I love best
When the evening rolls around
The sun has settled in the west
And the cows are all bedded down.

Then ol' Paint is relieved of his saddle
And he shakes off the dust and the sweat
I'll fetch him some oats, and some water
Then I'll go find what ol' Cooky has set.

When ol' Cooky has served up a good one
Roast beef, with gravy, an' taters, an' beans
Then topped it off with sweet apple puddin'
I'm just a'bustin' plumb out of my jeans.

When the campfire is nothin' but embers
And the last cup of coffee is gone
Now is the time for the boys to unwind
And fill the night with their song.

Then Kenny will bring out his Banjo
And his fingers will dance on the frets
While Skelly plays his Gibson guitar
- Boys, - this is as good as it gets.

Then old Grizz will recite us some poetry
Maybe tell us a story or two
'Bout cowboy ways in the good old days
When he was a greenhorn Buckaroo.

When the last of the songs has been sung
And the twang of the Banjo is still
When Skelly puts his Guitar away
Coyotes start their song from the hill.

Then I lay me down in my soogans*
And I thank my dear God for such bliss
For cowboy life and cowboy friends
Man, it can't get, - any better than this.

* Soogans, blankets or bedroll.

*****

COWBOY TALK

The Chuck wagon was closed; the campfire had burned down
The cows were all bedded, - lyin' quiet all a'round.
We had just settled down for another night camp
While night bugs danced 'round the old kerosene lamp

I lay on my bedroll - just a'watchin' the sky
And listenin' to Charley, and Slim, on the sly
Those two old cowboys were discussin' their past
The times that were slow and the times that were fast.

They had ridden together since heck was a pup
Both back in their teens when they first signed up
For forty odd years they had stuck through it all
From calvin' in the spring to the round up in the fall.

Slim was a'talkin' - just like he most always was
With Charley just listenin' an' with good reason because
You can't git a word in when Slim's on a roll
He'll save up for days, and then just let 'em all go.

"Charley," said Slim, when he commenced to begin
"It's shorly a wonder all th' places we've been
When we first started out on th' old Circle-Bar-Jay
Would'ja ever hav' thought we'd still be a'ridin' today?

Remember that wreck on th' old Chisholm Trail
When th' cattle got spooked by a lone coyote's wail?
I'd shorly been trampled if it hadn't been fer you
Now, what more could ya' ask from a real Buckaroo?

Then, that time down in Rio, at Th' Blue Moon Saloon
We started on friday, an' woke up in jail, monday noon
That drunk was a humdinger, an' I'll never forgit that
I lost a whole months wages an' my best four beaver hat.

Now that skunk in th' privy really wasn't somethin' I did
An', I wus sorry that he got ya', when you lifted th' lid
Th' boys wouldn't let ya' in th' bunkhouse that night
But I couldn't help laughin', you wus such a sad sight.

We've had lots of th' good times, an' maybe some of th' bad
All th' pranks that we pulled, an' th' fights that we had
Yes, we've had a few bad times, but we've had lots of fun
An', I'll tell ya, old Pardner, I've shor enjoyed every one.

All in all, Charley, it's been one hellu'va good life
But, now it's time that I got me a home, - an' found me a wife.
I've done my share of ridin' an' punchin' cows all a'round
Now, I'd like a gal I can talk to an' then jus' settle down.

I'd like a real purdy young woman to keep me good company
An' a real feather bed to sleep in, no more bunk-beds fer me
I'd like to raise me some boys, an' teach 'em good cowboy ways
An', maybe some girls, to cheer up, th' rest of my days.

I'll git an old rockin' chair, an' then rest in th' shade
Just'a soakin' up interest, fer all th' dues that I've paid
When yer young you can dream, 'bout that home on th' range
But, there's a time on th' trail, when yer due fer a change.

Now I've had it with cowboy life, an' I'm jus' plumb wore out
And it's time that I find out, what th' rest of life is about
When this drive is over, I'll pick up my pay, then I'm through
But I want ya to know, Charley, it shor ain't because of you."

Then Slim stopped for breath, and that gave Charley a chance
To reply in his fashion how he felt, 'bout this new circumstance.
"Old Pardner", said Charley, "All that you said might be true,
But Slim, there jus' ain't no woman, that could ever put up with you."

******

CHARLEY'S REVENGE

We were drivin' a herd to the Dodge City Rail
And had camped for the night, out on the trail.
The cook had closed up, and turned out the light,
Both Charley and Slim had turned in for the night.

Charley was a'snorin', - or just pretendin' to
Soon, so was Slim, and the rest of the crew.
But Charley, the faker, was just a'thinkin' on
A prank to fix Slim for that skunk in the John.

Slim's boots were settin' right close by his side
To be handy for that trip to the brush in the night.
There ain't no pain like sand burrs in your feet
When you're in a big hurry, an' you're still half a'sleep.

Now, Slim was not a "dally man", he always tied on
With the his lariat tied tight to his saddle horn.
Then Charley got the notion how it would be nifty
To repay his old Pard for that skunk in the privy.

So, he slipped out of his bedroll, easy and quiet
To the saddle at Slim's head and his lariat by it.
He took Slim's lariat and made a little loop,
Then he lassoed the ankle of old Slim's boot.

'Bout an hour 'fore sunrise, Slim felt that urge
That comes in the night after a late coffee splurge.
He slipped into his boots, and took off at a lope,
But he soon hit the end, of that thirty foot rope.

He let out a yell, when he landed flat on his back,
Stampedes have been started by a lot less than that.
But Slim found the fall was the least of his grief
'Cause all of that coffee spilled out in relief.

Now, if there's anything worse than burrs in the sands
It's burrs in your bottom, and wet in your pants.
Oh, - hell hath no fury like Slim had that night
And he came up a'lookin' for one hell of a fight.

He headed straight for Charley, plumb wild to get it on
But Charley's bed was empty, ------ Charley was gone!
The night guard reported on his next time around,
"Charley said somethin', 'bout havin' business in town."

*"Dally man": A roper who uses a loose rope, and takes a dally,
or a wrap around his saddle horn to stop and hold a roped calf.
"Tie man": A roper who ties his rope dirctly to his saddle horn
so the horse can hold a roped calf while he dismounts for the tie.*

******

A COWBOY'S LAMENT

It was only a couple of years ago
I rode out to the old Bar-D.
I heard they needed another hand,
And I thought it might as well be me.

But the Honcho jus' smiled at me kindly,
Then he said, "I'm sorry old Pard,
But you see I need a younger hand,
'Cause we're gon'a be ridin' hard."

Those words were like a bitter pill,
With a taste of gall on my tonque.
To think, at seventy, I couldn't ride,
Like I did, - when I was young.

Now today, when I look around me
At old friends that I've known so long,
I see the changes that time has made,
And I wonder, where the years have gone.

Now our cowboy days are over,
But we still remember those days,
When we started out as little boys
To learn the big cowboy ways.

But those days are gone forever,
Just as our youth has gone,
And live only in our memories,
To be recalled in our poem, and our song.

So here's to our cowboy memories,
And here's to our song, and our poem,
Of the tall tales told, of the days of old,
When the wide open range - was our home.

Now we sometimes get together,
Just us boys, - now much older men,
To speak our piece in lines of rhyme,
And relive, - our yesterdays, - again.

******

BLACKY

When I first got Blacky I was only ten
An I thought it was rather strange
That tears streaked the dust on fathers face
When he carried the foal in from the range.

He had found them there, down by the creek
Where his mare had birthed and died
And the foal was struggling for his life
Sucking a teat that was cold and dried.

Now, father said, it would be my job
And that he had lots of faith in me
To keep that little foal alive
To be the colt that he was meant to be.

At times it seemed there was just no way
That he could make it through the night
But my prayers, and tender loving care
Always made things turn out right.

Both day and night I cared for him
And I watched him slowly grow
From the weakling, father had given me
Into the colt I was proud to show.

At the fair he won the Blue Ribbon
And he stood as proud as he could be
But the pride I saw on fathers face
Just meant the world, and all to me.

As time flew by my pony had grown
The finest in all the world it seemed
And the joys that we shared together
Was more than a boy ever dreamed.

For thirty years Blacky was my best pard
A bond that only a cowboy and horses know
Then he passed to that great green pasture
Where the best of all good horses go.

There's another cross now, by the creek
That was carved with utmost loving care
Where his mother died to give him birth
And my Blacky is also now resting there.

Now each day I ride, down by the creek
Just to sit, and dream of days gone by
And wonder if Blacky and I shall ride again
In those great green pastures in the sky.

******

RATTLER

There ain' nothin' like a rattler
To make yor hoss shy high
Then yor a'lyin' on yor back
Just a'lookin' at th' sky.

But there ain't no time to worry
'Bout whut happened to yor hat
'Cause you cain't help but wonder
Just where that rattler's at.

You bounce up off th' ground
Like you had springs on yor back side
An never even stop to think
'Bout th' cactus a'stickin' to yor hide.

But now you got a'nother problem
'Cause yor hoss has galloped off alone
An' left you with that rattler
To ride ol' skank's mare home.

Now high heel boots with pointy toes
Wuzn't made for prairie walkin'
An' bull hide chaps in summer sun
Soon gits yor legs to gallin'.

Oh, you can cuss that danged ol' pony
An' swear to take th' hide off him
But when he shys high from a'nother rattler
You'll have it all to do agin.

******

DAD'S OLD BOOTS

I still remember my Mother, when I was just a lad.
Then I would often hear her, gently scold my Dad,
"Harley, how often must I remind you,
Leave those filthy boots outside the door?
Don't track half the corral into this house,
I've just mopped the kitchen floor."

Then Dad would smooth her ruffled feathers,
- That was his daily trial,
And soon he'd win her over,
With his charming, tender, smile.

But that was many years ago
And Father has taken his last ride.
Tho' years have passed, the memories last
- But tears are hard to hide.

Now, Mother sits at the kitchen window
Just staring, out beyond the pasture gate.
Then I hear her softly whisper,
- "I'd best warm over supper
It looks like Harley might be late."

I wonder if she really knows he's gone
- Or is she just pretending,
To hide the hurt she feels inside,
From a broken heart that's slowly mending.

But Dad's old boots are resting there,
- Just outside the kitchen door.
Again, I hear her whisper softly,
- "I wonder what's keepin' Harley?
He's never been this late before."

Now, on the other side, of the Great Divide
I see my Father, smiling, there.
And I see a pair of golden boots
At the top of that Golden Stair.

But some old habits just never die,
- And to that I can relate,
For I see those boots are resting there
- Just outside, - that Golden Gate.

******

Old Pard

An old cowboy stood by a crude wooden cross
That marked the new grave of his old Pard
And while tears betrayed the grief of his loss
Spoke these words that came from his heart.

"Today I have lost another old friend
Who used to ride the trails with me
And now I have almost reached the end
Of the old friends that used to be.

Of old friends I've known for many years
Who staunchly through both thick and thin
Through times of laughter, and times of tears
Stood by my side, when I needed them.

And I in turn was bound to greet
Their call for any of their needs
For friendship is a two-way street
That's paved with constant, friendly deeds.

Now, with the passing of the years
I too, it seems, have older grown
And wander back with smiles and tears
Through joys and sorrows we had known.

But memory blocks out the bad times
To recall the joys, that we shared always
And dwells only on the good times
- When we dream of our yesterdays.

So now I mourn for the one I've lost
And pledge to seek, and find another
With whom I can share at any cost
The bond that makes of man, a brother.

So here's to my old and my new friend
- To all friendships, tried and true
And to this friend I knew to the very end,
- Old Pard, I'll always - remember you."

******

THE GATEWAY TO THE WEST

In the Missouri city of St Louis
On the bank of the Mighty Miss
There stands a giant archway
A symbol of "The Gateway To the West".

For Missouri was the gateway
Through which the settlers came
- And this is the story
Of how Missouri got the name.

John Sutter ran a general store
In the Missouri city of St Jo'
Then he moved to California
To a place called Sacramento.

There on the American River
Sutter built his famous lumber mill
Then he hired a Missouri carpenter
And James Marshall filled the bill.

It was there in the sawmill tail race
Where the mill driving waters ran
James Marshall found a bit of gold
In the American River sand.

When the story reached St Joseph
The news was printed as it was told
And that story in the St Joseph paper
Spurred the rush for California gold.

Then many came to seek their fortunes
Others came looking for new land
Where they might find a brand new start
And Missouri is where it all began.

Some came up the Mississippi
From the town of New Orleans
Some came down the Great Ohio
Searching for their land of dreams.

Some, who hired the river boats
With the likes of Mickey Finn
Headed up the Wide Missouri
And were never seen ag'in.

St Louis was the river port
Where the crowded steamboats came
With families seeking new beginnings
As the wild, wild west was tamed.

They debarked there at St Louis
Bought supplies, a horse, and wagon
Then pushed on toward the sunset
Women walkin', skirts a'dragin'.

Drawn to the west Missouri border
To the towns of Westport, and St Jo'
Where the wagon trains were gathered
And headed westward, movin' slow.

But for some the search had ended
When they found their land of dreams
On these wide Missouri prairies
And on the Ozark mountain streams.

This caused a brand new problem
Of getting mail from here to there
As families divided by the savage miles
Sought for answers to their prayer.

Then William Russell, of St Joseph
Ran a newspaper "ad" one morn
For young, hard riding Broncos
And the "Pony Express" was born.

Binding East and West together
By couriers riding hard, and fast
Just to bring some welcome word
From family, and friends at last.

And so, the West was settled
By those just passing through
This land they Called Missouri
To their dream-land rendezvous.

That, my friends is how Missouri
Became "The Gateway To The West"
Where settlers moving westward
Came to start their westward quest.

******

THE PROPHET

A professor of the great white University
On a quest to the Western Indian land
Was appalled by the state of their diversity
And modes that he could not understand.

Then he chanced upon an ancient hogan
A hovel an Indian had once called home
- A place of dreams that now lay broken
A shell for memories, now long since flown.

A force there seemed to summon him
Like the lure of the ancient sirens call
By something strange that lay within
He was drawn by spirits of the aboriginal.

He stooped and peered into the hogans gloom
- And was struck with a ghostly fear
By a form that sat in the dim lit room
- A foreboding presence most austere.

An old Indian sat on the adobe floor
- On a woolen rug dyed an earthen hue
A withered hand beckoned the visitor
- "Come in, I have a message for you.

The plight that you see of our people
Is no different from that of your own
Though we are indeed a sad spectacle
You also have much for which to atone.

We too were once a great proud nation
And our land was a most sacred place
Then white men came with forked tongue
And our sacred land was soon defaced.

You cruely drove us from our home land
With wanton slaughter of both man and beast
Then claimed it all for your own land
Condemned us to barrens of worth the least.

Oh, you had your lofty goals for living
A place to worship your God as you pleased
You thought your God was all forgiving
- But now your God is most displeased.

Your nation is steeped in moral decay
You are slaves to the pleasures you seek
But soon you will return to the clay
And your soul to the Great Judgement seat.

Yes, you can see our deplorable reservation
And heap blame upon us for our sad dispair
But give some pause upon your own refection
And see the prophetic disaster lurking there.

Your squaws have no time for the hogan
And your children have no father there
You have spurned your nations slogan
There is no "In God We Trust" in prayer.

You have no statesmen for your leaders
- When their character is flawed
There is no respect for your elders
- And there is no respect for your God.

No nation can endure forever
When morals are trambled rough-shod
There must always be Godly endeavor
For no nation can survive without God."

******

Leroy Watts   Poet/Reciter
Rt 1 Box 155-A
Verona, Mo. 65769

Leroy is a Major Charter Member, and one of the founders of the Missouri Cowboy Poets Association. He is currently the Chairman of the MCPA Board of Directors. He was born in Joplin, Missouri in 1923, and spent much of his life in the mountains of Colorado and the deserts of Arizona. He has published a hard bound book, "Reminisin'", of his original poetic stories, a tape of his original "Cowboy Poems", and three booklets, "The Closet Poet", "Cowboy Talk", and "Ozark Cowboy Filosofies". Leroy has appeared at various Cowboy Poetry Gatherings throughout the Southwest. He and his wife, LaVern, are now retired in their own little world in the Ozark hills.

I STILL MISS HIM SOMETIMES

Do you ever wish
you could still talk to your Dad?
Just to say how you doin',
Or tell him about the day you've had.

You see my Dad's gone
it's been bout nine years now.
Yeah, I know he's gone,
but sometimes it don't seem like it somehow.

Why sometimes something good will happen,
and I feel so glad.
The first thing I think of, is
I got to go tell Dad.

So I saddle my horse
and point him that way.
Oh! I know he's going to be tickled
to hear what I got to say.

Then I remember he's gone
Well, What was I thinkin'?
Then a big ole lump will come up in my throat,
and I hold back the tears by blinkin'.

Ah! I know he's gone,
and I'm not one to pine.
But you see, I just forget
and I miss him sometimes.

I rode by his old place today
and reminisced for a while.
I could still see him sittin' on the front porch,
wearing that big smile.

One thing I guess
that makes me so sad,
is that I can't ever remember saying
I love you Dad.

Ah, he knew I loved him,
It was something I never had to say.
Besides, telling another man you loved him,
even your Dad, it just wasn't done out our way.

As I rode back toward my place
I thought what the heck,
I'm gonna' go tell my son I love,
and hug his neck.

******

WHEN MEN WORE HATS

The other day I was looking at some picture took back when I was a kid
And thought about the difference in the clothes we wore and the things we did

The men all had short haircuts, and long sleeve shirts
Most of the women's hair was long and so was their skirts

The men wore their Levis, and khakis, and overalls proud
There wasn't a pair of Bermuda shorts or an earring in the crowd

Some men wore high top leather shoes, others wore Wellington boots
No tennis shoes or sandals on these galloots

Most all the men wore hats, not necessarily western style
some had leather or wool caps, they wore once in a while

They used expressions like, "Gone like a wild goose in winter," "pull a Hank
     Snow,"
"Making a killing," and "Boys let her go"

All the stores closed on Sunday, the Blue laws saw to that
Back when women wore dresses and a man wore a hat

Folks could rest on Sunday or worship as they please
We hadn't hear of "love in's" or AIDS disease

People were proud our boys in uniform, if you can picture that
When women wore dresses and a man wore a hat

It's a different world now a days, we all dress different and that's a fact
But, I still think a woman looks better in a dress, and a man looks better in a hat

******

DOES YOUR HEART EVER SOAR?

Does your heart ever soar? Do you know how much it means
To have on a good pair of boots and fades old jeans?

Do you ever sing to your horse, while you set him astride
With the sun warm on your back, you're just glad to be in the saddle.

Did you ever just haul off and jump and shout real loud with glee?
For no other reason than you're just glad to be free.

Did you ever just talk to the Lord, did you ever just pray
To think Him for the sunshine and the beautiful day?

Think about it real hard and try to recall a time
When you were just happy to be yourself and let your troubles unwind.

You weren't worried about bills, the future or the chores.
You were just glad to be alive and breathing in God's great outdoors.

You may have been out with your dog or riding your favorite mule.
It may have been a day off work or a weekend away from school.

Have you ever felt this way partner? Can you remember back when?
What's that? You say you've never, or "my, how long has it been?"

Well sir, it won't make you feel better to bellyache or moan.
Get out in God's great outdoors. Take a walk even alone.

Look at the river, the trees and the flowers that God put on this green earth.
He put you here, too, Partner. He knew you before your birth.

You're more important to Him than the stars, and He has them
    numbered in the sky.
He said, "Surely you're more important than a sparrow,"
    and he Knows each one that falls to earth never again to fly.

So if you want inner peace and happiness of which there is no other kind.
The Lord said, "Knock and the door will open, seek him, and you
    will surely find.

******

A FEW GOOD MEN

Once when I was young
That was way back when.
I heard that the United States Marines
Were looking for a few good men.

Now I was fairly strong for my size
And sound of body and mind
Trustworthy, loyal, had good morals
Did right most of the time.

JFK told us, "Ask not what you country can do for you,
But ask what you can do for it."
I was fairly bright and not afraid to fight.
Yes, the Marine Corps would be a good fit.

So on February the 10th, 1966
I went to serve my country with pride.
Both my brothers were in during Korea,
I wouldn't burn my draft card and hide.

After boot camp at San Diego
They sent us on to Camp Pendleton.
There we met some East Coast Marines,
And hooked up with a few more good men.

With machine guns, rockets and mortars we trained,
Our emblem we proudly wore.
We believed, "The more you sweat in peace,
The less you bleed in war."

The mess halls weren't French restaurants,
That's to say the least.
But the sign in the mess hall read
"Everyday's a holiday, Every meal's a feast."

All of us were young Americans
Who knew that communism wasn't right.
With America's resources backing us
A few good men could never lose the fight.

We boarded the U.S.S. Henrico
Bound for Viet Nam.
We rode out Typhoon Ida
And landed when the waters calmed.

We had jungle warfare training in Okinawa
Then we left for Subic Bay.
We sweated hard in the jungles of The Philippines
But at night we were hard at play.

We were anxious to do our part in the war.
We didn't know they wouldn't let us win.
At the mouth of a river near Don Hoi,
I hit the beach with a few good men.

We fought in places that had names
Like 881, 861 North and South,
Hue City and Phu Bai,
Waiting for McNamara to help us out.

We fought at Dong Hoi when the ammo dump blew.
We fought at Khe Sanh and Conn Tien.
Many a mother lost many a son,
And the Marines lost a few good men.

We won our battles on the ground
Because our hearts were in the fight.
Never shirking the task or complaining,
Just doing what was right.

We kept our sense of humor.
We joked when times were tough.
We helped each other when we needed it,
A few good men kept each other up.

When you take a few good men
And put their backs against a wall
Without ammo, food or water
And no outside help at all,

A few good men will fix bayonets
And charge at a double time stride.
A few good men can fight and win
On nothing but Marine Corps pride.

For years we kept South Viet Nam free,
And on freedom you can't put a price.
If my country asked me to fight again,
Yes, I would do it twice.

A few good men would answer the call.
We would not hesitate.
We won the battles in Viet Nam.
The war was lost in the states.

There's only one stipulation I would make
Before returning to Viet Nam again.
I would have to fight as a marine
Alongside a few good men.

******

Jerry White   Poet/Story Teller/Humorist
1135 S, Ferguson
Springfield, MO   65807

Jerry White is a Major Member of the Missouri Cowboy Poets Associatio, and is the current MCPA Vice President for the term July 1, 2000 through June 30, 2002. Jerry was born in Ash Grove, Missouri, and raised on small country farms. He went to school in Ash Grove, Republic, Halltown, and graduated from high school in Billings, Missouri. Jerry served in the United States Marine Corps, and a veteran of the Viet Nam war. One of Jerry poems was first place winner in a Texas contest, and he enjoys sharing them with others at every opportunity.

NOT LONG AGO

Not long ago I camped by a creek
With the fire not far from my head,
My saddle and pad, a blanket rolled out
Are all that I had for a bed.

The stars lit up the midnight sky
And an owl far off gave a hoot,
The fire warmed the cool night air
And the wind helped dry out my boot.

Ole Buck was tethered close to camp
With lush green grass at his feet,
I was sippin' the last of my coffee
Thinkin' this life is real hard to beat.

We came along way since daylight this morn
The cedar breaks tested our skill
The one horned cow and the bull that made fight
Are the ones that tested our will.

We'll camp here for days and make this our home
Till the round up and brandin' are through,
The chuck wagon's stocked and water close by
And there's plenty of cookie's good stew.

Ole cookie's a stokin' the fire with wood
Cause cow chips give off a bad smoke,
And Shorty's got everyone laughin' real hard
He just got done telling a joke.

Life couldn't be better out here on the range
There's just nothing better to do,
Except when I'm dreaming of holding your hand
And whispering sweet nothings to you.

I started to doze and my nose gave a snort
Then my feet slipped off my bench,
My chair sped out from under my seat
And I found myself holding a wrench.

I picked myself up and chuckled a bit
And scratched my head through my cap,
Should I go on and finish my job
Or should I get back to taking my nap.

COOKIE'S PRAYER

Oh Lord I pray at the end of the day
in my bedroll here on the ground
that the campfire light will warm my night
and keep me safe and sound.

That my aches and pains
will all go away,
that I might rise
to see another day.

That my biscuits won't burn
and always rise high,
that my coffee won't weaken
as the day goes by.

I hope that the boys
will all like my stew
cuz cookin' good chuck
is all that I do.

If ya wander into camp
all wet, tire and cold,
I got hot coffee
for your hands to hold.

Put your back to the fire
and sit a spell,
have a hot plate of beans,
we'll find some stories to tell.

When you're all rested
and warm inside
and get back on your horse
to finish your night ride.

Make a round or two
and circle through camp
where you can stop for awhile
and dry off the damp.

I'm greatful oh Lord
for all that I've had,
life here on the range
isn't so bad.

I've got a thick bedroll
and good chuck to eat,
a home where the scenery
just can't be beat.

I'll build up the fire
and make some more brew
while you ride out on night herd
watchin' after the crew.

******

SLEEPLESS IN THE SADDLE

The campfires a fadin', the pots gettin' cold.
Ol cookie's shuttin' the lid.
My heads in my saddle, my backs to the ground,
I'm weary from all that I did.

I'll be in good hands out here on the ground
With the night riders watchful eye
I'll dream of the fair maiden from the dance back in town,
Her smile as I bid her good-by.

But all is not well, my sleep is cut short,
Our camp is coming alive.
The night rider signals, a cattle stampede!
The camp was quick to revive.

We were saddled in minutes and rode out of camp
Fanning our horses behind
We headed them off a ways out of camp,
The cattle were not hard to find.

But Tanner was missin' the youngest we had
He just hired on back in town.
We searched through the night, was a desperate attempt
In hopes the boy would be found.

At a bend in a dry wash all lathered and wheezin'
His pony had trodded his last.
Our faces all dropped, our hearts pounding hard,
At the thought of his life ending fast.

As we rounded that bend and tied up his pony,
We start to look for our friend,
There high on the bank we heard from the rocks
Where the heck have you guys been?

******

CHASIN' DREAMS

The guys I work with often tell
Of horses they once rode.
The bosses' pride they rode so well
And the ones that got'em throwed.

They like to brag of secret ways
To make one take the bit,
Or just how well they stuck it out
Till finished with its fit.

"I rode wild horses for the boss"
Is the story I'd always hear,
When I was young and full of spit
I didn't have no fear.

My bones been busted so many times
My chin split once or twice,
I've laid in in traction in a bed
With my leg all packed in ice.

Some stories grew from day to day
How they went from ranch to ranch,
Some only day worked here and there
Or went from branch to branch.

Each one had a unique tale
That kept you in suspense,
Of how he roped a maddened cow
That drug him through the fence.

Or stories of going down a hill
A pealin' off their shoes,
To drivin' cattle down a road
That made the 6 o'clock news.

My story's just a little different
So I'll start with the truth,
Upon a horse I never sat
When I was in my youth.

I'd dream of livin' way out West
And working from a saddle,
Of fightin' Indians in a raid
And drivin' long hor cattle.

It's been my privilege since that time
To ride with some of the best,
All friends of mine I call today
They don't brag like the rest.

The saddle time and cattle drives
Have all come true for me,
Upon a horse chasin' dreams
Is where I'll always be.

******

THUNDERING HERD

At the crack of dawn we rode out of camp
to parts unknown to us.
The horses were loaded with supplies we'd need
and the ride would be hard until dusk.

As the sun broke over the ridge at our backs
and we wound ou way through the draw,
a chill hit my neck and my hair stood on end
at the thunder that waved through us all.

It wasn't long till we realized
the size of the buffalo herd
that was shakin' the ground for miles around,
the sweat in my eyes made them blurred.

It was tense as we stopped in an out crop of rock
our eyes made contact without a word.
We thought we were safe so we settled in
to watch that thundering herd.

There were times it seemed it was letting up
but on and on they came,
till out through the dust came a towering bull,
and one more that put him to shame.

My eyes couldn't believe the size of those two,
the challenger and the king of them all.
The fight lasted on, but the king met his match
and the dust claimed him dead at the fall.

He strutted around on his new won ground
and got closer and closer to us.
We were packin' away from the danger we saw
when my old leather cinch bit the dust.

The young bull gained speed as he headed our way,
there's no way out of his path!
Ole Buck gave a leap, unloaded it all,
and right then I knew I wouldn't last.

That bull was breathing down my neck,
he was standing on my arm,
the smell of his breath as he past by my nose
meant my death or bodily harm.

Just then my body shook and gave its last jerk,
but my eyes were opening wide!
"Denny" I heard, ~you've got to wake up,
there's a buffalo standing outside!"

******

Dennis Williams   Poet/Reciter/Chuck Wagon Owner-cook
8613 Oxbow Ln
Neosho, MO.   64850

Dennis lives just West of Neosho, Missouri where he owns, and operates the Country House Buggy Shop. Dennis is one of the MCPA Chuck wagon cooks, and has published a book of poems and chuck wagon recipes, with drawings and instructions for building a chuck wagon box. He is a wheelwright, and a wagon and buggy maker. He manufactures new wheels and wagons, and restores and repairs old equipment. He is a member of the Western Chuck Wagon Assoction, and he cooks and entertains all over the Midwest. He and his wife Donna also do a lot of trail riding.

Through Dennis's profession as a wheelwright and wagon maker from the Southwest corner of Missouri, he has become well acquainted with ranching and cowboy life. His hobby of chuck wagon cooking and riding has led to spending many hours in the saddle, both in Missouri and other Western states. His relationship with others of his lifestyle has inspired him to write of those experiences in both story and rhyme. He now enjoys sharing his poetry with others, as well as cook their cowboy meals.

THE COWBOY AND THE SADDLE

He sat the half empty tin cup of coffee on the rock
As he used both hands to pull the boot over his sock
He felt the predawn breeze bite the back of his neck
While he watched a sparrow find a worm to peck.

For neigh on fifteen years he's made this his home
Herding five thousand head of cattle and being alone
Ain't nothing to do with people, it just ain't his way
The hustle, and bustle of the city every day.

Most wanta-a-be cowboys, leave his saddle alone
They can imagine the blisters they're gon'na know
He says a real cowboy's tough as steel
Them kind's things he don't admit he ever feels.

The sound the saddle makes is hard to describe
But it's music to a cowboy's ears, out on a ride
The way his horse moves just walkin' along
The cowboy on that saddle, has to start singin' a song.

Now this cowboy ain't as pretty as the Marlboro Man
But he can live like a coyote on the desert sand
He's long and lean, and knows ev'ry day's a battle
And knows he wouldn't be him, without his saddle.

******

Ol' JAKE

They claim Ol' Jake was a rounder,
A rider, roper an' such
They say his ho'ss, it stumbled
He just, plain ran out of luck.

We rode together for years
And his story I know too well
It's always here in my mind
It's just clear as a bell.

There's the eight of us drovers
Drivin' north on the Santa Fe Trail
Buck an' Patchy in the lead
When it started to rain, then hail.

We knew we was in trouble
When the winds got real quite
Them danged ol' cows got restless
We could see the fear in their eyes.

Might as well have been a gun shot
From my extra long barrel "Colt"
When that big oak tree was split
In two, by a lightin' bolt.

The cattle took off all crazy like
Look out men! Their gon'na stampede!
Strayin' to the four winds
Some nearly ran over me.

Headin' for a box canyon
Jesse and Pete took off to the West
Patchy and Buck made a wide turn
Followin' with the rest.

George and Harlin took out
For the strays that went East
And Ol' Jake got tangled up
With a couple of mighty beasts.

The lightin' cracked and thunder
Rolled____ across the hills
In that flash of light
I saw Jake take the spill.

Them two big bulls was fightin'
With horns that cut like a knife
When the storm blew over
Ol' Jake had lost his life.

They claim Ol' Jake was a rounder,
A rider, a roper an' such
They say his ho'ss, it stumbled
He just, plain ran out of luck.

******

CURLY RED

I could tell you of the bulls I've rode
And the times I didn't win
Winding roads, deep valleys
And rivers that never seem to end.

Life on the Blue Bayou and
Honeysuckle vines
But this particular story's
About Curley Red and a railroad line.

I was herdin' cows for the H bar C
I saw the smoke unravelin' out'a that stack
Heard the whistle blowin'
Runnin' wild down that lonely track.

It was an ol' 2-4-2
With a handful of cars
When a mama cow tryin' to cross the rails
Met with those heavenly stars.

I started my own spread and I hand fed that
Curley red baby bull 'til he could stand
And he's paid me back for savin' his life
Curley Red, grand daddy of the Flyin' W brand.

******

A COWHAND'S DREAM

Out of the moonlit winter dark
Comes the morning light
And the smell of fresh coffee
Brings an' open eye.

Now Ol' Cookie's bacon and eggs
Bisquits, gravy, and Mulligan stew
Starts the day right ...
Take a sandwich or two.

Grab my saddle and blanket
Throw it on that ol' horse
Tell 'em how good 'he' is
An' cinch 'em up tight, of course.

I'm gon'na ride all day
Got some fences to mend
It's a two hour ride
To the rivers first bend.

Crossin' the prairie ground
We come upon a rattlesnake
Let's back up ol' horse
There's other trails to take.

Down by the river
There's a doe with her fawn
As I get a cool drink from my hand
I looked again an' the doe was gone.

Standin' tall I reach for the sky
To give these ol' bones a stretch
An' some puffy white clouds
Pass by, so beautifully etched.

Ridin' down the fence
I watched the squirrels play in the trees
I stopped while a cow gave birth to her calf
I'm sure glad we're well into spring.

When I'd fixed some more holes
Made by the big bulls when they fight
I find myself wakin' up in my bunk
And the foreman yelling,
"Quit dreamin' of that cowhands life."

... Out of the moonlit winter dark
Comes the mornin' light
An' the smell of fresh coffee
Brings an open eye.

******

James Wilson   Poet/Reciter
302 W. Spring Street
Eldorado Springs, MO   64744

Jame Wilson is a Major Charter Member of the Missouri Cowboy Poets Association.

MCPA ANTHOLOGY